What to Do About…

What
to Do
About...

A COLLECTION OF ESSAYS
FROM *COMMENTARY* MAGAZINE

edited by NEAL KOZODOY

ReganBooks
An Imprint of HarperCollins*Publishers*

A subscription to *Commentary* magazine may be ordered by calling toll-free 1-800-829-6270 or by writing:

Commentary
165 East 56th Street
New York, NY 10022

HarperCollins books may be purchased for educational, business, or sales promotional use. For information please write: Special Markets Department, HarperCollins Publishers, Inc., 10 East 53rd Street, New York, NY 10022.

FIRST EDITION

Designed by Alma Orenstein

Library of Congress Cataloging-in-Publication Data
What to do about . . . : a collection of essays from Commentary magazine /
    edited by Neal Kozodoy. — 1st ed.
      p.   cm.
    ISBN 0-06-039154-5
    1. Conservatism—United States. I. Kozodoy, Neal. II. Commentary
(New York, N.Y.)
JC573.2.U6W53   1995
320.5'2'0973—dc20   95-23212

95 96 97 98 99 ❖/HC 10 9 8 7 6 5 4 3 2 1

CONTENTS

Contents

ACKNOWLEDGMENT

In preparing the *What to Do About . . .* series for publication in *Commentary*, we received both encouragement and critical financial support from the Bradley and Olin Foundations, which we gratefully acknowledge here. In preparing the manuscript for publication in book form, I received practical help of great value from my colleagues Brenda Brown and Gabriel Schoenfeld, who as always have my deep thanks.

—N. K.

Introduction

NORMAN PODHORETZ

Norman Podhoretz served as Editor-in-Chief of *Commentary* from 1960 until May 1995. He is now the magazine's Editor-at-Large, and a senior fellow at the Hudson Institute.

It is now nearly a half-century since Lionel Trilling—then well on his way to becoming one of America's leading literary and cultural critics—famously proclaimed that "In the United States at this time, liberalism is not only the dominant, but even the sole, intellectual tradition." Trilling called it a "plain fact" that there were "no conservative or reactionary ideas in general circulation." No doubt, he acknowledged, there were strong impulses "to conservatism or to reaction, . . . perhaps even stronger than most of us know." But these impulses did not, "with some isolated and some ecclesiastical exceptions, express themselves in ideas but only in actions or in irritable mental gestures which seek to resemble ideas."

Trilling's sweeping dismissal of American conservatism met with very wide acceptance in 1950 as an accurate assessment of the case, and it is still often cited as authoritative. Yet it was a wild exaggeration. Even among his fellow literary critics at the time, distinguished conservatives like Allen Tate and John Crowe Ransom—not to mention the expatriate T. S. Eliot—abounded, while

in other parts of the American intellectual forest, the likes of Leo
Strauss, Ludwig von Mises, Richard Weaver, James Burnham, and
Peter Viereck were on the scene and busy at their labors (as were
such counterparts in Europe as F. A. Hayek, Michael Oakeshott,
and Bertrand de Jouvenel). And far from being, as Trilling charged,
"bankrupt of ideas," the conservative movement in America was
already heavily pregnant with important books by Russell Kirk,
Eric Voegelin, William F. Buckley, Jr., Will Herberg, Clinton
Rossiter, Robert Nisbet, and a dozen more that would all be completed and published within the next 2 or 3 years.

Unlike many liberals in 1950, Trilling knew that such people
existed; he was even personally acquainted with a few and had
read a number of others. But in so contemptuously ignoring or
dismissing their work as self-evidently retrograde and irrelevant,
he, who in so many other respects dissented from the standard
attitudes of the liberal community, for once went along with the
conventional liberal wisdom.

Still, whatever may have been the state of affairs in 1950, today
no one would dream of saying that conservative ideas are not
worth bothering with. Indeed, a conservative counterpart of
Trilling today could easily turn the tables and claim that it is conservatism which is now the dominant and even the sole intellectual force in America. Yet this, too, would be an exaggeration, since
(as several of the essays collected here demonstrate) liberalism
retains its hold over most of our cultural institutions—the universities, the schools, the arts, and the major media of information
and entertainment.

It is, however, a hold exercised by an intellectually necrotic
class, which is less and less able to provide a defense of its own
ideas that seems persuasive to anyone but itself. Certainly it is hard
to imagine a comparable collection of essays coming out of the
liberal community that could match this one in intellectual power
and vitality. And judging by the inability of the liberals (especially
the intellectuals among them) to do anything more than hurl the
tired charges of racism and mean-spiritedness at their conservative
opponents, it is liberalism that today can be characterized, more
justly than conservatism was in 1950, as a series of "irritable mental gestures which seek to resemble ideas."

The sorry intellectual condition of liberalism is reflected in its dismal political fortunes: as almost everyone now recognizes, the amazing Republican sweep of 1994 represented a repudiation by the voters less of the Democratic party as such than of liberalism and all its works. But here again, things are not as simple as they may appear. For it is important to recognize that even in the social and political realms, and even today, liberalism remains the great shaping force it began to become under Franklin D. Roosevelt in the 1930's.

The reason liberalism retains this power is that in spite of lusty calls for rollback by its conservative opponents, the institutional legacy of Roosevelt's New Deal was left almost entirely intact when the Republicans under Dwight Eisenhower finally dislodged the Democrats in 1952, just as the next great wave of liberal reform, Lyndon Johnson's Great Society programs of the mid-1960's, survived the accession of Richard Nixon in 1968. Nixon's rhetoric may have suggested that he was intent on undoing the great society, but (for reasons that remain unclear) he actually pushed it so much further in the crucial area of affirmative action that he has a better claim than Johnson to being the father of racial quotas. Even Ronald Reagan, the most conservative President of modern times, was unable (and perhaps unwilling) to do much more than slow the growth of the liberal programs and policies he had inherited.

The new Republican majority that was swept into both houses of Congress on November 8, 1994 has no intention of restricting itself to so modest a goal. The Republicans who came before today's cohort may have settled for being "tax collectors for the welfare state" (which is how the current speaker of the House, Newt Gingrich, once characterized the current majority leader of the Senate, Bob Dole), but now most Republicans today seem really to want to dismantle the welfare state. And they are even more determined to sweep away the extensions of it that were enacted in the 1960's by Lyndon Johnson—a determination fed by the conviction that the plagues of family breakdown, crime, welfare dependency, and deteriorating schools, along with the Balkanization of our society into racial, ethnic, and sexual enclaves seeking special treatment and privileges, are in large measure the fruits of that poisoned tree.

I wish I could claim that when, in the early months of 1994, the editors of *Commentary* commissioned the series of articles which began appearing in the magazine in September of that year and have now been collected here, we did so because, foreseeing the imminent coming-to-power of this new breed of Republican counterrevolutionaries, we wanted to offer them something of greater depth to chew on than the Contract with America. But the truth is that no more than anyone else did those of us at *Commentary* expect so great a conservative victory so soon. What we did anticipate was that the major problems facing American society would continue to get worse; that public disgust would continue to grow with standard liberal answers to pathologies either iatrogenically created or exacerbated by those answers in the first place; and that the Clinton administration would get weaker and weaker as a result. The moment therefore seemed especially propitious for an effort to lay out what a responsible conservative alternative might look like in key areas of national life.

This would not, as we envisaged it, take the form of a compendium of conventional position papers. What we were after was a series of articles in each of which a writer who had lived with and studied a particular problem for a long time would reexamine its history, its nature, and its scope, clearing away false ideas and conventional rot as he went along, and only then going on to offer concrete proposals for dealing with it. In other words, the series would bring together the writers who were in great part responsible for building the intellectual foundations of a conservative alternative and would give them a chance to rethink and restate their ideas in the light of the latest developments.

That the moment had indeed arrived for such a series was confirmed by the response of these writers when we approached them to do the job. More often than not, an editor has to nag and plead and cajole to get the articles he wants out of people he thinks are best able to write them. But in this case, to our pleasant surprise, almost everyone we invited turned out to be enthusiastic about the project and most of them eager to contribute.

The articles they produced speak so lucidly and forcefully for themselves that there is no need for me to discuss them here.[1] But I can say this much: that they add up to perhaps the most astute and the most comprehensive diagnosis yet made of what ails American society, and that the proposals they offer point clearly to the direction this country will have to take if conditions are to improve. Beyond that, I would like to offer two observations about the series as a whole.

First, it is weighted very heavily in the direction of domestic problems, with only three out of fourteen articles focused on foreign affairs. Obviously this balance of interest reflects the current state of American political culture: we are all (liberals no less than conservatives) so fixated at the moment on the conditions of life at home that we have been paying relatively little attention to the question of the role we ought to be playing abroad.

Where conservatives in particular are concerned, the end of the cold war has also resulted in a breakup of the old anti-Communist consensus and the rough guidance it provided in grappling with the questions of how and where American power should be deployed. A few conservatives have responded by returning to the nativist isolationism that was once a hallmark of the movement, but no encouragement is given here to this tendency (which, disguised as "multilateralism," has also surfaced among liberals). To the conservatives represented in this book—who, I believe, are themselves representative of the prevailing ethos within the conservative movement today—the need for a strong American role in the world and a commensurately strong national defense remains a given, with the debate still centered mainly on the issue of limits. This was, of course, the case even during the cold war, but as is evident from the ten responses to Robert Kagan's article, there is now a sharply diminished enthusiasm among conservatives for the kind of Wilsonian interventionism that many of them embraced

---

[1] These articles did not, incidentally, include James Q. Wilson's piece on abortion or Robert Kagan's on foreign policy. Though both originally appeared in *Commentary*, neither was written specifically for the "What to Do About" series. Nevertheless, they both fit the bill so well that it seemed gratuitous to look for anything else on these subjects. Moreover, the responses to Kagan's article, besides being interesting in themselves, give a vivid sense of the range of conservative opinion on the American role in the world today.

in the headier ideological climate generated by the American conflict with Soviet Communism.

The second observation I want to make concerns my use of the term *conservative*. With one or two exceptions, the contributors to this volume have generally been known not as conservatives but as neoconservatives: that is, people "new" to conservatism in the sense that they began their political life somewhere on the Left, either as liberals or as radicals, and were then, in Irving Kristol's famous definition, "mugged by reality." But Kristol, in a less famous definition, added that neoconservatism also amounted to a new brand of conservatism. The older variety, he said, was dedicated to repealing the welfare state, whereas neoconservatism aimed only to keep it within reasonable bounds.

Yet neoconservatives today are no longer new in either of these two senses. By now, the older members of the group have been conservatives for 25 years or more, and there is already a second generation to the manner born. As is clear from this book, moreover, most neoconservatives (the old along with the young) have pretty well given up on the welfare state by which, as they now see it, American society has been mugged just as surely as they once were by reality. They may disagree over how best to phase out this or that feature of the welfare state, but there is no disagreement over the harm it has done and the desirability of working to get rid of it.

Perhaps, then, the time has come to retire the term *neoconservative*. For better or worse it has ceased to evoke a point of view distinctive enough to require its own special name. On the other hand, it is still useful in describing the style of intellectual discourse on such brilliant display throughout this book, and it remains an indispensable part of the story of how conservatism came to assume the dominant position occupied for so long by liberalism in the intellectual and political life of this country.

What to Do About

The Children

WILLIAM J. BENNETT

William J. Bennett served as Secretary of Education under President Reagan and as director of National Drug Control Policy under President Bush. He is now co-director of Empower America and a John M. Olin Fellow at the Heritage Foundation. Among his recent books are *The Book of Virtues* and *The De-valuing of America: The Fight for Our Culture and Our Children*.

At the dawn of the 20th century there was every reason to believe that ours would be (in the title of a best-selling book at the time) "the century of the child." From the early part of the 1900's through the 1950's, despite ups and downs, despite Depression and war, things got better in almost every area touching the welfare of American children: economic security improved, material earnings increased, medicine progressed, family structure was stable, children occupied a valued place in society, and our civic institutions were strong and resilient. In retrospect, it seems as if the midpoint of the century was a high point for the well-being of children.

By the 1960's, however, America began a steep and uninterrupted slide toward what might be called decivilization. Although every stratum of society has been affected, the worst problems have been concentrated within America's inner cities. No age group has remained untouched, but the most punishing blows have been absorbed by children.

In assessing conditions today, it is important to keep perspective: America is *not* in danger of becoming a third-world country; the vast majority of children do not live in sewers of disease and depravity; and most are not violent, sexually promiscuous, or drug-takers. At the same time, however, there is no question that as we approach the end of the last decade of this "American century," the condition of too many of our children is not good. The indicators are well known: low educational achievement, the decline of the two-parent family, moral confusion, and, for a sizable and increasingly large minority, abuse, neglect, and very bleak prospects for the future.

Consider some real-world facts:

- From 1960 to 1991, the rate of homicide deaths among children under the age of 19 more than quadrupled. Among black teenagers, homicide is now by far the leading cause of death.

- Since 1965, the juvenile arrest rate for violent crimes has tripled, and the fastest-growing segment of the criminal population is made up of children.

- Since 1960, the rate at which teenagers take their own lives has more than tripled.

- The rate of births to unmarried teenagers has increased by almost 200 percent in three decades; the number of unmarried teenagers getting pregnant has nearly doubled in the past two decades.

- Today, 30 percent of all births and almost 70 percent of all black births are illegitimate. By the end of the decade, according to the most reliable projections, 40 percent of all American births and 80 percent of all minority births will be out of wedlock.

- During the last 30 years there has been a tripling of the percentage of children living in single-parent families. According to some projections, only 30 percent of white children and only 6 percent of black children born in 1980 will live with both parents through the age of 18.

A useful historical reference point may be 1965, when Daniel P. Moynihan, then an Assistant Secretary of Labor, wrote *The Negro Family: The Case for National Action*. Then, one-quarter of all black children were born out of wedlock; one-half of all black children lived in broken homes at some time before they reached age 18; and 14 percent of black children were on welfare. Moynihan considered this "tangle of pathologies" to be a social catastrophe, and so it was. Today, however, were we to achieve such figures in even one of our major urban centers, we would consider it a stunning accomplishment.

As the figures above demonstrate, these problems are by no means limited to lower-class or minority populations. In addition to everything else, divorce, rampant in all social classes, causes over one million children annually to end up, at least temporarily, in single-parent families. And wherever they live, American children today, especially the teenagers among them, spend relatively minuscule amounts of time with either their fathers or their mothers—or their homework—and vastly greater amounts of time on other things, from crime to television.

A few years ago a special commission of political, medical, educational, and business leaders issued a report on the health of America's teenagers titled *Code Blue*. In the words of this report, "Never before has one generation of American teenagers been less healthy, less cared for, or less prepared for life than their parents were at the same age." According to the sociologist David Popenoe, today's generation of children is the first in our nation's history to be less well off psychologically and socially than its parents.

Nor is the concern limited to the experts. When asked in a recent Family Research Council poll, "Do you think children are generally better off today or worse off than when you were a child?," 60 percent of all Americans—and 77 percent of all black Americans—said children today are "worse off." They are right.

*   *   *

The greatest long-term threat to the well-being of our children is the enfeebled condition—in some sectors of our society, the near-complete collapse—of our character-forming institutions. In a free society, families, schools, and churches have primary responsibility for shaping the moral sensibilities of the young. The influence of these institutions is determinative; when they no longer provide moral instruction or lose their moral authority, there is very little that other auxiliaries—particularly the federal government—can do.

Among those three institutions, the family is preeminent; it is, as Michael Novak of the American Enterprise Institute once famously said, the original and best department of health, education, and welfare. But the family today is an agency in disrepair. Writes David Popenoe:

> This period [the 1960's through the 1990's] has witnessed an unprecedented decline of the family as a social institution. Families have lost functions, social power, and authority over their members. They have grown smaller in size, less stable, and shorter in life span. . . . Moreover, there has been a weakening of child-centeredness in American society and culture. Familism as a cultural value has diminished.

And so, too, has fatherhood. Each night in America, four out of ten children go to sleep without fathers who live in their homes, and upward of 60 percent will spend some major part of their childhood without fathers.

In the past, the typical cause of fatherlessness was divorce; its new face is homes headed by never-married mothers. This is "the most socially consequential family trend of our generation" (in the words of David Blankenhorn of the Institute for American Values), and it has seismic social implications. Moynihan warned 30 years ago that a society which allows a large number of young men to grow up without fathers in their lives asks for and almost always gets chaos. We have come to the point in America where we are asking prisons to do for many young boys what fathers used to do.

★   ★   ★

There are other signs of decay, particularly of the cultural variety. Television shows make a virtue of promiscuity, adultery, homosexuality, and gratuitous acts of violence. Rap music celebrates the abuse and torture of women. Advertisements are increasingly erotic, even perverse. And many of our most successful and critically acclaimed movies celebrate brutality, casual cruelty, and twisted sex.

None of these trends takes place in a moral or cultural vacuum. During the last 30 years we have witnessed a profound shift in public attitudes. The pollster Daniel Yankelovich finds that we Americans now place less value on what we owe others as a matter of moral obligation; less value on sacrifice as a moral good, on social conformity, respectability, and observing the rules; less value on correctness and restraint in matters of physical pleasure and sexuality—and correlatively greater value on things like self-expression, individualism, self-realization, and personal choice.

How does all this affect young children? A single, simple statistic tells much: while in 1951, 51 percent of Americans agreed with the statement, "Parents who don't get along should not stay together for the children," in 1985 that figure had risen to 86 percent.

The social historian Barbara Dafoe Whitehead has observed that the Hallmark company now offers two lines of divorce cards: one set for the newly single adults, the other for children of divorced parents. For the latter, a typical message is piercing in its casualness: "I'm sorry I'm not always there when you need me but I hope you know I'm always just a phone call away." By contrast, one adult card reads, "Think of your former marriage as a record album. It was full of music—both happy and sad. But what's important now is . . . *you*! the recently released *hot new single*! You're going to be at the *top of the charts*!" As Whitehead comments, "What had once been regarded as hostile to children's best interests is now considered essential to adults' happiness."

If the self, in the late Allan Bloom's withering assessment, has become "the modern substitute for the soul," we are also living in an era in which it has become unfashionable to make judgments on a whole range of behaviors and attitudes. This unwillingness to judge has resulted in unilateral moral disarmament, as harmful in the cultural realm as its counterpart is in the military. With the removal of social sanctions in the name of "tolerance" and "open-mindedness," and the devaluing of the idea of personal responsibility, is it any wonder, for instance, that in a recent survey 70 percent of young people between the ages of 18 and 34 said that people who generate a baby out of wedlock should not be subject to moral reproach *of any sort*?

It would be supererogatory at this late date to catalogue the role of government in giving form and force to these ideas and beliefs through law and policy. Suffice it to say that from the area of criminal justice, to education, to welfare policy, to the arts, to a whole tangle of sexual and family issues, government has increasingly put itself on the side of the forces of decomposition, not on the side of the forces of restoration. The consequence is that the moral universe we are sending our children into today is more harsh, more vulgar, more coarse, and more violent than the moral universe most of us grew up in—and they are less equipped to deal with it.

We should not flinch from admitting this unsettling truth: we live in a culture which seems dedicated to the corruption of the young, to assuring the loss of their innocence before their time. "It dawned on me recently," the anthropologist David Murray has written, "that we have now become the kind of society that in the 19th century almost every Christian denomination felt compelled to missionize."

If the problem is one of moral breakdown, it would be fatuous to suggest that it can be fixed by government intervention. There is, after all, one proposition which has been tested repeatedly over the last three decades and just as repeatedly been found wanting— namely, that we can spend our way out of our social problems. Instead of encouraging government, we need to relimit it—not only, or even primarily, for fiscal reasons, but because the "nanny state" has eroded self-reliance and encouraged dependency, crowding out the character-forming institutions and enfeebling us as citizens.

Still, there are a number of actions government *can* take that would amount to constructive and far-reaching, even radical, reforms. A number of these ideas have been on the table for quite some time, but as the results of the November 1994 elections suggest, Americans may be more ready for fundamental reform today than at any other point in recent history. So we suddenly find ourselves presented with an extraordinary opportunity.

Before getting down to particulars, I would stipulate two general points that should guide any discussion of public-policy solutions to the problems faced by children in America. One of them I borrow from an old principle of medicine: *primum non nocere*— first, do no harm. In many, many cases, the best thing government can do is (to quote Myron Magnet of the *City Journal*) "to *stop* doing what makes the problem worse."

As for the second point, it was well expressed by Alexander Hamilton, who in *The Federalist No. 17* questioned whether "all those things . . . which are proper to be provided for by local legislation [should] ever be desirable cares of a general jurisdiction." To state this in terms of our present situation, there are many responsibilities which would be better handled by states and localities but which have fallen under the jurisdiction of the federal government; they should be devolved back to the smaller "laboratories of democracy."

Within those constraints, government, at one level or another, does have a role to play in improving conditions for the young. Let us look at a few key areas, beginning with the link between welfare and illegitimacy.

Between 1962 and 1992, welfare spending in the United States increased by over 900 percent in 1992 dollars. At the same time, the poverty rate dropped by less than 5 percent—and illegitimacy rates increased over 400 percent. Children are the real victims in this national tragedy. They are being conditioned into the same habits of dependence they are surrounded by, resulting in an almost unbreakable cycle of welfare and "the tangle of pathologies" associated with it.

John J. DiIulio, Jr., of Princeton has put this last point well:

The problem *is* that inner-city children are trapped in criminogenic homes, schools, and neighborhoods where high numbers of teenagers and adults are no more likely to nurture, teach, and care

for children than they are to expose them to neglect, abuse, and
violence. . . . Children cannot be socialized by adults who are
themselves unsocialized (or worse), families that exist in name only,
schools that do not educate, and neighborhoods in which violent
and repeat criminals circulate in and out of jail. . . .

Quite a number of serious and thoughtful proposals have been
advanced for restructuring the entire system of welfare benefits, of
which Charles Murray's is among the most thoroughgoing.[1] In a
similar spirit, I would endorse full-scale and far-reaching plans to
send welfare back to the states, which have proved the best settings
for innovative reform and experimentation.

As for the problem of illegitimacy in particular, one year after
legislation is enacted I would recommend ending direct welfare
payments to women who have children out of wedlock; enforcing
existing child-support laws; and terminating the increase in benefits for women who have children while participating in welfare
programs. The success of such reforms, it seems to me, depends
critically on their sweep and magnitude; incremental steps will not
do the necessary job of altering fundamental assumptions and
expectations.

To turn to a point that has been heavily controverted since the
elections of November 8: in my view, situations will arise which
may warrant the removal of a child from the care of his parent(s).
To be sure, this should only happen in desperate circumstances and
as a last resort. But we cannot ignore the plain fact that there are
more and more horrifying cases of abuse, neglect, and parental
malfeasance.

While adoption is the best alternative in such circumstances,
the concept of orphanages, or group-care homes, should not be
dismissed. Such institutions pretty much disappeared from the
national scene when government began distributing money in the
expectation that poor parents, with federal assistance, would do a
better job of raising their children. But in far too many cases that
expectation has been resoundingly refuted by experience.

When parents cannot care for their children's basic material,
psychological, medical, and moral needs, it is time to look to other

---

[1]"What to Do About Welfare," See p. 200.

institutions. The orphanage—call it a boarding school without tuition—may then be in their best interest. Can anyone seriously argue that some boys would be worse off living in Boys Town than in, say, the Cabrini Green housing project in Chicago, considered by its residents a virtual war zone?

But adoption is certainly preferable. Only 50,000 children are adopted each year in the United States; half are healthy infants and half are older children or children with disabilities. At any given time, however, one to two million homes are waiting to adopt. Provided only the child is young enough, there is, in effect, no such thing as an unwanted child, and this goes even for babies who are not fully healthy. Unfortunately, most potential adopters (and adoptees) are hamstrung by needless barriers.

In addition to the high cost of a private adoption, often as much as $10,000, many couples are automatically excluded from consideration due to race, financial background, age, disability, or home size. Other potential adopters are scared away by lax confidentiality laws, nonbinding adoptions, and the expanded rights of the biological father to reclaim legal custody.

The barriers to adoption are only one side of the problem. Availability is also severely limited. Unwed mothers are often denied information about adoption in prenatal counseling; others decide to abort their pregnancy for economic reasons. (Indeed, it may be partly for this reason that abortion has increasingly become a problem of juveniles: of the one million teenage pregnancies each year, about 400,000 now end in abortion.)[2] Finally, and perhaps most importantly, with the stigma of illegitimacy all but gone in this country, for many young, unwed, pregnant women single motherhood has become a more attractive option than giving a child up for adoption.

---

[2]Although abortion *per se* is not one of my subjects in this article, let me register here my belief that 1.5 million abortions a year—of which the overwhelming majority are performed on perfectly healthy women in order to prevent the birth of perfectly healthy children—is a national catastrophe. There is no doubt that such a number must also have a coarsening effect on adults' attitudes toward children and what they need from us.

Again, there is a limit to what government can do. But again, too, the greatest hope lies in reforms at the state level, such as:

- prohibiting the use of race and/or ethnicity as a disqualification for would-be foster or adoptive parents (in practice this has affected whites seeking to adopt nonwhite babies)

- expediting adoption procedures for infants and children who have been abandoned by their parents and are living in limbo in hospitals, group homes, and/or foster care

- terminating parental rights and thus making a child available for adoption if by the age of 6 months—in the case of infants born with positive toxicology—maternal drug use has not ceased, or if a child has been severely abused by its parents

- enacting model legislation that will require courts to consider the best interests of the child first in all cases concerning custody

- establishing uniform rules making voluntary surrender/adoption irrevocable at any point past 72 hours after birth

- restricting payments to biological parents by adoptive parents to necessary expenses related directly to the pregnancy and adoption

- ensuring that adoptive families are treated with the same respect as other families, free of the fear of intrusion by the state or other parties after an adoption has been finalized.

Then there is divorce—which, in terms of damage to children, can be the most devastating circumstance of all, yet which is conspicuous by its absence from the agenda of policy-makers.

As Karl Zinsmeister of the *American Enterprise* has written: "We talk about the drug crisis, the education crisis, and the problems of teen pregnancy and juvenile crime. But all these ills trace back predominantly to one source: broken families."

The statistics, indeed, are chilling. Children of single-parent families are twice as likely to drop out of high school, or, if they remain in school, have lower grade-point averages, lower college aspirations, and poorer attendance records than the general population. Girls living with only one parent are two-and-a-half times more likely to become teenage mothers. When it comes to crime, according to some studies, 70 percent of juveniles now incarcerated in state-reform institutions have lived either in single-parent homes or with someone other than their natural parents, and 75 percent of adolescent murderers come from single-parent homes.

The divorce rate has nearly doubled since 1960—not coincidentally, the same period in which no-fault divorce laws became popular. Previously, before a divorce was granted, the law had required a showing of fault, such as cruelty, abuse, adultery, or desertion. The recision of these conditions not only significantly increased the number of divorces but transformed marriage into a simple business contract.

Though the incidence of divorce cannot significantly be addressed through public policy, its effects can perhaps be curbed to some degree. My suggestions include braking mechanisms when children are involved, such as mandatory and substantial "cooling-off" periods as well as mandatory counseling; reinstituting fault as an absolute requirement for divorce and in determining the terms of a settlement; and classifying all property as family property, which would affect the distribution of assets in cases where children are involved.

This brings us to institutions outside the home, starting with the schools. Parents all over the country are increasingly aware that the public-education system in America is an embarrassment. As the federal government has taken over more responsibilities for the nation's schools, the quality of education has plummeted. The response of the education establishment and of the teachers' unions to this situation, and to the growing movement for greater parental involvement and local control that has arisen in response to it, has been to advocate pumping more money into the system. This has only served to perpetuate and even escalate the problem.

The signs of failure are everywhere, and need not be reiterated here.[3] Fortunately, there are many potentially good solutions—though more money is not among them. Instead, and yet again, a devolution is in order: the first step toward genuine education reform should be to rein in the federal government. In my judgment, legislation is called for which would restore decision-making responsibilities to state and local authorities, enabling the federal government to give states a block grant with virtually no strings attached. The state, local school districts, and parents would then be in a better position to make their own decisions regarding curriculum, books, standards, discipline, etc. Not only would this lead to a system more accountable to parents, but it would encourage innovation and experimentation.

The next step is to implement reforms at the state level which would foster excellence in the education system. These include open enrollment; charter schools; privatization; performance-testing for students and teachers; a merit-pay system for teachers and administrators; and, above all, school choice, complete with vouchers redeemable at public, private, and religious schools. And to prevent a future trend toward regulatory authority, the federal Department of Education should be dismantled. The limited functions of the department should be carried out by the executive branch in an office of education policy.

What about crime? Between 1985 and 1991, the annual rate at which young men aged 15 to 19 were being killed increased by 154 percent, far surpassing the rate of change in any other group. Twenty percent of high-school students now carry a knife, razor, firearm, or other weapon on a regular basis. As James Q. Wilson recently pointed out, "Youngsters are shooting at people at a far higher rate than at any time in recent history."[4] Or, in the words of Senator Bill Bradley, "The murderers are younger, the guns more high-powered, and the acts themselves occur more and more randomly." This problem will almost certainly get worse before it gets

---

[3]Chester E. Finn, Jr., in "What to Do About The Schools" (see p. 100), provides a long list of the appalling details.

[4]"What to Do About Crime," see p. 282.

better, as by the end of the decade there will be a half-million more American males between the ages of 14 and 17 than there are today, 30,000 of whom will probably become high-rate offenders.

The justice system spends $20 billion a year to arrest, rehabilitate, and jail juvenile offenders, only to watch 70 percent of them commit crimes again. Here, too, money is evidently not the panacea. Genuine reform of our juvenile-justice laws, which for the most part should take place on the state level, would involve keeping records of juvenile arrests, fingerprinting offenders, and making these records available to adult courts to prevent juvenile criminals from being treated as first-time offenders when they reach the age of 18. I would also strongly recommend legislation at the state level to allow juveniles, 14 or older, to be charged as adults for certain crimes—such as murder, rape, armed robbery, and assault with a firearm.

Genuine reform would also establish consistent, graduated punishments for every offense. It would insist on building and maintaining the facilities needed to keep violent offenders off the streets. It would speed up the criminal-justice system by enacting and enforcing realistic trial provisions. It would prohibit irresponsible judges from unilaterally imposing measures (such as "prison caps") which release violent and repeat offenders back onto the streets. It would require offenders to pay restitution to their victims. And it would create extended sentences in institutional boot camps for repeat offenders and those who failed to participate in the community-service and public-works programs to which they had been sentenced.

A special subcategory of the overall crime problem is drugs. From the mid-1980's until 1991, significant progress was made on the drug front, with researchers tracking a sharp decline in overall use. But in 1991 use began to rise, and drugs are still a major problem among the young.

According to the latest study from the University of Michigan's Institute for Social Research, one in four students has used illegal drugs before reaching high school; among 8th graders, 13 percent say they have smoked marijuana in the last year, *double* the rate of 1991; and over 40 percent of all 10th graders and nearly 50 percent of all 12th graders have used some illicit drug, including LSD, inhalants, stimulants, barbiturates, and cocaine and crack. This, in the words of the study's principal investigator, Lloyd D. Johnston, is "a problem that is getting worse at a fairly rapid pace," and it is being abetted by a decline in peer disapproval and a general softening of teenagers' attitudes toward drug use.

While the Clinton administration has not formally abandoned the war against drugs, it has abandoned it for all practical purposes. This could have a dire effect on what has already been achieved, incomplete as that is. If we mean to continue our efforts, we will need to do a number of things. They include allowing communities to choose their own antidrug priorities by combining federal antidrug support with that from states and localities; putting the U.S. military in charge of stopping the flow of illegal drugs from abroad, and giving the military control over the entire interdiction process; establishing trade and diplomatic sanctions and eliminating aid to cocaine-source countries that fail to reduce their production of cocaine by 10 percent per year, and by at least 50 percent in 5 years; and requiring the Attorney General first to identify all major drug-trafficking organizations known to be operating in the United States and then to create a plan to dismantle them.

Drawing up laundry lists of public policy may seem a tedious and academic exercise. It is nevertheless an instructive one, if for no other reason than that it glaringly exposes how *little* has been done, on the most commonsensical level, to address the terrible problems that confront us, and that have accumulated in both number and intensity over the past 30 years. In this sense, thinking concretely about specific, practical reforms offers the hope that, by a concerted national effort, we might yet begin to alleviate some of the worst manifestations of these ills, and even, in time, to reverse course.

And yet, to repeat, even if we were to enact each and every one of the desired reforms in each and every area, we would still be a long way from having healed the broken families of America.

Smart, intelligent public policies can and do make a difference. But political solutions are not, ultimately, the answer to problems which are at root moral and spiritual.

"Manners," wrote Edmund Burke two centuries ago,

> are of more importance than laws. Upon them, in a great measure, the laws depend. The law touches us but here and there, and now and then. Manners are what vex or soothe, corrupt or purify, exalt or debase, barbarize or refine us, by a constant, steady, uniform, insensible operation, like that of the air we breathe in. They give their whole form and color to our lives. According to their quality, they aid morals, they supply them, or they totally destroy them.

Can government supply manners and morals if they are wanting? Of course it cannot. What it can supply, through policy and law, is a vivid sense of what we as a society expect of ourselves, what we hold ourselves responsible for, and what we consider ourselves answerable to. There can be little doubt that in this last period of time the message our laws have been sending our young people and their parents has been the profoundly demoralizing one that we expect little, and hold ourselves answerable for still less.

By changing and improving our laws, we might not thereby bring about, but we would certainly *help* to bring about, a climate that would make it easier rather than harder for all of us to grow more civilized; easier rather than harder for us to keep our commitments to one another; easier rather than harder for us to recapture the idea of personal and civic responsibility. This, in turn, would make it easier rather than harder for us to raise our children in safety to adulthood—something which at the moment we are not doing very well at all.

What to Do About

The First Amendment

ROBERT H. BORK

Robert H. Bork, who served from 1982 to 1988 as a federal judge on the court of appeals for the D.C. circuit, is John M. Olin Scholar in Legal Studies at the American Enterprise Institute and the author of *The Tempting of America: The Political Seduction of the Law* and *Antitrust Paradox: A Policy at War With Itself.*

The text of the First Amendment is quite simple: "Congress shall make no law respecting an establishment of religion, or prohibiting the free exercise thereof; or abridging the freedom of speech, or of the press, or the right of the people peaceably to assemble, and to petition the government for a redress of grievances." These are not words that would lead the uninitiated to suspect that the law, both with regard to religion and with regard to speech, could be what the Supreme Court has made of it in the past few decades.

Where religion is concerned, for example, a state may lend parochial schoolchildren geography textbooks that contain maps of the United States but may not lend them maps of the United States for use in geography class; a state may lend parochial schoolchildren textbooks on American colonial history but not a film about George Washington; a state may pay for diagnostic services conducted in a parochial school, but therapeutic services must be provided in a different building.[1]

At this moment, the most prominent issue involving the religion clauses of the First Amendment stems from the decision in *Engel* v. *Vitale* (1962), and subsequent cases, prohibiting prayer, Bible reading, or even a moment of silence in public schools. In addition to declaring that these are all violations of the First Amendment, the Court has held unconstitutional even school practices that are neutral as among different religions on the ground that, under the First Amendment, religion may not be preferred to irreligion. Since the vast majority of Americans are believers, these holdings are fiercely resented by most of them as attempts to impose secularism on their children, and school prayer remains a simmering political issue.

The new Speaker of the House of Representatives, Newt Gingrich, has responded to these concerns by proposing to offer a constitutional amendment to permit the prayer the Court forbids. The current draft of the amendment reads:

> Nothing in this Constitution shall be construed to prohibit individual or group prayer in public schools or other public institutions. No person shall be required by the United States or by any state to participate in prayer. Neither the United States nor any state shall compose the words of any prayer to be said in public schools.

Whatever one may think of the language here and of the idea of an amendment specifically directed to school prayer, left untouched are far more serious judicial deformations of the true constitutional relationship between government and religion. For the Supreme Court has been secularizing not just the public schools but, so far as it is able, our entire culture. We have grown

---

[1]This list comes from then-Associate Justice Rehnquist's dissent in *Wallace* v. *Jaffree* (1985).

so accustomed to this trend that it may come as a shock to realize that it does not reflect the intention underlying the religion clauses.

The First Amendment's establishment clause—"Congress shall make no law respecting an establishment of religion"—clearly precludes recognition of an official church, and it can easily be read to prevent discriminatory aid to one or a few religions. But it hardly requires the conclusion that government may not assist religion in general or sponsor religious symbolism. An established religion is one which the state recognizes as the official religion and which it organizes by law. Typically, citizens are required to support the established church by taxation. The Congress that proposed and the states that ratified the First Amendment knew very well what an establishment of religion was, since six states had various forms of establishment at the time; ironically, one reason for the prohibition was to save these state establishments from federal interference.

The history of the formulation of the clause by Congress[2] demonstrates that it was not intended to ban government recognition of and assistance to religion; nor was it understood to require government neutrality between religion and irreligion. And as we shall see, it most certainly was not intended to erase religious references and symbolism from the actions and statements of government officials.

Had the establishment clause been read as its language and history show it should have been, the place of religion in American life would be very different from what it now is. But in modern times, the Supreme Court has developed a severe aversion to connections between government and religion. Nowhere is that more evident than in the Court's alteration of its fixed rules to allow such connections to be challenged far more easily than other claimed violations of the Constitution.

[2]See Walter Berns, *The First Amendment and the Future of American Democracy;* Robert Cord, *Separation of Church and State;* and C. Antieau, A. Downey, and E. Roberts, *Freedom from Federal Establishment.*

Major philosophical shifts in the law can occur through what may seem to laymen mere tinkerings with technical doctrine. Thus, the judiciary's power to marginalize religion in public life was vastly increased through a change in the law of what lawyers call "standing." Orthodox standing doctrine withholds the power to sue from persons alleging an interest in an issue only in their capacities as citizens or taxpayers. An individualized personal interest, some direct impact upon the plaintiff, such as the loss of money or liberty, is required. But in 1968, in *Flast* v. *Cohen*, the Supreme Court created the rule that taxpayers could sue under the establishment clause to enjoin federal expenditures to aid religious schools.

Though the opinion offered a strained explanation that would fit some suits under other parts of the Constitution, the Court has managed to avoid allowing such suits with still more strained rationales. Every single provision of the Constitution from Article I, Section 1 to the 37th Amendment is immune from taxpayer or citizen enforcement—except one. Only under the establishment clause is an ideological interest in expunging religion sufficient to confer standing.

The unhistorical severity of establishment-clause law was codified in the Supreme Court's opinion in *Lemon* v. *Kurtzman* (1971). To pass muster, the Court held, a law must satisfy three criteria: (1) the statute or practice must have a secular legislative purpose; (2) its principal or primary effect must be one that neither advances nor inhibits religion; and (3) it must not foster an excessive government entanglement with religion.

So few statutes or governmental practices that brush anywhere near religion can pass all of those tests that, were they uniformly applied, they would erase all traces of religion in governmental affairs. But there are too many entrenched traditions around for *Lemon* to be applied consistently. While a case challenging the use of a paid chaplain in Nebraska's legislature was pending in the Supreme Court, the appeals court on which I then sat gathered to hear a challenge by atheists to the practice of paying the chaplains who serve Congress. We and counsel stood while a court officer intoned, "God save the United States and this honorable court," an inauspicious beginning for the plaintiffs since the ritual, followed in the Supreme Court as well, would appear to violate all three prongs of *Lemon*.

Our case was later rendered moot because the Supreme Court approved the Nebraska legislature's chaplain in *Marsh* v. *Chambers* (1983). Justice William Brennan, dissenting, argued that the state's practice could not pass the *Lemon* test since it hardly had a secular purpose, and the process of choosing a "suitable" chaplain who would offer "suitable" prayers involved governmental supervision and hence "entanglement" with religion. The Court majority, however, relied on the fact that employing chaplains to open legislative sessions conformed to historic precedent: not only did the Continental Congress employ a chaplain but so did both houses of the first Congress under the Constitution, which also proposed the First Amendment. In fact, they also provided paid chaplains for the Army and Navy.

Presumably for that reason, Chief Justice Burger, who had written *Lemon*, did not apply it in *Marsh*. And quite right he was. The Court often enough pays little attention to the historic meaning of the provisions of the Constitution, but it would be egregious to hold that those who sent the amendment to the states for ratification intended to prohibit what they had just done themselves.

But if the *Lemon* test should be ignored where there exists historical evidence of the validity of specific practices or laws that could not otherwise pass muster, then it is a fair conclusion that the test itself contradicts the original understanding of the establishment clause and is destroying laws and practices that were not meant to be invalidated.

As matters stand, *Lemon* makes it difficult for government to give even the most harmless or beneficial forms of assistance to religious institutions. New York City, for example, implemented a program, subsidized with federal funds, under which public-school teachers could volunteer to teach in private schools, including religious schools. The program offered instruction to educationally deprived children in remedial reading, mathematics, and English as a second language. The teachers were accountable only to the public-school system, used teaching materials selected and screened for religious content by city employees, and taught in rooms free of religious symbols. The teachers were generally not members of the religious faith espoused by the schools to which they were assigned. There was no evidence that any teacher complained of interference by private-school officials or sought to teach or promote religion.

The court of appeals said this was "a program that apparently has done so much good and little, if any, detectable harm." Nevertheless, constrained by *Lemon*, that same court held the program an impermissible entanglement, because the city, in order to be certain that the teachers did not inculcate religion, had to engage in some form of continuing surveillance. The Supreme Court, in *Aguilar* v. *Felton* (1985), affirmed on the same ground. The educationally deprived children were then required to leave the school premises and receive remedial instruction in trailers.

To cite another example, the Satmar Hasidim, who observe a strict form of Orthodox Judaism, organized the village of Kiryas Joel in Orange County, New York, where only members of the sect lived. Children were educated in private religious schools which did not offer any special services to the handicapped. The handicapped pupils were thus forced to attend public schools outside the village. But their parents soon withdrew them because of "the panic, fear, and trauma" the children suffered in leaving their own community and being with people whose ways were so different and who taunted them. The New York State legislature then enacted a statute making Kiryas Joel a separate school district which ran only a secular special-education program for handicapped children; the other children of Kiryas Joel remained in the private religious schools. When the separate school district was, predictably, challenged, the trial court held that the statute violated all three criteria of *Lemon*. Dividing six to three, the Supreme Court affirmed in *Board of Education of Kiryas Joel* v. *Grumet* (1994), though the various opinions articulated different rationales.

Those parts of Justice David Souter's opinion in which a majority of the Court joined found an establishment-clause violation because the unusual nature of the statute gave "reason for concern whether the benefit received by the Satmar community is one that the legislature will provide equally to other religious (and nonreligious) groups" and because the statute delegated political power to a religious group. Justice Stevens, joined by Justices Blackmun and Ginsburg, concurred with the remarkable statement that in protecting the handicapped students from "panic, fear, and trauma," "the state provided official support to cement the attachment of young adherents to a particular faith."[3]

This was only one of many decisions detecting the "establishment of religion" in the most innocuous practices. A lower court held that it was unconstitutional for a high-school football team to pray before a game that nobody be injured. Another court held that a Baltimore ordinance forbidding the sale of nonkosher foods as kosher amounted to the establishment of religion. A federal court decided that a school principal was required by the establishment clause to prevent a teacher from reading the Bible silently for his own purposes during a silent reading period because students, who were not shown to know what the teacher was reading, might, if they found out, be influenced by his choice of reading material.

The list of such decisions is almost endless, and very few receive Supreme Court review, not that that would be likely to change things. After all, the Supreme Court itself decided in *Stone v. Graham* (1980) that a public school could not display the Ten Commandments. (The school authorities were so intimidated by the current atmosphere that they attached a plaque stating that the display was intended to show our cultural heritage and not to make a religious statement; no matter, it had to come down. It also did not matter that the courtroom in which the case was heard was decorated with a painting of Moses and the Ten Commandments.)

So, too, in *Lee v. Weisman*, decided in 1992, a five-Justice majority held that a short, bland, nonsectarian prayer at a public-school commencement amounted to an establishment of religion.

---

[3]For a more detailed account, see "The Curious Case of Kiryas Joel," by Jeremy Rabkin, *Commentary*, November 1994.

The majority saw government interference with religion in the fact that the school principal asked a rabbi to offer a nonsectarian prayer. Government coercion of Deborah Weisman was detected in the possibility that she might feel "peer pressure" to stand or to maintain respectful silence during the prayer. (She would, of course, have had no case had the speaker advocated Communism or genocide.) Thus was ended a longstanding tradition of prayer at school-graduation ceremonies.

The law became a parody of itself in *Lynch* v. *Donnelly*, a 1984 decision concerning Pawtucket, Rhode Island's, inclusion of a crèche in its annual Christmas display. The Court held that the display passed muster, but only because, along with the crèche, it also included such secular features as

> a Santa Claus house, reindeer pulling Santa's sleigh, candy-striped poles, a Christmas tree, carolers, cut-out figures representing such characters as a clown, an elephant, and a teddy bear, hundreds of colored lights, and a large banner that reads "*Season's Greetings.*"

The display of a menorah on a public building has been subjected to a similar analysis. In other words, the question to be litigated nowadays is whether there is a sufficient number of secular symbols surrounding a religious symbol to drain the latter of its meaning.

Modern establishment-clause jurisprudence is often justified by reference to the views of Jefferson and Madison, but the truth is that their opinions on this subject were idiosyncratic among the Founders. Jefferson's often-quoted phrase about the "wall of separation" between church and state appears in a letter he wrote to the Danbury Baptist Association, and most historians agree that he was not expressing the views of those who enacted the Bill of Rights. As for Madison, the constitutional scholar Walter Berns points out:

> It is sufficient to recall that as President he vetoed a bill to grant a charter of incorporation to the Episcopal Church in Washington,

D.C. [a routine practice at the time], and opposed the appointment of chaplains in the Army and Navy and the granting of tax exemptions to "Houses of Worship"; he even objected to presidential proclamations of days of thanksgiving. . . . The extent to which others did not share all his views is reflected in the fact that he found it necessary to yield to the pressure and issue such a proclamation.

In short, Jefferson and Madison held radical and unrepresentative positions on what constituted the establishment of religion. By following their opinions, the Supreme Court has mutilated the establishment clause as it was understood by those who made it law.

Indeed, no rigid separation of religion and government such as *Lemon* prescribes is even conceivable. For governments regularly and inevitably take actions that do not have a secular purpose, whose principal effect is to advance religion, and which entangle them with religion.

Aside from the examples already given, there are property-tax exemptions for places of worship, which do not have a secular purpose and do advance religion. Government, in the form of boards, courts, and legislatures, determines what qualifies as religion in order to award draft exemptions for conscientious objectors, aid to schools, and the like. In order to see that education is properly conducted, states must inspect and demand certain levels of performance in religious schools. Federal employees receive paid time off for Christmas, and the National Gallery preserves and displays religious paintings.

In short, our actual practices cannot be made consistent with the complete separation of religion and government.

There may be some who are dubious about the claim that the judiciary's rulings are hostile or damaging to the place of religion in society. To them, I recommend Justice Potter Stewart's dissent in *Abington School District* v. *Schempp*, a 1963 decision in which the majority struck down rules that required Bible reading without discussion at the beginning of each school day. Said Stewart:

[A] compulsory state educational system so structures a child's life that if religious exercises are held to be an impermissible activity in schools, religion is placed at an artificial and state-created disadvantage. Viewed in this light, permission of such exercises for those who want them is necessary if the schools are truly to be neutral in the matter of religion. And a refusal to permit religious exercises thus is seen, not as the realization of state neutrality, but rather as the establishment of the religion of secularism, or at the least, as government support of the beliefs of those who think that religious exercises should be conducted only in private.

Similar conclusions could be drawn concerning the effects of decisions erasing religious speech and symbolism from our public life and denying nondiscriminatory aid to religious institutions. Nathan Lewin, who argued the case for the village of Kiryas Joel, wrote, justly I think:

> The *Kiryas Joel* decision proved once more that a majority of the Justices of the Supreme Court—like most judges of lower courts in the United States—are either hostile to religion or do not understand what religious observance is all about.

The case is very different with the speech and press clauses of the First Amendment.[4] Since this part of the amendment has less legislative history than the religion clauses, its plausible meaning must be deduced from other materials. But we can dispose at once of the notion that because the First Amendment states that "Congress shall make no law ... abridging the freedom of speech," it imposes an absolute bar to any regulation of speech. Nobody supposes that, not even judges who announce "absolute" positions. There are well-recognized exceptions of time, place, and manner: Congress, for example, can have a person prosecuted for haranguing its members from the visitors' gallery, and it has been held constitutional, under a congressionally enacted code of military conduct, to imprison an officer for inciting troops to disobedience.

[4]The law of the press clause is quite similar to that of the speech clause, so in the interest of brevity I will deal only with the speech clause here.

Still, the existence of the amendment implies that there is something special about speech, something that sets it apart from other human activities that are not accorded constitutional protection. Justice Brandeis tried to specify what that something was in his impassioned concurrence in *Whitney v. California* (1927). He wrote, though more colorfully, that the benefits of speech are: (1) the development of the faculties of the individual; (2) the happiness to be derived from engaging in the activity; (3) the provision of a safety valve for society; and (4) the discovery and spread of political truth.

The list is not entirely satisfactory. The first two benefits do not distinguish speech from a myriad of other unprotected activities that develop human faculties or contribute to happiness. The safety-valve function suggests that prudence requires letting people blow off steam so they do not engage in actions that threaten stable government, yet prudence to preserve stable government is necessary in many ways, none of them important enough to be mentioned in the Constitution.

The "discovery and spread of political truth," however, does set speech apart from other human activities. Only speech can deal explicitly, specifically, and directly with politics and government. In a previous writing, I too casually accepted Brandeis's qualification of the truth to be discovered and spread as "political," and I therefore mistakenly arrived at the proposition that only explicitly political speech should be protected by the speech clause.

Of course, political speech does have a special claim to protection: a representative democracy would be nonsense without it. But there is both a practical and a theoretical objection to limiting protection to explicitly political speech. The practical objection is that other forms of speech could find protection if the speaker added the admonition that we pass a law on the subject, whatever it was. The theoretical objection is that speech is both valuable and unique, whatever kind of truth it seeks to discover and spread. There is thus reason to conclude that the protection offered by the speech clause extends to many other types of speech that express ideas.

On the other hand, the modern Court has gone wrong, in my estimation, by accepting as a major part of the speech clause's rationale the desire of the individual to find happiness through self-expression. This is, as noted, inconsistent with the fact that many other forms of happiness-seeking are not protected. The idea that speech is the preferred form of happiness-seeking is merely an intellectual-class bias. There is no ground in constitutional law or philosophy for supposing that the fulfillment obtained through, say, dealing in financial markets is inferior to the fulfillment sought in writing a novel.

Acting on the basis of the self-expression rationale, the Court decided that a young man could not be punished for wearing into a courthouse a jacket with words on the back urging, with a four-letter verb, that an implausible sexual act be performed on the selective-service system. "One man's vulgarity," the Court opined, "is another's lyric."

The same rationale also led directly to the Court's decision in *Texas* v. *Johnson* (1989) that the clause protects not merely what it addresses, "speech," but actions that express moods and attitudes, such as burning the American flag. The burner could have expressed his hatred for America in as many and as eloquent words as he could muster and have been protected by the true core of the speech clause. But his lawyer said that burning the flag was important because its offensiveness drew attention in ways that mere words would not. We must await the Court's reaction when somebody, on the same theory, decides to protest the laws relating to sex by engaging in indecent exposure.

More recently, the Court wrestled with the question of whether Indiana's general ban on public nudity could be applied to naked dancing in the Kitty Kat Lounge. The answer, in *Barnes* v. *Glen Theatre, Inc.* (1991), was that it could, but the astonishing fact was that eight Justices thought a First Amendment question was presented because nude dancing "expresses" eroticism and sexuality. The ninth, Justice Scalia, thought the First Amendment was not implicated, but only because the statute was of general application and not aimed at dancing in the altogether.

In general, pornography and obscenity can hardly be thought to lie at the center of the First Amendment, but efforts by communities to limit their spread have been frustrated repeatedly by appeal to the speech clause.

To be sure, in 1973, by a vote of five to four in *Miller* v. *California*, the Court seemed to allow some minimal control of pornography. It stipulated that three things had to be determined before pornography could be banned or its purveyors punished:

> (a) whether the "average person, applying contemporary community standards" would find that the work, taken as a whole, appeals to the prurient interest . . . , (b) whether the work depicts or describes, in a patently offensive way, sexual conduct specifically defined by the applicable state law, and (c) whether the work, taken as a whole, lacks serious literary, artistic, political, or scientific value.

Yet when Cincinnati prosecuted a museum for displaying Robert Mapplethorpe's photographs of one naked man urinating in the mouth of another and of himself naked with the butt of a bullwhip in his rectum, expert witnesses proclaimed that the pictures had serious artistic merit, and the jury acquitted. It is hard to imagine that the Supreme Court would have found fault with this verdict. In any event, *Miller* has done little to help communities that have been searching for some way to control the torrent of pornography that earlier decisions loosed upon them.

With regard to speech advocating violence and the violation of law, the Court has been no more helpful. This failure largely reflects the great influence of the famous dissents of Justices Holmes and Brandeis. The crux of their position was that such advocacy could not be punished unless there were shown a clear and present danger of success or imminent, serious harm. There is some doubt even about the provisos, for Holmes could bring himself to write, in *Gitlow* v. *New York* (1925), and Brandeis joined him, that,

> If in the long run the beliefs expressed in proletarian dictatorship are destined to be accepted by the dominant forces of the community, the only meaning of free speech is that they should be given their chance and have their way.

This, in a case where the defendant proposed violent action by a minority in order to impose a dictatorship. But why were the "dominant forces of the community" who wrote the law imprisoning Gitlow not permitted to have their way? How could Justices who 6 years earlier in *Abrams* v. *United States* voted to protect speech because thought should be tested in the "competition of the market" vote now to protect speech calling for violence to abolish the market? Berns sums up the matter neatly: "The only meaning of free speech turns out to mean that it is worse to suppress the advocacy of Stalinism or Hitlerism than to be ruled by Stalin or Hitler. The reasons for this are not, one might say, readily apparent."

The Holmes-Brandeis mood (it was hardly more than that) culminated in 1969 in *Brandenburg* v. *Ohio*, where the Court announced that

> the constitutional guarantees of free speech and press do not permit a state to forbid or proscribe advocacy of the use of force or law violation except where such advocacy is directed to inciting or producing imminent lawless action and is likely to incite or produce such action.

If we take seriously Brandeis's observation that speech assists the discovery and spread of political truth, however, it should be obvious that advocacy of force or the violation of law has no value. Such speech does not aim to convince a majority of a truth. Rather, it advocates violence or lawlessness to overturn the republican form of government which the Constitution embodies and guarantees to the states or to cancel the laws which legislative majorities have enacted.

The late constitutional scholar Alexander M. Bickel, a staunch friend of the First Amendment, questioned the worth of the Holmes-Brandeis market metaphor:

> If in the long run the belief, let us say, in genocide is destined to be accepted by the dominant forces of the community, the only meaning of free speech is that it should be given its chance and have its way. Do we believe that? Do we accept it?

Bickel went on to ask

> whether the best test of the idea of proletarian dictatorship, or seg-
> regation, or genocide is really the marketplace, whether our expe-
> rience has not taught us that even such ideas can get themselves
> accepted there.

The Brandeisian response would be that the cure for evil
speech is good speech; yet to engage in debate about such ideas is
to legitimate them, to say that they have their place in public discourse. As Bickel wrote, "Where nothing is unspeakable, nothing is
undoable."

Bickel implicitly raised a difficult question. The advocacy of
genocide, to use his example, would fall within the category of
political speech, the core of the speech clause. It is preposterous,
nevertheless, to suppose that those who wrote and ratified the
First Amendment wanted every conceivable idea, no matter how
vicious, to be proposed for a vote. The problem for judges is to
draw a line between the ideas Bickel mentions and silly regulations, such as campus speech codes, that try to outlaw offensiveness. The courts have carved out exceptions to the protection even
of political speech. Developments in an increasingly fragmented
and angry society may force judges to rethink the legacy of
Holmes and Brandeis.

Those who take the position that speech advocating violence,
law violation, and forcible overthrow should be constitutionally
protected often attribute their views to the Founders. But the fact
is that the Founders held no such position. Jefferson and his follow-
ers took literally the amendment's statement that Congress should
make no law, but they did so not on civil-libertarian grounds but
out of a devotion to the sovereignty of the states. Even in the fierce
debates that swirled around the Alien and Sedition Acts, the Jeffer-
sonians' opposition to federal power was accompanied by the assertion that the states already had such laws. The Founders were clear
that government had the right to punish seditious speech; they disagreed only about which government had the power to do it.

★   ★   ★

The tendencies of the Supreme Court's unhistorical applications of the First Amendment are fairly clear. The late social critic Christopher Lasch asked what accounted for our "wholesale defection from standards of personal conduct—civility, industry, self-restraint—that were once considered indispensable to democracy." He concluded that though there were a great number of influences, "the gradual decay of religion would stand somewhere near the head of the list." Despite widespread religious belief,

> Public life is thoroughly secularized. The separation of church and state, nowadays interpreted as prohibiting any public recognition of religion at all, is more deeply entrenched in America than anywhere else. Religion has been relegated to the sidelines of public debate.

As religious speech is circumscribed in the name of the First Amendment, however, the Court—in the name of that same amendment—strikes down laws by which communities attempt to require some civility, some restraint, some decency in public expression. The Ten Commandments are banned from the schoolroom, but pornographic videos are permitted. Or, as someone has quipped about the notorious sculpture by Andres Serrano, a crucifix may not be exhibited—unless it is dipped in urine, in which case it will be awarded a grant by the National Endowment for the Arts.

The result of all this is an increasingly vulgar and offensive moral and aesthetic environment, and, surely, since what is sayable is doable, an increasingly less moral, less happy, and more dangerous society.

The Supreme Court should therefore revisit and revise its First Amendment jurisprudence to conform to the original understanding of those who framed and enacted it. Religious speech and symbolism should be permissible on public property. Nondiscriminatory assistance to religious institutions should not be questioned. Communities, if they so desire, should be permitted to prefer religion to irreligion. There is no justification whatever for placing handicaps on religion that the establishment clause does not authorize.

*   *   *

As for the speech clause, it should be read to apply to *speech*, not to nonverbal expression, and it should protect the dissemination of ideas, not the individual's desire for self-gratification. Would this allow for greater regulation of obscenity and pornography? Probably, though there will always be a professor around, and a judge or jury to believe him, that the purest pornography has redeeming artistic merit (just as, it must be admitted, there is always the chance that genuinely meritorious works will be banned). Perhaps, too, the flood of pornography has already changed community standards and habituated us to an environment that would once have seemed unacceptable. Perhaps it is too late, perhaps there is no way back. But the Court ought not to prevent communities from trying to find one.

Finally, the wholesale protection of the advocacy of violence and law violation—a judicial construct not grounded in history—should be rescinded. The effects of incitements to violence will often be unknowable; nor need they be imminent to be dangerous. If, for example, speakers incite racial hatred and advocate violence against another race, as happens all too often nowadays, those utterances may well lead to actual violence, but it will be impossible to prove a direct connection to the speeches.

The rule of *Brandenburg* also contemplates judging the effect of each particular speech. Yet even though no individual speech may have the effect of producing violence, cumulatively such speeches may have enormous influence. Whether or not it is prudent to ban all such advocacy is a different question, one that should be addressed by legislatures and prosecutors rather than courts. There is no good reason to put advocacy of violence and law violation in the marketplace of ideas.

How much chance is there that the Court will undertake such sweeping reforms? Not, it would seem, a great deal. The Court, particularly when it deals with the Constitution, and more particularly when it deals with the First Amendment, is as much a cultural and political institution as it is a legal one. It has always responded to dominant class values, and in our day that means the cultural elite: academics, clergy, entertainers, journalists, foundation staffs, bureaucrats, and the like. These folk tend to be hostile or indifferent toward religion and to sanctify the autonomous individual as against the community—precisely the attitudes underlying contemporary First Amendment jurisprudence.

That having been said, it must also be recognized that there have been strong dissents to the modern decisions, particularly to the decisions deforming the religion clauses. It is entirely possible, therefore, that we may at least expect piecemeal improvements, especially given the more conservative climate that was reflected in the 1994 elections.

What to Do About

Immigration

LINDA CHAVEZ

Linda Chavez is president of the Center for Equal Opportunity, a Washington, D.C., think tank, and author of *Out of the Barrio* (Basic Books, 1991).

Despite overwhelming opposition from the media, from leaders of the religious and civil-rights communities, from the education establishment, and even from prominent conservatives like Jack Kemp and William J. Bennett, California voters last fall enthusiastically adopted Proposition 187, which bars illegal aliens from receiving welfare, education, or health benefits except for emergency medical treatment.

The anger toward illegal immigrants had grown steadily among Californians in recent years, fueled both by the huge number of illegal aliens living in the state—nearly two million, or about half of the country's entire illegal population—and by the state's lingering economic recession. And the resentment had deepened as the apparent costs of providing benefits to illegal aliens rose; for the fiscal year 1994–95, that figure is estimated to stand at $2.35 billion. California, moreover, had gone far beyond what was required by federal law in granting benefits to illegal aliens, including in-state tuition in the Cal-State University system and free prenatal care.

As if all this were not tinder enough, in mid-October 70,000 mostly Latin demonstrators marched through downtown Los Angeles waving Mexican and Guatemalan flags and shouting *Viva la Raza*. Tracking polls, which had shown Proposition 187 ahead by only 5 points just prior to the demonstration, registered a four-fold jump in the three days immediately following.

Proposition 187's success has inspired activists in several other states to consider similar measures, but their plans may be derailed if the law is declared unconstitutional. (A federal court has enjoined California from enforcing Proposition 187, pending the outcome of a suit.) Nonetheless, the proposal's popularity has launched a long-overdue national debate on immigration—legal as well as illegal.

Like so much American social policy, immigration policy is a monument to the law of unintended consequences. Although assurances to the contrary were offered by the legislators responsible for the last major overhaul of the nation's immigration law, the 1965 Immigration and Nationality Act, that law profoundly altered both the makeup and the size of the immigrant flow. Until 1965, most immigrants came from Europe; today, some 80 percent of those legally admitted are from Asia or Latin America. The new law also significantly increased the pool of eligible applicants by giving preference to family members of immigrants already here.

But these changes might not have had such striking effects had they not coincided with dramatic developments in civil-rights law and with the expansion of the welfare state. As it is, immigration now intersects with two of the most troubling issues of our time: race and entitlements.

In 1994 (the last year for which figures are available), over 800,000 legal immigrants were admitted to the United States and an estimated 300,000 illegal aliens settled here, more or less permanently. Over the last decade, as many as ten million legal and illegal immigrants established permanent residence—a number

higher than at any period in our history, including the peak immigration decade of 1900–10.

To be sure, these numbers are somewhat misleading: because
our population is so much larger now than it was at the beginning
of the century, the rate of immigration is much lower, barely one-
third of what it was then. And while the proportion of persons living in the United States who are foreign born is high by recent
standards—about 8 percent in the last census—it is still lower than
it was for every decade between 1850 and 1950.

The numbers alone, however, do not fully describe the dimensions of the immigration issue. Americans are not just concerned
about the size of the immigrant population; they are worried
about the kind of people who are coming, how they got here, and
whether they are likely to become a benefit or a burden to our
society. There is deep suspicion that today's immigrants are fundamentally different from earlier waves. In recent polls, 59 percent of
Americans say that immigration was good for the country in the
past, but only 29 percent think it is a good thing now. Former
Colorado Governor Richard Lamm, who favors restricting immigration, summed up this national ambivalence: "I know that earlier
large waves of immigrants didn't 'overturn' America, but there are . . .
reasons to believe that today's migration is different from earlier
flows."

Immigration enthusiasts (among whom I count myself, albeit
with some important reservations) like to point out that Americans have never been eager to accept new arrivals, for all our
rhetoric about being an "immigrant nation." As Rita Simon of the
American University Law School noted recently, "We view immigrants with rose-colored glasses, turned backward." Perhaps, then,
there is nothing much new in the worries so many people express
about whether this generation of immigrants will indeed assimilate to American norms. But comforting as the thought may be
that today's Mexicans, Vietnamese, Pakistanis, and Filipinos are the
equivalent of yesterday's Italians, Jews, Poles, and Irish, it fails to
take into account the tremendous transformation America itself
has undergone in the last half-century.

*   *   *

The America to which Europeans immigrated—first northern Europeans in the 19th century and then southern and eastern Europeans in the first quarter of the 20th—was a self-confident, culturally homogeneous nation. There was never any question that immigrants would be expected to learn English and to conform to the laws, customs, and traditions of their new country (although even then, some immigration restrictionists questioned whether certain groups were capable of such conformity). And immigrants themselves—especially their children—eagerly wanted to adapt. Public schools taught newcomers not only a new language, but new dress, manners, history, myths, and even hygiene to transform them into Americans who sounded, looked, acted, thought, and smelled the part.

In those days there were no advocates insisting that America must accommodate itself to the immigrants; the burden of change rested solely with the new arrivals. To be sure, by their sheer numbers they managed subtly to alter certain features of their new country. Because of them, the United States is less Protestant than it would otherwise have been; no doubt American cuisine and art are richer; and the pantheon of American heroes from Christopher Columbus to Joe DiMaggio to Albert Einstein is more diverse. Still, until fairly recently, Americans—native-stock or of later lineage—understood what it meant to be American, and it meant roughly the same thing regardless of where one's ancestors came from.

We are far less sure what it means to be American today. Thus the question "What to do about immigration?" is inextricably wound up with how we define our national identity.

Some critics of immigration—most notably John O'Sullivan, the editor of *National Review,* and Peter Brimelow, author of *Alien Nation*—believe that national identity must be defined in explicitly racial and ethnic terms and that the current high levels of non-white immigration will drastically alter that identity. O'Sullivan argues:

A nation is an ethno-cultural unit—a body that begins its life as a cultural in-gathering but, by dint of common history, habits, tastes, shared experiences, tales, songs, memories, and, above all, intermar-

riage, becomes progressively more like an extended family—that is,
more ethnic—over time.

As long as America's core remained overwhelmingly WASP, so
this argument goes, it was possible for Italian Catholics or Russian Jews or Japanese Buddhists to become American. Both
O'Sullivan and Brimelow fear, however, that the large numbers of
nonwhites who are now coming in will undermine the assimilative
capacity of the nation; they both cite Census Bureau projections
that the majority of the U.S. population will become nonwhite
(or more accurately, non-Hispanic white) by the year 2050; and
they both blame current immigration policy for this portentous
outcome.

But is race or ethnicity really the issue? If so, O'Sullivan and
Brimelow can relax. Yes, the majority of immigrants admitted to
the United States in the last 20 years have been relatively dark-
skinned Mexicans, Filipinos, Vietnamese, Chinese, Koreans, etc. Yet
by the year 2050, their great grandchildren are unlikely to look
much like them. Intermarriage rates in the United States have
never been higher; nor have mixed-race births. The Population
Reference Bureau (PRB) recently touted this development in its
monthly newsletter in a front-page article, "Interracial Baby
Boomlet in Progress?" Births to mixed Japanese/white couples
now exceed those to all-Japanese couples. There are now so many
ethnically mixed persons in the United States that the Census
Bureau is debating whether to create a special classification for
them. (Perhaps it should consider calling the category "American.") Not even groups with strong traditions or religious prohibitions against intermarriage seem exempt from the trend. About
half of all American Jews, for example, marry non-Jews.

Nor is the inclination to intermarry diminishing among more
recent immigrant groups. One-third of young, U.S.-born Hispanics marry non-Hispanics; and perhaps more significantly, nearly
half of all Hispanics consider themselves white. Peter Brimelow
dismisses this phenomenon, noting that those of Mexican origin,
who make up nearly two-thirds of the entire group, are predominantly Indian. But he misses the point. By defining themselves as
white, Hispanics are identifying with the majority. In a recent sur-

vey, a majority of Hispanics said the group with which they felt they had most in common was whites, and so did Asians.

In short, the problem of national identity is not primarily connected with heredity or ethnicity. It is, rather, a function of culture. But on this score, the evidence is decidedly less reassuring.

From the White House to Madison Avenue to Main Street, the idea has taken hold that the United States is a multicultural society. Many doubt that such a thing as American culture even exists. When I recently told a university audience that American blacks, Hispanics, Asians, and whites have more in common with one another than they do with their contemporaries in any of their ancestral homelands, the students literally gasped in disbelief. "I don't know what you mean by 'American culture,'" one young Puerto Rican woman told me. "I have a right to my own culture and language." She said this, however, in perfect English, leaving me wondering just what culture and language she might be referring to.

But if the irony of her situation escaped this particular student—whose coloring and features suggested predominantly Spanish ancestry—her political statement was clear. A European-looking, English-speaking Hispanic who chooses to reject American culture, she represents the flip side of the large number of brown-skinned Hispanics who see themselves as white. It is hard to know how many such persons there are, but their numbers are surely growing as ethnicity becomes increasingly politicized.

Into this confusing mix come immigrants who, unlike these *ersatz* ethnics, truly are culturally different from those around them. And such are the misgivings of the rest of us that we no longer seem able or willing to help these newcomers become Americans. Public schools, which worked to acculturate previous immigrant groups, now see it as their mission to preserve immigrant languages and culture. The Los Angeles school system, which educates more Latino immigrant children than any in the nation, prides itself on teaching these youngsters primarily in Spanish for three years or more. Denver public-school officials recently ordered one local high school to stop teaching 450 Hispanic youngsters in English, and transferred out 51 Asian students so that the school could concentrate on its Spanish bilingual program. The demand for Spanish-speaking teachers is so great that districts from Los Angeles to Chicago have begun importing instructors from Mexico, Spain, and Puerto Rico; in 1993, Mexico signed an agreement with California to provide both teachers and 40,000 textbooks for the state's Spanish-language classrooms.

Yet bilingual education did not originally grow out of the pressures of immigration. It started as a small, federally funded program to help Mexican-American children (largely native born) in the Southwest, and it was already in place years before the large influx of Spanish-speaking immigrants in the 1970's and 1980's. Its chief sponsor, former Senator Ralph Yarborough (D-Tex), declared that the purpose of his bilingual-education bill was not "to create pockets of different languages throughout the country . . . but just to try to make [Mexican-American] children fully literate in English." By 1975, however, civil-rights enforcement agencies in Washington were insisting (on the basis of a Supreme Court ruling involving the Civil Rights Act of 1964) that school districts teach "language-minority" youngsters, mostly Mexican-Americans and Puerto Ricans, in Spanish or face a cutoff of all federal funds.

In the early stages of the program, the overwhelming majority of students in bilingual classes were U.S.-born; today, nearly 60 percent still are. What is more, many of these children are more fluent in English than Spanish—no one knows exactly how many, because most states use an arbitrary cutoff score (usually the 30th or 40th percentile) on a standardized English test to place Hispanic youngsters in Spanish-language programs, rather than testing to see whether they are more fluent in English or in Spanish.

Bilingual voting ballots, which are now mandated by the federal government, were also an outgrowth not of immigration but of civil-rights legislation—in this case, the 1975 Amendments to the Voting Rights Act of 1965—and they too were aimed at a U.S.-born population: namely, Mexican-Americans living in the Southwest. The main impetus behind the amendments was to give Washington the same power to oversee federal elections in areas where Hispanics lived as the original Act gave it over the Deep South, where egregious efforts were being made to prevent blacks from voting.

Since few Spanish-speaking immigrants naturalize and since few can therefore vote, the 1975 Amendments have had little effect on them. But thanks to additional amendments adopted in 1982, and a series of court decisions, the Voting Rights Act is now used mainly to create districts which pack in as many Hispanics (or blacks) as feasible in order to assure the election of minority candidates. This practice has received widespread publicity because of the often bizarrely gerrymandered districts that result, but what is less well-known is that immigrants—including illegal aliens—often make up the majority of persons entitled to representation in these new Hispanic districts.

So far, at least, the Act has not been invoked to create safe districts for Asians, although in principle they qualify under the same "language-minority" designation as Hispanics. The law already requires federal ballots to be printed in Chinese, Vietnamese, and Korean, among other languages; and the huge increase in the Asian immigrant population in California probably means that the courts will before long use their presence to justify the need for safe seats for Asians. Since Asians are too widely dispersed for simple ethnic gerrymandering to suffice, we may expect the courts to order new remedies such as cumulative voting. This technique, which allows voters to cast multiple ballots for a single candidate in a multi-member, at-large race, would, for example, enable Asians comprising only 14 percent of the electorate in a given city to elect one representative on a six-member city council even if no whites voted for the Asian candidate.

The manipulation of both the Bilingual Education Act and the Voting Rights Act points to a central problem of our present immigration policy: the current confluence of ethnic-based entitlements and the large influx of newcomers eligible to receive them creates an ever-growing demand for such programs.

One solution, favored by those who want to restrict immigration for other reasons, is to cut off the flow of immigrants. Yet while this might diminish the clientele for ethnic entitlements, the programs would continue to serve the native-born populations for whom they were originally created. For it is not immigrants who clamor for these programs. Asian immigrants, for one, have largely eschewed bilingual education in favor of English-immersion programs. Even some Latino immigrant parents have staged protests in California, New York, and New Jersey upon discovering that their children were being taught in Spanish; others simply withdraw their children, sending them to parochial schools that teach all students in English.

The other solution to the problem of ethnic entitlements, of course, would be simply to end them for everyone. There are many good reasons for doing this, even if immigration were to cease altogether. Race- and ethnic-based entitlements have been a bane of American social policy for the last quarter-century. They have divided Americans, increased group hostility, and perverted the whole notion of color-blind justice. Furthermore, they are the foundation on which the entire edifice of multiculturalism is built. Without the enticement of racial and ethnic preferences in education, employment, voting, and elsewhere, group identity, instead of intensifying in recent years, might have diminished.

Multicultural education has become the main instrument to help preserve group identity. But multicultural education is no more a byproduct of increased Latin and Asian immigration than are bilingual education and ballots, ethnic voting districts, and affirmative action. In fact, multicultural education first came into being largely to address the demands of blacks for proportional representation in the curriculum—though by now it has spread (some would say, metastasized) to the point where all students are encouraged to think of themselves primarily as members of groups rather than as Americans.

Thus, when California recently adopted a new textbook series for kindergarten through 8th grade, ethnic protesters turned out at school-board hearings in San Francisco, Los Angeles, San Diego, Oakland, and other cities, insisting upon changes not only in the treatment of blacks but also in the way the series dealt with Indians, Hispanics, Jews, Muslims, and even conservative Christians.

Critics of immigration like O'Sullivan and Brimelow believe

that multiculturalism would, in O'Sullivan's words, "be easier to dismantle if immigration were reduced." But the California story suggests that, if anything, it is ethnic diversity itself that might actually hasten the demise of multiculturalism. Like a house of cards that has grown too unwieldy, multicultural education may collapse of its own weight if it is required to include the distinct stories of each of the hundreds of different groups now in the schools.

But the unraveling of multicultural education, salutary a prospect as it may be, is hardly a good reason for maintaining our current immigration policy. Clearly, that policy needs changing in ways that are consistent with our national interests and values. I would argue, indeed, that our immigration policy should *reinforce* our national identity—which is not necessarily the same thing as our racial or ethnic composition.

What, then, should we do? Let me deal with legal immigration first.

• *Change the system to one that favors skills.* The basis of the current system is the principle of family reunification, adopted in 1965 with the expectation that this would maintain the ethnic balance of the U.S. population as it existed at the time. Of course things have not worked out that way. But questions of ethnic balance aside, there is nothing sacrosanct about family reunification as a guiding principle of immigration policy, and we should not be deterred from changing it out of fear that such a move might be interpreted as racist.

In any case, the problem with the current immigrant pool is not that there are too many Latinos and Asians *per se*, but that too many of the people we now admit are low-skilled. Mexicans come with only about seven years of schooling on average, and less than a quarter have obtained high-school diplomas. Such newcomers face a much more difficult period of adjustment and bring fewer benefits to the U.S. economy than would more highly skilled immigrants.

It is true that under current criteria, which include only

140,000 slots for skills-based admissions, immigrants are twice as likely to hold Ph.D.s as are U.S.-born persons. But they are also more likely to be high-school dropouts. We ought to admit more of the former and fewer of the latter, and regardless of their country of origin. As it turns out, immigrants from Africa and Asia have among the highest average levels of education. Nearly 90 percent of all African immigrants are high-school graduates—a figure 15 percent higher than that for Canadian immigrants. And Indians, Taiwanese, and Iranians have among the highest proportions of college or graduate degrees.

• *Encourage immigrants to assimilate.* Immigration policy entails more than laws regulating who gets admitted and under what criteria. It also involves—or at least should involve—how we incorporate immigrants into our society. On that score, we are doing much more poorly now than we did in the past, in part because we have given up on the notion that we have an obligation to assimilate immigrants. Regardless of what other changes we make in immigration policy, we must reverse course on this issue. If immigration to the United States ceased tomorrow, we would still have twenty million foreign-born persons living here, plus their children. Assimilation is essential for them, as well as for the rest for us, if we are to stop the further fragmenting of our society.

First and foremost, this means encouraging immigrants and their children to learn English, which in practical terms means abolishing bilingual education in favor of English-immersion programs in the public schools. By now we have nearly 30 years of experience demonstrating that bilingual education helps children neither to learn English nor to do better in school. Latino immigrants in particular have been badly served by bilingual education—and by their putative leaders, usually U.S.-born, who are the main lobby behind this expensive, ineffective, and wasteful program.

But bilingual education is not the only culprit. With so many services available in their native language, immigrants have fewer incentives today to learn English than they did in the past. Private services—native-language newspapers, advertising, etc.—fall outside the scope of public policy. But *government* services ought to be provided only in English. A common language has been critical to

our success in forging a sense of national identity. Our public policies should preserve and protect that heritage. If the courts continue to obstruct local and state efforts to make English the official
language of government, we should pass a federal constitutional
amendment to ensure it.

• *Limit welfare benefits.* Although immigrants as a whole are
somewhat more likely than natives to receive welfare, the opposite
is true of those of working age (15 to 64). In addition, immigrants
have higher labor-force-participation rates than natives, with Hispanic men having among the highest—83.4 percent compared
with 75 percent for non-Hispanic whites. If we modify our admission criteria to favor more highly skilled immigrants, welfare
among working-age immigrants should drop below even the current rate of about 3 percent, alleviating much of the concern
about immigrants and welfare.

The problem is high dependency rates among refugees and
elderly immigrants. Among the former, this is a direct result of
U.S. policy, which guarantees cash and medical assistance to all
persons admitted under the refugee-resettlement program. Having
been admitted, they are then attracted to states with relatively high
benefits, and this tends to encourage long-term dependency. Thus,
in California, some two-thirds of Laotian and Cambodian refugees
and more than one-third of Vietnamese refugees remain on welfare after more than five years in the United States.

While dealing comprehensively with this situation entails the
much larger issue of welfare reform, it is possible to make a dent
in it by redesigning programs to limit the number of months
refugees can receive assistance. One of the most promising possibilities would be to turn over responsibility for such assistance to
private agencies, such as Catholic Charities, Lutheran Immigration
and Refugee Service, and the Council of Jewish Federations,
which have proved more successful at moving refugees off welfare.
In Chicago, 74 percent of refugees in an experimental private
resettlement project found work within six months of arrival, and
only 2 percent remained on welfare after thirteen months, compared with more than 40 percent in the state-administered program.

The problem of elderly immigrants is more complicated. In

1990, 55 percent of elderly Chinese immigrants in California who had arrived between 1980 and 1987 were on welfare, as were 21 percent of elderly Mexican immigrants. Because they have worked too few years or at insufficient wages to qualify for adequate Social Security benefits, most such recipients obtain Supplemental Security Income (SSI).

But many of these immigrants are the parents of resident aliens who brought them here under family-reunification provisions. Anyone who sponsors an immigrant must guarantee that he will not become a public burden, and is required to accept full financial responsibility for up to five years. Simply enforcing these provisions would greatly alleviate the problem of welfare dependency among elderly immigrants. (Among recipients in California that should not pose a problem, since 50 percent of their children's households in 1990 had incomes over $50,000, and 11 percent over $100,000.) We might also consider lengthening the number of years sponsors are required to provide support to family members; Canada currently requires a ten-year commitment.

All these reforms are addressed to the policies governing legal immigration. What about illegal immigration?

Like welfare dependency among immigrants, illegal immigration is not so big a problem as many people imagine (in one recent poll, two-thirds said they thought most immigrants are illegal aliens). Estimates of overall numbers vary widely, with some commentators hysterically claiming more than ten million illegal aliens. But the more reliable Census Bureau estimates about four million, with (as noted earlier) another 300,000 or so added each year.

In theory, no amount of illegal immigration is acceptable, since the phenomenon represents our failure to maintain secure borders, a prerequisite of national sovereignty. In practice, however, it is unlikely that we will ever completely eradicate illegal immigration: our borders are too long and porous and our society too free and prosperous. But there are steps we can take that would significantly reduce the current flow.

• *Stop illegal aliens at the border.* There is no mainstream support for mass roundups and deportations of the type used in the

1930's and 1950's to roust illegal aliens; nor could such a program withstand legal challenge. Therefore, the only way to reduce the flow is to contain it at the border. The frontier between Mexico and the United States is 2,000 miles long, but only about 250 miles of it are traversable. Most illegal aliens enter in a handful of places near metropolitan areas—about 65 percent around San Diego and El Paso.

We know that it is possible to reduce the flow significantly with more Immigration and Naturalization Service (INS) personnel and better equipment and technology. A recent two-month, $25-million experiment in beefed-up border control near San Diego halved the number of illegal crossings; similar experiments in El Paso produced comparable results. While the most determined may seek alternative routes of entry, for the large majority rough terrain will limit the opportunity.

• *Deport alien criminals.* Apprehending and deporting illegal aliens who have successfully gotten past the border requires more resources and more draconian enforcement measures than most Americans would be willing to endorse; but there is overwhelming support for deporting those arrested for criminal acts in the United States. In order to do this, however, local law-enforcement officials must be able to ascertain the status of persons in their custody, which they cannot now do easily. A pilot program in Phoenix, which allows police officers 24-hour access to INS records, might prove an effective model for enhancing local police efforts and making more deportations feasible.

• *Outlaw sanctuaries.* Several cities, including San Francisco, Sacramento, and Chicago, have enacted ordinances banning city employees from contacting the INS if they know someone is in the country illegally. These ordinances are an outrage and show utter disregard for the rule of law. Any city that chooses to obstruct immigration enforcement should lose all federal funds.

• *Deny welfare benefits to illegal aliens.* This is what California voters thought they were enacting with Proposition 187. In fact, in most states illegal aliens are already prohibited from receiving welfare and any but emergency medical treatment, but the authorities lack adequate means to verify the legal status of recipients.

Consequently, a pilot program instituted in the early 1980's, the Alien Status Verification Index, should be expanded and upgraded with access to on-line INS data bases so that the status of welfare recipients can be checked.

A potentially more intractable problem is that U.S.-born children of illegal aliens are eligible, as citizens, for Aid to Families with Dependent Children (AFDC) and other welfare benefits. Indeed, one out of four new AFDC recipients in California is a child of illegal-alien parents. The only way to prevent them from receiving benefits is to deny them citizenship in the first place, which would probably require a constitutional amendment. I would not suggest that we travel this route, at least not until we have exhausted all other means of keeping illegal aliens out. But neither should we consider the mere discussion of the issue taboo, as it is in most public-policy circles today. Especially now, when U.S. citizenship entails many more rights and benefits than responsibilities, it should not be beyond the pale to reconsider what entitles a person to obtain it.

• *Repeal employer sanctions.* While we are looking at ways to prevent illegal immigration, we ought to acknowledge that the linchpin of our current policy—punishing the employers of illegal aliens—has been a miserable failure. The Immigration Reform and Control Act of 1986, which established such sanctions, did virtually nothing to reduce the flow into the country. If anything, it probably contributed to the problem of welfare dependency among the four million illegal aliens already here, by making it more difficult for them to support themselves.

In typical fashion, those who falsely promised that employer sanctions would fix the illegal-alien problem now think they can tinker with the existing provisions to make it work. Senator Alan Simpson proposes a national identity card; the U.S. Commission on Immigration Reform thinks a national computerized work registry will do the trick.

But the purpose of both would be to enable employers to become better policemen for the immigration system, when they should never have been put in that position in the first place. Nor should the rest of us have to put up with more regulations and infringements on our privacy. It is simply wrong to burden the

98.5 percent of persons who are legally in the country with cumbersome and probably ineffective new requirements in order to try to punish the 1.5 percent of persons who have no right to be here.

These recommendations probably will not satisfy the most ardent foes of immigration, like the Federation for American Immigration Reform (FAIR), the most influential restrictionist organization now operating. But many restrictionists are confused or just plain wrong about the nature of the immigration problem.

FAIR, for example, focuses almost exclusively on two issues: the size of current immigration, and its economic consequences. But neither of these is the heart of the matter.

FAIR's roots are in the population-control and environmentalist movements: this explains its preoccupation with numbers. Its founder, John Tanton, is a past president of Zero Population Growth and chairman of the National Sierra Club Population Committee. FAIR's two most prominent demographer-gurus are Garrett Hardin and Leon Bouvier, both of whom have been actively involved with population-control groups. Their primary concern is that immigrants—no matter where they are from or what their social and economic characteristics—add to the size of the population. (Bouvier has actually said that he believes the ideal U.S. population would be 150 million persons, though he has not clearly spelled out what he would do with the other 100 million of us who are already here.)

It is true that immigrants account for about half of current population growth in the United States. Nonetheless, U.S. population growth as a whole is relatively modest, at 1 percent per year. Even with immigrants, including the more fecund Latins, we are in no danger of a Malthusian population explosion.

FAIR's other chief concern, the economic impact of immigration, probably has more resonance in the general debate; but here, too, confusion reigns. For years economists have discussed the consequences of immigration—legal and illegal—without coming to a definitive consensus. On one side are those like Julian Simon of the University of Maryland, who argue that immigration is a big plus for the economy, actually improving the standard of living of the native born. At the other end of the spectrum are those like Donald Huddle of Rice University, the author of an influential 1993 study for the Carrying Capacity Network, a population-control group in Washington. Huddle estimates that immigrants (legal and illegal) cost more than $42.5 billion a year in net public assistance and displace more than two million American workers, incurring $12 billion a year in additional public-assistance costs for those displaced.

Huddle's figures have been widely disputed, including most recently in a General Accounting Office study. Even George Borjas of the University of California, San Diego, easily the most influential academic critic of current policy, estimates that immigration brings economic benefits to the United States in the range of $6 to $20 billion annually—small, but still a net positive gain. More importantly, Borjas acknowledges that these benefits could be increased significantly if we changed our policy to attract more skilled immigrants.

No economic model, however, can adequately capture the more subtle benefits that Americans have clearly derived from immigration, and not just from the flows that brought many of our grandparents and great-grandparents here. As Francis Fukuyama[1] and others have argued, most immigrants still seem to personify the very traits we think of as typically American: optimism, ambition, perseverance—the qualities that have made this country great. The ranks of successful immigrant entrepreneurs are legion; in Silicon Valley alone, recent immigrants have built many of the major technology companies, including Sun Microsystems, AST, and Borland International.

Immigrants have also transformed urban America over the last decade, from Korean grocers in New York to Salvadoran busboys and janitors in Washington, Mexican babysitters and construction workers in Los Angeles, Cambodian doughnut-shop owners in Long Beach, Haitian cooks in Miami, Russian taxi drivers in Philadelphia, and Filipino nurses and Indian doctors in public hos-

[1]"Immigrants and Family Values," *Commentary*, May 1993.

pitals practically everywhere. As they always have done, immigrants still take the difficult, often dirty, low-paying, thankless jobs that other Americans shun. When they open their own businesses, these are frequently located in blighted, crime-ridden neighborhoods long since abandoned by American enterprise. And their children often outperform those who have been here for generations. This year, as in the last several, more than one-third of the finalists in the Westinghouse high-school science competition bore names like Chen, Yu, Dasgupta, Khazanov, Bunyavanich, and Hattangadi.

The contrast between the immigrant poor and the American underclass is especially striking. As the sociologist William Julius Wilson and others have observed, Mexican immigrants in Chicago, despite their relative poverty and much lower levels of education, show few of the dysfunctional characteristics of unemployment, crime, welfare dependency, and drug use common among the city's black and Puerto Rican underclass. In cities like Los Angeles and Washington, where American blacks and Latino immigrants inhabit the same poor neighborhoods, the despair of the former seems all the more intense by contrast to the striving of the latter—as if one group had given up on America even as the other was proving the continued existence of opportunity.

For all our anxiety about immigrants, then, in the end it is Americans of all classes who are caught in the middle of a national identity crisis. It is still possible to turn immigrants into what St. John de Crèvecoeur called "a new race of men," provided the rest of us still want to do this. But if we, the affluent no less than the poor among us, cease to believe that being an American has any worth or meaning, we should not blame immigrants, most of whom entertain no such doubts.

What to Do About

National Defense

Eliot A. Cohen

Eliot A. Cohen is professor of strategic studies at Johns Hopkins University's Paul H. Nitze School of Advanced International Studies and the author (with John Gooch) of *Military
Misfortunes: The Anatomy of Failure in War*, as well as numerous
articles on national-security affairs. From 1991 to 1993 he
directed a Defense Department study of the role of aviation
in the war with Iraq; for the resulting five-volume *Gulf War
Air Power Survey* he received the Air Force's highest civilian
decoration.

Old Ideas

Great struggles leave their marks on the institutions that wage them.

The ambience of the cold war saturated every element of our
defense establishment, including the intellectual establishment that
grew up around it. Our ways of thinking, our assumptions about
the world, our views of statecraft and of the American role in the
world—all bore, and still bear, the imprint of the duel with Communism. American defense planners have found it far easier to
scrap some of the hardware of the cold war than the software, the
intellectual algorithms for thinking about defense.

When a staff officer prepares a briefing justifying a defense budget
with carefully constructed scenarios of Iraq invading Saudi Arabia,
he does so using a frame of reference shaped by the cold war, even if
the Russians no longer figure as the enemy. When administration
representatives discuss the need to "contain" regional opponents,

they think in categories concocted by George Kennan and Paul Nitze at the dawn of the contest between East and West. When defense contractors offer studies to the Defense Department on "deterrence after the cold war," they unwittingly perpetuate concepts of American strategy that have decreasing relevance to the real troubles of the new age. It will be many years before self-conscious examination of the intellectual legacy of the cold war, and the smack of reality contradicting it, breed new ways of thinking.

One of the least fortunate aspects of all this has been an oversimplification of our own strategic history. When American strategists in the late 1980's and early 1990's first set out to consider a new posture for the post-cold-war period, they were haunted by the specter of a rapid and ruinously complete demobilization of U.S. forces. This, they said, was a peculiarly American temptation.

Thus, Richard Cheney, Secretary of Defense during the Bush administration: ". . . historically we've always gotten it wrong. We've never done it right. You can't find a time in this century when we've been through one of these cycles where we did, in fact, take the force down in an intelligent fashion." In making this assertion, Cheney was merely echoing the anxieties of other American military writers who have discerned repeated "cycles" in America's strategic posture from extreme underpreparedness, to a belated rush to arms in the face of emergency, and back again.

In fact, however, the essential American story is far more complex than this. From the time of colonial settlement, to the Founding, and throughout the 19th and early 20th centuries, our strategic record was far better than is commonly supposed, and certainly superior to that of most of the European states with which we had to contend. Moreover, even in the 20th century the so-called "cycle" disintegrates on closer inspection. In the immediate aftermath of World War I, for instance, the United States returned to adequately equipped regular services, with a considerably larger establishment than that of 1914, and a Navy on the edge of parity with that of Great Britain. America's serious inter-war military troubles began only in the late 1920's and early 1930's, when the Great Depression struck.

★   ★   ★

In more recent times, American military thinkers have found themselves transfixed not only by the theory of "cycles" but by four particular uses of force: three failures, and one success. The failures are Vietnam, Lebanon, and Somalia; the success is the Persian Gulf war. Many officers (and not a few civilians) read into these cumulative experiences the following half-truths or, in some cases, falsehoods: wars can be won easily if civilian authorities will set clear objectives and then get out of the way; the press is invariably hostile to the military, and should, where possible, be excluded or manipulated by it; the American people lack the stomach for casualties, and will only support war if it is conducted with the utmost speed.

Careful reflection reveals a far more complicated set of truths. The military in Vietnam had much more discretion (particularly in the South) than is usually acknowledged. When the use of force is likely to have political repercussions (i.e., always), some measure of civilian control is entirely appropriate. The press is no more hostile to the military, at least initially, than it is to any other institution of government or private enterprise; it is, in any event, an inescapable feature of modern life. And the sensitivity over casualties shown in the Gulf war stemmed far more from military officers (for a variety of reasons) than from the public, whose sons and daughters had no fear of conscription to induce in their parents a moderating aversion to bloodshed.

The cold war put an even greater premium on apodictic statements than is the norm in politics. The first task in rethinking American strategy after the cold war, then, is to develop a healthy mistrust of the shibboleths and folk wisdom of the American national-security debate. To revise our strategy in accordance with our needs will require not merely an attempt to limn our future, but a careful and, insofar as is possible, dispassionate examination of our past. This requires no small effort; most American policy analysts and decision-makers have little interest in serious study of our history, and too few military historians think they have much to contribute to an understanding of our present and future.

The Strategic Environment

For many people today, the world is a dismal place; the atrocities of war in cities from Bihac to Aden and from Sukumi to Kigali remind us of that. The trends in other parts of the world—where Japan anxiously eyes a Korean peninsula soon to be kitted out with nuclear weapons, or ethnic Russians think of secession from an economically moribund Ukraine—are not terribly encouraging. But from a purely *American* point of view, the world is, and for some length of time promises to be, a more secure place than it was during the cold war. For now, Americans have the luxury, as peoples very rarely do in their history, to rethink their fundamental national-security policy.

The new strategic environment has three dominant characteristics: international disorder; a revolution in military affairs; and a crisis of demotic culture. Let us consider each in turn.

That the cold war imposed an order on international politics and provided a strategic rationale for American behavior is a truism. It also imposed a global logic on American defense policy: the essential decisions, in such a world, were decisions *not* to engage the Soviet Union or its clients. Although American leaders distinguished between areas of greater and lesser importance to the United States, they often did so on the basis of cost and benefit, rather than intrinsic interest.

After the cold war, American interests have become altogether hazier; they have also in some measure contracted. To take only two cases: during the contest with the Soviet Union, Somalia and Yugoslavia had some importance as *points d'appui* for military power. The United States could not be indifferent to what happened in those countries, because of repercussions for the balance of power in their respective regions. Although the immediate *military* consequences of a shift of either of those countries from one camp to the other would have been small, the geopolitical and certainly the psychological effects would not.

Today, the situation is different. The United States has no immediate strategic interest in either country. Its prestige does not ride on the outcome of clan warfare in Mogadishu or Sarajevo, at least as long as Washington refrains from making foolish pronouncements about what it will do in either place. Our interest in the resolution of these civil conflicts is firstly humanitarian and only secondarily, and in the long term, strategic. (The long-term consequences of the Yugoslav civil war could prove exceptionally ugly in the Balkans more generally, but that should properly concern inhabitants of Berlin, Paris, and Rome far more than residents of Atlanta, St. Louis, and Los Angeles.)

The stumblings of the Clinton administration conceal a far deeper problem in the conduct of American foreign policy than the failures of a particularly inept group of politicians. The calls often heard at home and abroad for a foreign-policy "vision," along the lines of containment in the cold war, miss the point. It is highly unlikely that anyone can or will respond. The contrast between the situation now and that of 45 years ago reflects not only the superiority of the statesmen then (a fact, to be sure); it reflects the ambiguity of a world that faces challenges far more complex, if for the moment less ominous, than those of 1945–50.

The geopolitical challenge to American policy in those years was simple: the emergence of Soviet power and its expansion in Europe. The economics of that confrontation were also fairly straightforward: the American economy accounted for a staggering 50 percent of global production, and the European countries had most of the human resources necessary to rebuild their economies. Even so, it required several direct challenges, including Communist coups, for American statesmen to devise the responses—containment, the Marshall Plan, and the rearmament prompted by National Security Council Memorandum Number 68 and the Korean war—that the times demanded.

Today the geopolitical problems before us are far more diffuse, and the remedies far less obvious. There is, and can be, no global scheme for American foreign policy, save for the vague objective of promoting an open international trading and communications order. American statesmen have no dragons to slay, or even to tame; partners may be competitors, but no state poses a direct challenge to our security or that of our allies. Moreover, in this new world our economy, although thriving, commands barely a quarter of the world's gross product, a portion likely to shrink as growth continues to spread in Asia.

So much for the new element of international disorder. A second broad development is what defense thinkers call the "revolution in military affairs." We are in the early stages of a transformation of warfare which, like changes in the economy more generally, will be driven by the new technologies of information.

Until quite recently—say, the 1970's—military technology essentially resembled that of World War II, albeit vastly improved and upgraded. The advent of the microchip and various advanced materials (e.g., for the construction of stealth aircraft) now promises a far more radical change in the conduct of war.

Thus, armed forces in advanced states can deploy unparalleled capabilities to see and track opponents, and to deliver precise conventional fire. The Global Positioning System (GPS) satellites, for example, put accurate navigation within the grasp of human beings almost anywhere on the planet. Satellites, unmanned aerial vehicles, and remote acoustic, infrared, and other sensors have transformed the gathering of intelligence.

Above all, the networking of military organizations by electronic communications will radically alter their efficacy, even as it creates new opportunities for warfare by electronic means as varied as electromagnetic pulse weapons (which disable electronic devices by brute force) and computer worms or viruses (which do the same by stealth).

Conventional warfare in the 21st century may look very different from warfare today. It may be preceded by periods of covert warfare involving electronic sabotage. Fighting may consist of barrages of accurate long-range cruise and ballistic missiles, while mobile forces such as ships or tanks may find themselves caught in webs of "intelligent" minefields that can detect their presence in a half-dozen different ways. Rather than fighting as individual platforms, ships and planes will increasingly fight as networks, and what constitutes the high ground in such contests will be an advantage in information as much as in terrain. Attacks on command posts and on the other side's "eyes" will be accompanied by efforts to hide through the use of camouflage and deception.

The revolution in military affairs will have a number of effects. It will enable new competitors with the United States to amass certain kinds of military power relatively quickly. For example, until recently satellite pictures that could discriminate among objects one meter long were the stuff of supersecret national organizations. Today, they are on the verge of becoming routinely available commercial products from American and overseas space vendors. Again, in the Gulf war only the United States had, in any quantity, receivers that could allow precise geolocation using the GPS. Such receivers are already widely available commercially, and within a few years will fit comfortably in a shirt pocket.

Furthermore, the end of the cold war has meant that the vast pool of scientific talent and military technology in the former Soviet bloc has become available for export around the world. And as some countries, particularly in Asia, have become wealthier, they have acquired a taste for the latest in military hardware. In the 1960's, the Northrop Corporation could enrich itself by selling the reliable but relatively low-technology F–5 fighter to America's allies. Today, countries like Malaysia will buy only the latest in American military technology.

These developments do not necessarily undermine the American military edge. The American defense budget still towers over all others. At some $244 billion a year, it is roughly 7 times that of any major European country and about 6 times that of Japan. Minor troublemakers like Iran and Iraq do not spend 5 percent of what the United States spends on military power. In addition, during the cold war the United States amassed a vast capital stock which retains enormous value. Our constellation of intelligence-gathering systems in outer space and on earth, massive platforms like aircraft carriers and ships, and a technological establishment of astounding sophistication is unparalleled anywhere. Finally, only the United States has the know-how and logistical assets (including such mundane items as transport and refueling aircraft) to conduct large-scale and global operations.

In this respect in particular, analogies with the late 1940's are erroneous; the American lead in military technology is far more extensive today than it was 50 years ago. Advances in civilian technology may eventually subvert that lead, but whether that will occur depends very largely on decisions to be made over the next decade.

Strategists rarely discuss the cultural dimensions of strategy, but these are in fact a third conditioning force in the strategic environment. For the willingness to use military power and the capacity to amass it depend heavily on a country's culture.

During the cold war, strategic planners could take pretty much for granted the willingness of Americans to engage in world politics, and to contend with the Soviet Union for global hegemony. Even when Americans were not willing, in John F. Kennedy's words, to pay *any* price, or to bear *any* burden, they certainly accepted a military burden unprecedented in our peacetime history. This included assigning between 4 and 10 percent of our gross national product to defense (the historical norm had been closer to 1 or 2 percent); peacetime conscription; the creation of a vast military establishment, including a large standing army; and acceptance of various real and potential infringements on civil liberties. These last included a hedge of laws to protect secrets and the creation of large agencies of government with the ability to spy on Americans overseas and, to a lesser extent, at home as well.

The price was surely worth it, but a price it was. True, Americans have shown no particular eagerness to shed these burdens and structures completely; it may be one of the lesser surprises of the end of the cold war that Americans have become accustomed to world power, and have no intention of giving it up. But it is equally true that Americans will look on global responsibilities with a colder eye, particularly if exertions of military power seem to be efforts on behalf of allies too miserly or timid to fend for themselves.

At the same time, it has become apparent that the United States, and perhaps the West more broadly, are undergoing a crisis of cultural self-confidence similar to those of the 1930's and the 1960's.[1] The dimensions of this crisis are difficult to sketch, but they surely include the rise of criminality in most Western societies, the erosion of traditional means of socialization (family, church), and a perceptible decay in popular culture. The replacement of fare like *The Andy Griffith Show* by *Beavis and Butthead* is a telling symbol of a deeper and more distressing trend. One quanti-

---

[1] For evidence, one need only look at the spate of articles in *Foreign Affairs* (September/October 1993) triggered by Samuel P. Huntington's "The Clash of Civilizations," Summer 1993.

tative indicator is the rise of illegitimacy which (in the United States, at any rate) also translates into a rise of one-parent families. In 1970, births to unmarried women in the United States were 11 percent of all births; today, they are 28 percent.

These cultural trends affect national security in various ways. Among other things, they have induced American leaders to turn inward in the attempt to cope with a society that has lost much of its self-confidence. The election campaign of 1992, the first since 1936 which did not feature foreign affairs as a prominent issue, was an important sign of this change.

To be sure, the significance of the change has so far not penetrated a foreign-policy establishment that continues to hold earnest seminars on American policy vis-à-vis countries 10,000 miles away while ten blocks away thugs have driven all but the pluckiest, most foolhardy, or heavily armed citizens from the street. Indeed, the contrast between the formidable military power of the United States and its violent and disorderly cities suggests the hubris of an ambitious effort to police the world.

In the future, then, we can expect the American public to look askance at foreign adventures that aim to do for others what we have not yet done for ourselves. We can also expect politicians to learn from the experience of George Bush: no amount of success overseas will compensate for failure to solve problems at home.

The diseases afflicting American civilization have not escaped the notice of other nations. Americans tend to discount the cultural hostility of foreign intellectuals and politicians as mere window-dressing. In particular, many American intellectuals shrug off religious belief as a passing obstacle to the development of secular, humanistic, and libertarian societies. Living as we do in the oldest constitutional democracy on the planet, we often assume that American ways—our package of individual liberties and a legalistic political system—must inevitably spread to all countries. These American assumptions will probably fail in the next century. They not only attract the anger of fundamentalist groups in the Islamic world; they have also begun to elicit hostile reactions from other societies, including the far more successful states of Asia.

Conceivably, we may have passed the high-water mark of the spread of American culture around the world, as the United States finds itself increasingly at odds with countries resentful of our attempts to impose a world order that to them looks far from benign or attractive.

Indeed, in what may be the greatest strategic revolution of all, two concepts that the United States itself applied to the Soviet Union—deterrence and containment—may be applied to it. Other countries (plus substate and transnational actors) may seek not to contend with the United States for global hegemony, but to keep it out of their spheres of interest and influence. In such struggles, even modest amounts of force, if wielded dexterously and with determination, can thwart the objectives of a morose and troubled American giant.

Missions

In a "Bottom-Up Review," published early in its term, the Clinton administration described the forces it believed the country would require. Based on a cold-war-style analysis, it called for ten Army and three Marine divisions, twelve aircraft carriers, and thirteen active Air Force wings. Civilians occasionally sneer at generals for preparing to fight the last war; here, the analysts played the generals' part, albeit with an elaborate theoretical superstructure.

The chief premise of the Bottom-Up Review was that the conflicts for which the United States should prepare itself would be reruns of the Gulf war of 1991. This proposition, dubious enough for the next five to ten years, becomes absurd if one looks further ahead. And in any case, the projected budget will simply not allow an armed force of that size, or at least one that could be adequately paid, trained, and consistently modernized.

The Pentagon has confessed that over the next five years it will fall $40 billion short of the force called for in the Bottom-Up Review; the Government Accounting Office, probably closer to reality, makes the gap out to be $150 billion. The 1.4-million-strong force envisioned in the Bottom-Up Review, then, will not survive. In the next ten to fifteen years, the armed forces will shrink to perhaps a million men and women, about 40 percent that of the cold war.

Adjusting to the new size means giving up old structures and

radically changing ways of conducting business. Some of the services are deeply reluctant to do so. The Marine Corps, for example, is clinging to a force level of over 170,000 men and women—
a third the size of the Army—the maintenance of which will blot
out funds for the sorely needed modernization of the Marines'
equipment.

Not only will the U.S. military be smaller than at any time
since 1940; it will have to change in other ways as well. In particular, it will have to reduce its reliance on permanent forward
deployment of combat units, a policy that was sustainable in an era
of a two-million-man force but that will impose insuperable
strains on a force half that size. And a smaller military will have to
concede that some missions are simply too big for it to handle
alone. Indeed, one of the chief strategic choices that the United
States faces is that between unilateral and multilateral capabilities.

American defense policy *should* emerge from answers to the
question, What kind of world does the United States wish to
mold? But it is more likely to emerge from answers to easier questions: What calamities does the United States wish to avert? and,
What goals are worth even a modest fight?

From such considerations, four "missions" emerge:

First, the United States will have to think hard about *defense
proper*. Since World War II, American strategists have regarded
defense with only episodic interest. After a vigorous effort in the
area of continental air defense in the 1950's and the attempted
development of ballistic-missile defenses in the 1960's, this strategic option lapsed into a state of somnolence. The Reagan administration's Strategic Defense Initiative never attracted wide support,
and came under severe criticism for the stress it would place on
the 1972 Anti-Ballistic Missile treaty with the Soviet Union.

Defense in the narrow sense, however, is a long and honorable
American strategic tradition. Three waves of fortification—one
from the Federalist period through the War of 1812 and its immediate aftermath, another in the 1840's, and a third in the 1880's—
provided the United States with admirable protection for its ports.
In the early 20th century, much of American military planning
focused on the protection of installations such as the Panama
Canal.

During the cold war, the balance of American strategic think-ing and military action shifted decisively to the offense, and for good reason: nuclear weapons seemed an overwhelmingly offen-sive military tool, and political considerations mandated a forward strategy in Europe, Asia, and the Middle East. But that has now changed somewhat. The proliferation of long-range ballistic (and, later, cruise) missiles will make it increasingly possible for even small and relatively weak powers to strike at the United States. The technologies of low-level warfare—everything from car bombs to computer-hacking—make it easier to cross the oceanic distances that to this day insulate the United States from many traditional security concerns. The bombing of the World Trade Center in New York in 1993 was, most likely, a sign of things to come.

Large segments of the American military will resist conversion to essentially defensive roles. For one thing, the dominant combat-arms organizations have grown up as forward-deployed, expedi-tionary forces; this is their definition of what soldiering is. For another, many defensive missions are intrinsically more compli-cated and less promising than offensive ones; it is easier to build and operate a long-range missile than to defend against it, easier to launch long-raid special operations than to prevent them (and more fun as well).

A second broad mission of the armed forces will be that of *insurance*. The United States today faces no imminent threats, except for the serious but nonetheless contained prospects of war in the Korean peninsula and renewed Iraqi adventurism in the Persian Gulf. But it does face a world of tremendous uncertainty.

Defense planners have attempted to bound such uncertainty by suggesting standards like those contained in the Bottom-Up Review, which calls for the United States to prepare to fight two nearly simultaneous "major regional contingencies." Of course, subsequent examination has showed that American forces would have logistical difficulty enough in sustaining one contingency, and that two would exceed our capabilities. But even if the artificial standards of the Bottom-Up Review did represent achievable tar-gets, this is the wrong way of thinking about our requirements.

The essence of insurance is the preservation of certain *competencies*, upon which future forces could be built should they be needed.

To begin with, the United States may, at some juncture, need to deploy substantial land forces overseas, as it did during the Gulf war. In the short term, this is not too likely: following a resolution of the division of the Korean peninsula, it will become less likely still. In general, it should be the task of local allies to defend themselves on the ground, while the United States supplies various kinds of support from air, sea, and space. In a pinch, the United States might provide the high-technology core of a ground expeditionary force, and the technology and organizations capable of higher-level command and control.

The heavy portion of the U.S. Army should therefore preserve and indeed hone its expertise in ground combat, preparing to serve as the decisive nucleus for multinational forces or, if necessary in the long term, for a larger American force. Such a nucleus would not only be smaller than the Army of today, it would be different. It would consist exclusively of regular forces, as opposed to the Army's current practice of relying heavily on reserve units to support regular units, which makes the force less deployable (because of the political costs associated with reserve mobilizations). It would also be different by virtue of its dependence on other states in the event of a major contingency.

Another broad area of insurance lies in the realm of nuclear weapons. During the cold war, questions of nuclear strategy occupied center stage in the American policy debate. Today, our nuclear forces are the stepchild of a government eager to see them go away, and of a military establishment that has always viewed them with a certain amount of distaste. "The nuclear weapon is obsolete. . . . I want to get rid of them all," said one Air Force four-star general recently. The Navy and Army, in particular, have been delighted to see these awkward devices removed from their European arsenals, for they required specialized handling, posed tremendous operational problems, and made each service, in different ways, unpopular with local allies.

But the genie cannot be so easily put back into the bottle. Many small states will take from the Gulf war the lesson that the best counter to American conventional strength lies in the possession of a nuclear arsenal. To deter the use of such weapons (and, perhaps, chemical and biological ones as well), and if necessary to preempt nuclear forces, the United States will require a small but always modern nuclear force of its own. This ultimately also requires a low-level testing-and-development program, particularly for tactical weapons. By failing to develop and publicly defend small, clean nuclear weapons that might be useful for preemptive destruction of the small, crude arsenals of potential enemies, the Clinton administration may be making one of its most damaging long-term mistakes.

A third mission for the armed forces is the *maintenance of world order*. To a degree not found in any other country, the United States combines military, economic, and cultural power. It will wish to use that power in three ways: to limit, to punish, and to excise.

By *limitation* I mean the denial of certain kinds of capabilities to other countries. For example, the United States, as guarantor of an open commercial order, will wish to prevent other countries (or substate actors) from blocking or interfering with the free use of the sea and air lanes. What follows from this is, say, the ability to detect and destroy ships, aircraft, or submarines laying mines in the Straits of Hormuz or the Magellan Straits.

The idea of using military power to *punish* does not normally appeal to Americans. But in the future the United States may not wish to change a political situation on the ground through the direct use of force—by occupying a country and pacifying it. Rather, it may wish to affect the calculations of a local trouble-maker, or simply lay down a marker for future troublemakers. For example, were the United States to have used military power in the former Yugoslavia early on—at the time of the shelling of Dubrovnik in the fall of 1991—it would have done best not to have placed tens of thousands of troops on the ground but to have used its air and naval power to make the Serbian government suffer at home.

During the cold war, the use of military power for punitive purposes acquired a bad name. To hawks, it smacked of timidity in

engaging one's real opponents, and perhaps of a suspect enthrall-
ment to academic notions of force as a mere means of signaling.
To doves, it seemed innately cruel and impossible to reconcile
with a concept of just war. To both it appeared highly unlikely to
be effective. Indeed, the experiences of the Vietnam war seemed to
bear out the suspicions of hawks and doves alike.

Here again, however, it is time to reexamine our strategic
assumptions. Punitive strategies failed during the cold war because
the opponents against whom they were directed were in the grip
of a messianic ideology and because they had at their disposal the
resources of a superpower and a dozen major clients. Such strategies frequently failed as well because the largely peasant societies
against whom they were directed were less vulnerable to the kind
of punishment (chiefly bombing and blockade) that the United
States could deliver.

Today circumstances are quite different. In the next decade or
two, the United States will find itself engaged in what the British
once called imperial policing: the maintenance of some rough
order in unruly parts of the world. Our future opponents will not
have a superpower patron to rebuild their dams and power plants,
or to buy them a comprehensive air-defense system. They will
probably be more porous societies than the old Communist
states—more aware of the world through the mass media—and
probably less totalitarian domestically. They will have more sophisticated economies, which means they will have more to lose, and,
no less important, they will know that the key to survival lies in
some kind of engagement in the world economy, even if not in a
completely open fashion.

Within broad limits, strategies of punishment will work to
moderate the behavior of such states—to curtail (if not to stop
completely) efforts to subvert a neighbor or to mistreat an ethnic
minority. In addition, the technologies of precision-strike open up
new operational concepts for punishment. It is probably feasible,
for instance, to damage or destroy most of a country's major road
and rail bridges. To be sure, temporary bridges, rafts, and the like
will enable the country to continue to function, and even to move
armed forces around. But the economic dislocation will inflict
considerable pain on society and, ultimately, government.

Finally, the maintenance of world order will require a capability to *excise* certain kinds of capabilities, specifically weapons of mass destruction. In 1991, when the United States went to war against Iraq, it lacked the intelligence and, in some cases, the specialized procedures to attack storage sites for the Iraqi nuclear- and biological-weapons programs. When the war began, American planners had only two Iraqi nuclear targets on their hit lists; by the time International Atomic Energy Agency inspectors had finished their work, *sixteen* main facilities had been identified.

From a purely technical point of view, locating and destroying the capability of countries to use weapons of mass destruction is likely to be an extremely difficult task; this is particularly true in the case of biological weapons, which can be manufactured in small laboratories and distributed clandestinely. But should we ever witness the actual use of such weapons, there will be no choice but to move swiftly, and even at high cost, to prevent their repeated use.

The fourth and last mission of the armed forces will be *coalition-maintenance*. The United States is unique not only in its raw military power but in its ability to call on a wide variety of allies for assistance. These allies, in turn, often make claims on our own military capacity. It is in the American interest to provide key elements of support both to our core allies (for example, the British) and to occasional partners with whom we may have a more mixed relationship.

Indeed, one feature of the new international politics is a far greater ambiguity in our alliances. Thus, while American aircraft operated from Italy to surveil Yugoslav air space, American soldiers in Somalia were wondering whether their Italian colleagues were tipping off the Somali warlord they were attempting to track down.

But it would be almost as foolish to walk away from assisting allies when it is in our interest to do so as it would be to ignore such events when they occur. The United States will want allies for many reasons: to ensure political support at home and minimize opposition abroad to certain uses of force; to tap unique skills or local knowledge; to minimize our own weaknesses; and to shift some of the burdens of world policing to others. At the same time, there are some things that the United States does so well, or some goods it has in such quantity, that other countries will have to go on depending on us for support.

Choices

These, then, are the likely purposes of American military power: defense, insurance, the maintenance of world order, and the maintenance of coalitions. What choices will the American government have to make if a much smaller military is to serve these purposes adequately?

The first question for consideration is that of forward presence. During the cold war, the United States became accustomed to stationing vast forces overseas—a third of a million in Europe alone, more than a half-million all told in the mid–1980's. Since the end of the cold war the United States has still kept a substantial force stationed overseas (more than 300,000 men and women all told) and has made increasingly frequent temporary deployments of troops for peacekeeping (as in Macedonia), so-called peacemaking (as in Somalia), and humanitarian intervention (northern Iraq and Rwanda). We have also staged training or showing-the-flag exercises designed to reassure friends or build relations with other countries (e.g., deployments to Kuwait).

This trend has given no sign of abating, as the occupation of Haiti by 10,000 American troops made clear. Meanwhile, the administration promises to send tens of thousands of American troops to Yugoslavia in support of a peace settlement there, and diplomats talk loosely of a brigade or two on the Golan Heights in support of an Israeli-Syrian peace treaty.

It may be some time before the truly pernicious effects of this overstretching are felt. But one effect is already evident, in the strain imposed on service marriages and on morale. Specialized units suffer particularly: for example, airborne warning-and-control crews deploy overseas 170 days a year, whereas the normal limit is 120. The more forces are tied down in missions that are incidental to war-fighting, the less time and opportunity they will have to develop their combat skills.

One might argue that such activities may serve the purposes of American foreign policy, and provide a sense of mission and purpose for the men and women who undertake them. And it may be argued that in the next decade or two it will be less important that American forces sharpen their skills for all-out warfare.

Nonetheless, such activities exact a price on the organizations that sustain them—including a monetary one. The Haiti escapade will cost at least $250 million in direct costs, not to mention a billion dollars of planned aid to that pathetic demi-island. The deployment to Somalia alone cost $2.2 billion from 1991 through 1994, and the emergency movement of aid and troops to Rwanda in 1994 gobbled up several hundred million dollars within a couple of months. The recent suspension of all Naval-reserve training because of a shortage of funds to pay reservists is one of the smaller consequences of these unforeseen expenditures. Such costs come on top of less visible drains, like the Clinton administration's effort to take $300 million from the defense budget as a contribution to the United Nations' peacekeeping efforts.

What is all too little realized is that these sums come out of the operations and maintenance accounts of the armed services, and have begun cutting into the ability of American forces to train and to keep their equipment in good operating condition. Humanitarian adventurism induces an insidious kind of muscle fatigue, consuming sinew in what appears to be a beneficial exercise.

It is a cliché of American strategic thinking (and one to which I largely subscribe) that the United States will henceforth fight increasingly as a member of a coalition. But we will find ourselves choosing among different kinds of coalitions—those brought together under the banner of the United Nations; those locked in formal mechanisms of military cooperation such as NATO; and those constructed on an *ad-hoc* basis.

During the Gulf war the Bush administration set a precedent which appears likely to last, and according to which the United States will frequently use the cover of the United Nations for its military actions overseas. The United States has benefited both at home and abroad from the air of legitimacy this authority has pro-

vided. But if the atmosphere at the United Nations were to deteriorate—for example, if China should choose to exercise its veto
in the Security Council—the United States might wind up
embarrassed by these precedents. The proper course is likely to be
one of pragmatic use of the United Nations if it will provide the
necessary support, but a periodic reaffirmation (and even demonstration) of American willingness to act even without its endorsement. A reflexive appeal to the United Nations for legitimacy
even in cases abutting the American mainland—as has occurred in
Haiti—sets precedents that will be used to confine and restrict
American power in the future.

NATO remains the most durable and important of formal
American coalitions. In the long run, however, unless Russia
reemerges as a threat to the security of Europe, NATO is bound
to deteriorate slowly. Europe, as it expands, is likely to have more,
not less, difficulty in agreeing on a common foreign and defense
policy; the debacle in Bosnia is ample evidence of that. So, too, are
the persistent disagreements between Germany and some of its
Western neighbors on the expansion of both NATO and the
European Union to the East.

Europe's difficulty in acting collectively does not diminish
American interest in keeping NATO alive, but alive less as a command structure in time of war than as a means of harmonizing
procedures and familiarizing soldiers with one another in times of
peace. NATO's most useful work takes place when soldiers, sailors,
and airmen agree on standardized means of issuing orders, controlling air traffic, or managing naval operations.

From this common basis NATO members can operate in *ad-
hoc* coalitions on the fringes of Europe, even if not under NATO
auspices. The Gulf war, in which the United States managed to
coordinate the activities of a half-dozen air forces with the procedures and planning tools devised for use in Europe, demonstrated
the value of this experience.

To generalize from the case of NATO: American coalition
operations should most often take place through the medium of
temporary or local alliances, operating in some cases under a diffuse authority granted by larger organizations, but not dependent
upon them.

*   *   *

If the path to America's future coalitions is relatively clear, one cannot say as much for military acquisition. The issue here is not so much *how* the Pentagon develops and buys hardware (William Perry's Defense Department deserves credit for trying to streamline a cumbersome process) as in *what* it buys.

There are three broad trade-offs. One is between what one might call mega- and micro-systems. The United States did very well in the cold war with exceedingly large and complex military platforms—aircraft carriers, for example, but also such marvels of modern military technology as the B–2 bomber, the JSTARS surveillance aircraft, or even the M–1 Abrams tank.

For a time, in the 1970's, military reformers argued that the United States was ill-advised to build larger and more complex systems. They pressed instead for the purchase of cheaper aircraft like the single-engine F–16 fighter, or simple diesel-electric submarines, rather than the far more costly F–15 or the Navy's standard nuclear-powered submarine. The "military reformers" were proved wrong, at least insofar as hardware was concerned. In the Gulf war, the more sophisticated aircraft such as the F–111 and the F–15 far outperformed the F–16.

Ironically, however, the tide may have turned in the reformers' favor after they have been driven from the field, thanks to the "revolution in military affairs" discussed earlier. In brief, and to repeat, the advent of "smart weapons"—cruise missiles that can fly hundreds of kilometers and hit with an accuracy of a few meters; off-road mines that can listen for moving vehicles and attack them; remotely-piloted vehicles that can locate targets and bring in artillery fire; cheap glide bombs that can pick their own targets or hit predesignated ones—has wrought a transformation in warfare. Just as massive mainframe computers have lost a great deal of ground to networks of smaller computers engaged in parallel processing, so, too, the future of military technology may turn away from the mega-systems and toward networks of smaller and cheaper systems linked together by the new information technologies.

This trend toward warfare by micro-system points to a second trade-off, between quality and quantity. As the defense budget falls, the tendency will be to concentrate on smaller numbers of high-value platforms. These are not only aesthetically more satisfying and imposing, but politically more comprehensible. But the true indices of power in the future may lie in the possession of large numbers of cruise missiles and sensors. For as impressive as the performance of individual pieces of equipment may be, the key to their effective use will be their deployment in *quantity*.

This will be so because of those elements of war which Clausewitz termed "friction": malfunctioning of equipment, inadequate intelligence, and enemy countermeasures.

Thus, the January and June 1993 punitive attacks on Baghdad used 69 Tomahawk land-attack missiles and ate up $75-million worth of ordnance for uncertain, if not negligible, effects. To have real military and hence political effect, American generals will need to be able to launch hundreds of strikes repeatedly over time against enemy targets. Not only will scarce defense dollars have to go to keeping adequate stocks of munitions; the United States will have to be willing to spend large sums on manufacturing technology in order to drive down the costs of individual rounds. Further refinements to a Tomahawk cruise missile may matter much less to its utility as an instrument of military power than to reducing its cost from $1.2 million to a tenth of that figure.

Large-scale acquisition of the new technologies will be difficult in the face of pressure to keep up substantial forces and to maintain their operations tempo. Indeed, it is acquisition of new hardware that is taking the hardest hits from the Clinton cutbacks. Furthermore, the imperatives of day-to-day operations create pressures contrary to those of a sound, long-term strategy.

From a long-term point of view, for instance, it might be worth having the Navy invest in so-called "arsenal ships"—large, stealthy, semi-submersible vessels densely packed with missiles in vertical launch tubes. Such vessels—which might carry hundreds of rounds, plus reloads—could lurk hundreds of miles from their targets, reprogram their missiles using information transmitted by satellite, and open fire. Yet although an arsenal ship might be a handy vessel to have for actual war-fighting, it is considerably less valuable for showing the flag or administering a blockade.

In the same vein, it makes sense to purchase more than the

twenty B–2 bombers now on order by the U.S. Air Force, and in general to do everything possible to make up for the retirement of older bombers such as the Air Force's F–111 and B–52, and the U.S. Navy's A–6. Bombers, however, have little utility for shows of force, and none at all for humanitarian rescues or peacekeeping operations.

The last set of choices before the American defense establishment concerns its most important constituent elements: the armed services. Over the last decade, a consensus has emerged that equates the services with parochial and self-seeking behavior, at odds with the requirements of joint action in war and sound administration in peace. The Goldwater-Nichols Reorganization Act of 1986, itself the product of several years of debate prompted by congressional dissatisfaction with the Department of Defense's internal management, crystallized this disenchantment.

From Goldwater-Nichols there emerged a system that put increasing power in the hands of the chairman, and even the vice chairman, of the Joint Chiefs of Staff, together with the Joint Staff itself, which increasingly came under the direct control and supervision of the chairman. When Congress in 1994 created a commission to examine the roles and missions of the armed services, it complained once again about duplication of effort by the services, and the supposed inefficiencies of their mutual competition.

One might infer from much of the contemporary debate that the ideal armed service would consist of one kind of soldier wearing one uniform. Canada actually experimented with such a system in the mid–1960's, and soon discovered that even in its tiny military there was a natural breakdown among land, sea, and air services. It further discovered that morale suffered from even apparently minor matters like the discarding of traditional uniforms, a decision reversed twenty years later in 1985. (The U.S. Navy relearned this lesson in 1977 when it reinstated the cherished bell-bottom trousers and white sailors' caps taken away in 1971 by a chief of naval operations zealous for efficiency.)

Soldiers, sailors, and airmen inhabit very different worlds, and have very different cultures. This differentiation of service cultures is inevitable, bred by the physical environments in which soldiers, sailors, and airmen operate. It is also highly desirable. There may be no compelling operational requirement for a distinct Marine Corps (armies can conduct amphibious operations with adequate training), but the Marines' élan and professionalism, combined with the peculiar organizational forms they have evolved, make them a unique and invaluable asset. Even when they do the same things the Army does, they do them differently, and occasionally better. And as anyone who has associated with both services knows, each often attracts its own kind of people.

We take it for granted in business that customers will get better service from three or four competing franchises than from a monopoly; we do not call the existence of several national newspapers a deplorable failure of rationalization, or regard the existence of bicameral legislatures as evidence of inefficient government. In the same way, it is a good thing and not a bad thing to have services compete with one another for such missions as counterinsurgency or theater ballistic-missile defense.

In any case, much of the so-called duplication of the services does not represent unnecessary effort. If the Air Force controlled all combat aircraft, we would probably still have pretty much the same number of airplanes at sea on aircraft carriers, albeit supported by an organization far less familiar with the operating environment than the Navy. Because of the technological flux that characterizes military developments, it makes good sense to let competition, and not a master plan, shape the choices about which organizations take on which new missions.

This does not mean, however, that the current array of services is inevitable or desirable. There may be a case for expanding the number of the services by creating one devoted solely to space and long-range missile operations. And it is surely desirable to shape the competition among the services, which, after all, do not produce their own revenues.

But it must be remembered that it is the services that have the longest-term view. Goldwater-Nichols gave more power to the theater commanders-in-chief (the so-called CINC's), including a voice in making budget decisions. By the nature of their tasks, however, theater commanders, and to some extent even the chairman of the Joint Chiefs of Staff, have to look to immediate operational concerns and problems—whether, for instance, there is enough airlift to send soldiers to a trouble spot tomorrow. By contrast, a chief of staff of one of the services worries about equipping the force ten years from now.

One supposedly obsolete element of the service structure is the continued existence of service secretaries—civilian heads of the different departments. Too often these posts go to valued presidential campaign contributors, or to figureheads who enable an administration to score points with assorted constituencies. For their part, the uniformed services know very well how to lull their nominal civilian superiors with endless rounds of ceremonial speeches and enjoyable excursions—driving tanks, flying airplanes, conning a submarine.

Yet the secretaries of the services are potentially the most important figures for asserting civilian control over the military. They control (in theory, at any rate) the service personnel and promotional systems. They can, and sometimes do, know the general officers far better than a busy Secretary of Defense or his deputy. And if they do their job well, they can turn military tourism into an intimate knowledge of the working conditions, spirit, and needs of both officer and enlisted ranks.

Admittedly, most civilian secretaries do not measure up in all these ways, but occasionally some do. John Lehman, Secretary of the Navy during the Reagan administration, and Don Rice, Secretary of the Air Force during the Bush administration, though very different men, are examples of just how much important work a competent service secretary can do.

Civil-Military Relations

One reason good service secretaries are needed now more than ever is that American civil-military relations seem to be undergoing long-term deterioration. This has been noted by a number of observers and is evident in dozens of incidents: the failure of Admiral Frank Kelso, chief of naval operations, to retire despite the request of his superior, Secretary of the Navy John Dalton, that he do so; the instruction by General Barry McCaffrey, commander of

the U.S. Southern Command, that his subordinates report to him
and not (as the law requires) to the ambassadors in their respective
countries. The Clinton administration has managed at once to
show a lack of understanding of the military and on occasion even
a contempt for it, while meekly submitting to insubordinate
behavior by all too many of its members.

But the problem goes far deeper. It was evident in the willingness of Colin Powell, former chairman of the Joint Chiefs of Staff,
publicly to oppose government policy in Yugoslavia, and it
appeared in the generally hostile attitude of military staffs to both
press and civilian policy-makers during the Gulf crisis. It has been
reported as well in the writings of thoughtful officers like Colonel
Charles Dunlap, Jr., especially in his disturbing (and prizewinning)
fantasy, "The Origins of the American Military Coup of 2012."[2]

What are the sources of the contemporary distemper? One is
the trauma of Vietnam. Only 40 percent of draft-age men served
in the military during that war; of this group, only a quarter (that
is, 10 percent of all draft-age men) went to Vietnam, and a rather
small minority of these saw combat. The artful public reconcilia-
tion of the Reagan years, replete with parades and the construction of a Vietnam memorial, together with the mere passing of
time, has smoothed over the overt consequences of that war. But if
one probes deeper, down to the organizational culture of the
American defense establishment, one finds scars that will not fade.

For American soldiers—even for those who did not serve during the war—Vietnam is an *ur*-memory. Believing as they do that
the United States had never before lost a war, American officers
feel a certain humiliation at the failure of American arms to
reduce to submission an impoverished country with barely a tenth
of our population. Many, and probably most, are convinced that
this failure stemmed in large part from the interference of civilians
in the conduct of the war, and from the failure of politicians to
assign clear guidelines for waging it.

The debacles of the Lebanon intervention in the early 1980's

---

[2]*Parameters,* Winter 1992–93. See also Dunlap's article "Welcome to the
Junta: The Erosion of Civilian Control of the U.S. Military," *Wake Forest Law
Review,* Summer 1994.

and the Somali intervention a decade later, though far smaller in scale, have only confirmed these lessons. Quixotically conceived and erratically executed acts of social work masquerading as strategy, such as the Haitian occupation, reinforce soldiers' suspicion that politicians do not understand the military instrument's limitations, or comprehend the damage that misuse does to it. And officers are very well aware that the Vietnam experience corroded the morale, discipline, and professional expertise of the military itself. It took at least a decade to repair the damage.

On the other side, politicians, particularly those of the Vietnam generation who evaded service there (probably the majority in both parties of that age cohort), are often shy of exerting strenuous civilian control. Accepting, as many do, the military assessment of the war—an evaluation that actually has less merit than one might think—they fear the penalties of putting a now-popular military in harm's way under any but benign circumstances. For both soldiers and politicians, the model of the Gulf war is the one to follow: conducting a war for nominally limited and concrete (although in reality ambiguous) objectives, with overwhelming force, against an enemy who has been completely isolated and who, indeed, practically invites attack.

There is a further factor to be considered here. The American government, and in some ways even the military itself, poorly comprehended the enormous relative advantage we had over the Iraqis in the Persian Gulf. For military technology is becoming increasingly obscure, and military assessment increasingly recondite.

In the old days one could in some fashion count items—battleships, tanks, heavy bombers—and have a rough sense of what kind of power they purchased. Today, one missile may look very much like another, and a great deal of combat takes place invisibly, in the jamming of radars or the cloaking of planes, ships, and tanks by exotic materials and design. And as fewer and fewer politicians bring any kind of military experience of their own to bear, civilians find themselves increasingly dependent on military staffs. At the same time, civilian leaders put a premium on finding senior officers who mouth the right formulas about matters of gender and race.

This mixture of politicians' incomprehension on the one hand, and their desire for sycophancy on the other, poses long-term risks. One can imagine the emergence out of this of an officer corps, leading members of which identify themselves, if not with political parties, then with politicians. Indeed, in the 1992 election this occurred, as retired officers lined up behind presidential candidates with little thought to the pernicious consequences of their actions.

The evolution of warfare itself may produce further challenges. As we have seen, one of the few burgeoning areas of military thought and activity is "information warfare"—the conduct of conflict through the manipulation (and not merely the interception or exclusion) of information. Future tools of information warfare will include satellite television broadcasts, the disruption of financial systems, the forging of all kinds of electronic messages, and the corruption of data bases. It is the kind of activity that mischievous teenagers and greedy computer wizards have engaged in for decades now. The military, being as large and efficient as it is, can carry such activities to new heights, and increase the role played by the American military in a variety of everyday transactions.

At a lower level, other kinds of frictions will occur. Elite commando units worry about their members—trained in the black arts of breaking and entering, not to mention other, far nastier criminal skills—going bad. It has rarely happened, in part thanks to successful screening and training; but as the military breeds more information warriors, one wonders if such screening will continue to be effective. The temptations of computer hacking are far wider and stronger (among other things, it is much less violent and can be far more lucrative) than, say, assassination for pay. Far more worrisome, however, is the possibility that a military fighting the shadowy battles of "information warfare" may find itself engaging the country in foreign-policy tangles of a particularly messy kind.

None of this is to suggest that the United States has a rogue military, or anything like it. Quite the contrary. In many ways this is the most acutely self-aware armed force the country has ever known, and one which (in part) worries a good deal about its relationship with the broader society. As the Gulf war demonstrated, its leaders are far more politically astute and sensitive to the imperatives of foreign policy than their predecessors of bygone generations.

The difficulty is much more on the other side, in the absence of a civilian class familiar with military matters and comfortable with military people. As a generation that served in the military yields its place in public life to one whose members not only have not served but probably do not know anyone who has, an unfortunate gap grows. It is the civilians, not the soldiers, who have abdicated their responsibilities.

How to remedy matters? One recourse may be to increase the intermixing of civilians and soldiers by sending more civilians—not just civil servants but journalists, congressional staffers, business people, and others—for year-long stints in the country's war colleges. Another might be the deliberate creation and preservation of routes for brief active duty or longer-term reserve duty by young men and women who will, later on, become this country's civic leaders. Yet another course might be a more extensive use of programs that place soldiers in educational and even business institutions for a year or two at a time.

One of the chief legacies of the cold war was a narrowing of debate about national defense to an obsession with weapon systems (should we buy cheap single-engine fighters or more costly twin-engine fighters?) or simply the bottom line of the defense budget. This cramping of debate resulted from the existence of an altogether desirable consensus about the essential parameters of the defense problem. All responsible people agreed that the United States should have a very large military, that it should be forward-deployed, that it should be embedded in NATO, and so on.

That consensus helped win the cold war. But it has resulted in the atrophy of our capacities for a debate of the kind that occurred at the turn of the century, when the United States became a great power, or in the late 1940's, when the United States accepted its status as a superpower.

In the absence of events forcing our hand, we may find it hard to engage in such comprehensive self-scrutiny, and it is even conceivable that in the short term we will pay no large penalty. In a longer view, however—say, twenty years—matters may be different. If Francis Fukuyama's famous verdict turns out to be right, and we do in fact reach the end of history, defined as the rise of essentially pacific liberal-democratic states, all this concern about defense will seem an atavism, a survival of an older and bloodier age. The greater wisdom, however, may rest with Winston Churchill, who once wrote:

> Certain it is that while men are gathering knowledge and power with ever-increasing and measureless speed, their virtues and their wisdom have not shown any notable improvement as the centuries have rolled. The brain of a modern man does not differ in essentials from that of the human beings who fought and loved here millions of years ago. The nature of man has remained hitherto practically unchanged. Under sufficient stress—starvation, terror, warlike passion, or even cold intellectual frenzy, the modern man we know so well will do the most terrible deeds. . . . We have the spectacle of the powers and weapons of man far outstripping the march of his intelligence; we have the march of his intelligence proceeding far more rapidly than the development of his nobility. We may find ourselves in the presence of the strength of civilization without its mercy.

In the wreckage of Saddam Hussein's extensive nuclear program, in the dimly glimpsed transactions of Russian plutonium merchants, in the anonymous ferocity of those who bomb office buildings in New York and Argentina, one catches flashes of what "the strength of civilization without its mercy" may look like.

Beyond these menaces of the next decade, others may await us. Soon science will open up fantastic new possibilities—say, in the development of biological weapons and in the manipulation of human life itself—that some men or states will almost certainly turn to evil ends. Surely, it would be rank folly to shrug aside the possible rise of a Napoleon, a Hitler who would cunningly exploit "perverted science," as Churchill called it. And lesser men—the Milosevics, Husseins, and Aidids—will make trouble enough.

All the more reason, then, to break the habits of the cold war and prepare to meet a possibly less dangerous but almost certainly more turbulent age.

What to Do About

The Arts

JOSEPH EPSTEIN

Joseph Epstein is a long-time contributor to *Commentary* and the editor of the *American Scholar*. He is the author of eight books of essays, the most recent of which is *With My Trousers Rolled*, and a collection of short stories.

Arts that lack a particular distinction or nobility of style are often said to be styleless, and the culture is judged to be weak or decadent.

—MEYER SCHAPIRO

"Art for everyone": anyone regarding that as possible is unaware how "everyone" is constituted and how art is constituted. So here, in the end, art and success will yet again have to part company.

—ARNOLD SCHOENBERG

Nobody with a serious or even a mild interest in the arts likes to think he has lived his mature life through a bad or even mediocre period of artistic creation. Yet a strong argument can be made that ours has been an especially bleak time for the arts.

One of the quickest ways of determining this is to attempt to

name either discrete masterpieces or impressive bodies of work
that have been written, painted, or composed over the past, say, 30
years. Inexhaustible lists do not leap to mind. Not only is one
hard-pressed to name recent masterpieces, but one's sense of anticipation for the future is less than keen. In looking back over the
past two or three decades, what chiefly comes to mind are fizzled
literary careers, outrageous exhibitions and inflated (in all senses of
the word) reputations in the visual arts, and a sad if largely tolerant
boredom with most contemporary musical composition.

People who look to art for spiritual sustenance have been dip-
ping into capital—they have, that is, been living almost exclusively
off the past. In literature, less and less do the works created since
the great American efflorescence earlier in the century seem likely
to endure. (One thinks of 1925, that *annus mirabilis* for the American novel, which saw the publication of F. Scott Fitzgerald's *The
Great Gatsby*, Theodore Dreiser's *An American Tragedy*, John Dos
Passos's *Manhattan Transfer*, Sinclair Lewis's *Arrowsmith*, and Willa
Cather's *The Professor's House*.) In visual art, the line is drawn—if
not for everyone—at Abstract Expressionism, after which no powerful school or movement seems to have arisen, and so many reputations seem, as the English critic F.R. Leavis remarked in another
connection, to have more to do with the history of publicity than
with the history of art. In serious music, *performing* artists continue
to emerge, but the music they perform is almost exclusively that of
past centuries; the greatest appetite of all remains for the works
created between J.S. Bach (1685–1750) and Maurice Ravel
(1875–1937). True, dance, under such geniuses as George Balan-
chine and Martha Graham, has had a fine contemporary run. But
no one, I think, would argue against the proposition that the only
works of art capable of stirring anything like extensive excitement
in the nation just now are movies, which, given their general quality, is far from good news.

In explanation, and partially in defense, of this situation it has
been suggested that we are living in a time when sensibility has
been fundamentally altered; and, it is sometimes also argued,
advancing technology—the computer, the video—only figures to
alter it further. The artistic result of this putative shift in sensibility
goes under the banner of postmodernism. Although the word

means different things to different people, generally postmodernism in the arts includes the following: a belief that a large statement, in everything from poetry to architecture, is probably no longer persuasive; a self-reflexiveness, a playfulness, and a strong reliance on irony, which the advocates of postmodernism find a refreshing and fair exchange for spirituality in art; and a contempt for criticism, traditionally understood as the activity of making discriminations, distinctions, and, especially, value judgments.

At the same time that some argue for a change in sensibility, suggesting in turn the need for a change in the nature of art, others feel that if art is not to lose its standing entirely, more than ever it needs to give itself directly to social and political purposes. We have driven around this block before, of course, most notably in the 1930's when novelists and poets, painters, and even musicians were scolded for insufficient engagement in the political struggles of the day. Then, these criticisms were directed by Communists and fellow-travelers; today they are made under the aegis of an ideology that finds its chief outlets in environmentalism, sexual liberation, a lingering anticapitalism, and an inchoate but determined multiculturalism.

The paramount enemy for such people, then as now, is disinterested art that attempts to transcend political and other sorts of human division. This is art of the kind Marcel Proust had in mind when he wrote that it "gives us access to higher spiritual reality resembling the otherworldly metaphysical speculations of philosophy and religion." This is art which, among its other effects, seeks to broaden horizons, to deepen understanding, and to enhance consciousness as well as to convey the ultimately unexplainable but very real exaltation that is integral to heightened aesthetic pleasure.

By such measures, most contemporary art has fallen down badly on the job. Art still functions to confer social status on what today one might call the educated classes, as witness the large crowds that attend certain museum shows and operas and concerts given by performers who have been declared superstars. But high art (except the political kind) has more and more been relegated to a minority interest and is under attack for doing what it has always done best. Much of high Western art is now even judged, *mirabile dictu*, to be politically less than correct.

*   *   *

Some of this might have been predicted—and, in fact, it was. More than 40 years ago, in an essay entitled "The Plight of Our Culture,"[1] the late Clement Greenberg wrote that "high culture has lost much of its old implicit authority." In that essay, Greenberg ran through those brutal simplicities—as he rightly called them—known as highbrow, middlebrow, and lowbrow.

Highbrow art, from Homer through Rembrandt to Schoenberg, had always made the greatest demands on its audience—and those demands, it had always been understood, resulted in the highest rewards, both philosophical and aesthetic. In its modern forms, highbrow art, wrote Greenberg, tended to be synonymous with avant-garde art, which made even stricter demands. Avant-garde art was often about itself, and the avant-garde artist, turning inward, was interested above all in solutions to the problems his particular art presented: problems of surface and perspective in painting, of tonality and dissonance in music, of language and depth psychology in literature.

Because of this it had become more and more difficult to admire a modern artist's work apart from his technique. As Greenberg had put it in an earlier essay, as the avant-garde became highly specialized, so "its best artists [became] artists' artists, its best poets, poets' poets," and this, not surprisingly, had "estranged a great many of those who were capable formerly of enjoying and appreciating ambitious art and literature, but who are now unwilling or unable to acquire an initiation into these craft secrets."

Lowbrow art presented no difficulties of definition: it was mass art, produced for and aimed at the lowest common denominator, and promising nothing more than entertainment. But then there was middlebrow art, where the problems, for Greenberg and others, arose. Middlebrow art promised both to entertain and to educate, and attempted to pass itself off as highbrow by its appearance of seriousness. Yet the middlebrow was not finally serious; it was instead merely earnest, which was not at all the same thing. Middlebrow art was always teaching, if not preaching. (In our own time, it has been chiefly preaching political lessons.) And middle-

[1]*Commentary,* June 1953.

brow art was responsible for deploying one of the most self-serving myths of our age, the myth of the artist as a permanent rebel against society.

Writing in a special issue of the British magazine *Horizon* in 1947, Greenberg called for a frankly highbrow elite that would help bring about an art characterized by "balance, largeness, precision, enlightenment." We have had, he wrote, "enough of the wild artist." What we need now are

> men of the world not too much amazed by experience, not too much at a loss in the face of current events, not at all overpowered by their own feelings, men to some extent aware of what has been felt elsewhere since the beginning of recorded history.

Nearly a half-century later, all one can say of Clement Greenberg's aspirations for art is that none of them has come into being, whereas most of his worst fears have. Middlebrow art is taken so much for highbrow in our day that the very category of highbrow is in doubt. My own personal, shorthand definition of a middlebrow is anyone who takes either Woody Allen or Spike Lee seriously as an artist. And most of the country, it will not have gone without notice, does.

One of the consequences of the debasement of art is that fewer and fewer people are able to make the important distinctions which high art itself requires for its proper appreciation. An institution that has played a large role in bringing this situation about is the university. Formerly free from the tyranny of the contemporary—the tyranny, that is, of being up to the moment—the university now takes great pride in being a center for the creation of contemporary art. Over the past three or four decades, the university has become something akin to a continuing WPA program by furnishing an ever-larger number of artists—chiefly writers but painters and musicians, too—with jobs.

This might not be so bad, but, with all these artists on hand, the university now also provides a fairly strong diet of contemporary fare in its curriculum. Once, it was not thought necessary to teach the works of contemporary writers, painters, and composers;

if a student was a reasonably cultivated person, or had the desire to be such a person, he could learn about such things on his own. No more. Some artists even teach themselves.

Although many universities continue to offer traditional subjects in the arts, the university has, at the same time, caved in to the demand for courses that fit the politics of a large number of the people who teach there: feminism, Marxism, Lacanism, the new historicism, deconstructionism, semiotics—"the six branches of the School of Resentment," as the literary critic Harold Bloom has called them. Thus, in the contemporary university literature and painting are often put through the meat grinder of race, class, and gender. This is well known. What is perhaps less well known is the odd way it has skewed the arts themselves.

To give an example of how the skewing works, the week before President Clinton's inauguration I was called by the (London) *Daily Telegraph* for my opinion of the poet Maya Angelou, who had been chosen to read a poem at the inaugural. I told the reporter that I had no opinion of Maya Angelou, for I had read only a few of her poems and thought these of no great literary interest. Ah, he wondered, did I know anyone who might have an opinion that would be interesting to English readers? I conceded that I knew of no one who read her. When asked how that might be, I responded that what the reporter had to understand was that in the United States just now there were a number of authors who were not actually for reading but only for teaching, of whom Angelou, who herself teaches, lectures for vast fees, and probably has more honorary degrees than James Joyce had outstanding debts, is decidedly one.

By teaching so many contemporary writers and simultaneously laying itself open to the political aspirations of multiculturalism, the university has had a serious hand in helping to discard the idea of standards, which is absolutely essential to high art. The politics of many university teachers have played a key role in this, with the result that today we no longer have in force the only distinction in the arts that really matters—that between the good and the bad, the well made and the shoddy. Once one starts playing this particular game, the essential, the only really relevant, fact becomes not the quality of an artist's work but which category it fits into: black composers, women painters, gay/lesbian poets, and the rest of the multicultural mélange.

All but a handful of people who currently work in the arts—writers, painters, musicians, arts administrators, and patrons—seem to go along with this program. Multiculturalization has for many seemed a way out of the wrenching dilemma of wishing to seem as democratic as possible while knowing in one's heart that serious art is nothing if not thoroughly meritocratic and, in the best sense, finally and irremediably elitist.

"In art the ideal critical ethic is ruthlessness," wrote the music critic Ernest Newman. "The practice of art should not be made easier for the weaklings; it should be made harder, so that only the best types survive." Such notions are troubling to people of tender liberal conscience. The arts are now somehow construed to carry the message that they are themselves a means to progress, and progress implies encouraging the downtrodden; clearly, the last thing such people want to be caught acknowledging is that the arts are not—at least not necessarily—for everyone.

The misguided belief that art is one of the forms that progress takes is connected with the notion that the avant-garde itself is a kind of movement, or party, for progress—an appealing notion for people who wish the arts to do things they were never meant primarily to do: to fight censorship, to give groups pride in what is called their "identity," to increase the awareness of AIDS, to fight inequities of every kind. As Clausewitz said that war was diplomacy carried on by other means, so art is seen as social justice and political enlightenment carried on by other means.

The avant-garde of an earlier time, beginning in the 1890's and proceeding through the early decades of the 20th century—the "banquet years" of French painting, music, and writing—was (again) an avant-garde of technique. It was impelled by a spirit of experimentation; it attempted to provide fundamentally new ways of seeing, hearing, and understanding: postimpressionism, atonal music, stream of consciousness, and free verse were names given to some of these experiments. Whether or not one admires the results, the utter seriousness as well as the aesthetic purity of the enterprise cannot be mistaken.

The practitioners of what must now somewhat oxymoronically be called the old avant-garde were true revolutionaries. They wished to—and often did—change the way we intuit and understand and feel about the world around us. They *truly* altered sensibility. For a complex of reasons, their revolution has been halted. While new experiments in style and technique continue, the avant-garde has largely turned away from technique and toward content.

Obscenity, homoerotic exhibitionism, sadomasochism, political rage—these have been the hallmarks of the advanced art of our day. In a way never intended either by Matisse, whose early paintings so upset the Parisian audience, or by Stravinsky, whose *The Rite of Spring* caused its audience to bust up chairs in the hall in which it was performed, the avant-garde artists of our day are knocking themselves out to be outrageous. An avant-garde magazine puts a woman's vagina on its cover and runs the tag line, "Read My Lips"; child pornography, if set out "tastefully," is not thought beyond the bounds of respectability; neither is a production of *Tannhäuser* with the title character as a TV evangelist and Venus as a hooker. If the political revolutionaries of an earlier day cried, "Burn, baby, burn!," the artistic revolutionaries of ours exclaim, "Squirm, baby, squirm!"

The targets for such art, it ought to be clear, are middle-class respectability, the family, heterosexuality, organized religion, and finally high culture itself. The aesthetic standard by which this art asks to be judged is the degree to which it succeeds in hitting its targets. As a panel for the National Endowment for the Arts (NEA) once put it, a work that is "challenging and disturbing . . . precisely . . . shows us that it is worthy of consideration." The more outrageous the art, the more worthy of notice and protection.

Consider by contrast how T.S. Eliot, a great avant-garde poet himself, saw the role of the artist:

> The artist is the only genuine and profound revolutionist, in the
> following sense. The world always has, and always will, tend to sub-

stitute appearance for reality. The artist, being always alone, being heterodox when everyone else is orthodox, is the perpetual upsetter of conventional values, the restorer of the real. . . . His function is to bring back humanity to the real.

Yet the contemporary, putatively avant-garde artist is neither alone nor heterodox. He is today almost invariably part of a larger group—a feminist, a gay liberationist, or a spokesman for an ethnic or racial group—and his thought, far from being heterodox, is, within both his own group and what is called the "artistic community," more rigidly conformist than a Big Ten sorority. He is published in the fashionable magazines, exhibited by the toniest galleries, awarded Pulitzers and other prizes, given federal grants, and generally rewarded and revered.

The politicizing of art, setting it on the side of all the politically correct causes, has rendered it more acceptable even as it has become less artistic. A commercially successful painter named David Salle, a man with a good feel for the ideological winds, was quoted last year in the *New Yorker* apropos the politics of contemporary artists:

> Because in art-politics to be homosexual is, *a priori*, more correct than to be heterosexual. Because to be an artist is to be an outsider, and to be a gay artist is to be a double outsider. That's the correct condition. If you're a straight artist, it's not clear that your outsiderness is legitimate. I know this is totally absurd, that I'm making it sound totally absurd. But the fact is that in our culture it does fall primarily to gays and blacks to make something interesting. Almost everything from the straight white culture is less interesting, and has been for a long time.

How could we possibly get into a condition in which what David Salle says, absurd as it assuredly is, can nonetheless be taken as axiomatic truth? We did it by accepting the quite false notion of the artist as an outsider and extending it to the point where the farther "outside" one represents oneself as being, and the more victimized, the greater one's standing as an artist.

I first came across the name of the dancer Bill T. Jones in an

article in the *New York Times Magazine*, where he was described as
the "HIV-positive son of migrant workers," which, in current *New
York Times*-speak, means a man beyond any possible criticism.
Recently Jones and what he represents have come in for some
trenchant comment in, of all places, the *New Yorker*, a magazine
where only a few weeks earlier he had been the subject of a fawn-
ing profile. Arlene Croce, the magazine's distinguished dance
critic, wrote a powerful piece demurring from the general celebra-
tion and entering the opinion that "the cultivation of victimhood
by institutions devoted to the care of art is a menace to all art
forms, particularly performing-art forms."[2]

Croce's article, "Discussing the Undiscussable," takes up the
question of how the art of victimhood—so depressing, so manipu-
lative, so intimidating, and ultimately so uncriticizable—has risen
to such a high place in contemporary culture. She understands
that some of its appeal is a combination of false empathy and real
snobbery on the part of its audience: "There's no doubt that the
public likes to see victims, if only to patronize them with
applause." But she makes the larger—and, I think, valid—point
that the behavior of government, specifically through the NEA,
has had a great deal to do with the situation she deplores.

In 1984 I was appointed a member of the National Council of
the NEA, a body on which I sat for 6 years. One of the most
impressive moments I can recall from my years on the Council was
when the director of the music program mentioned that a particular orchestra had had its grant reduced by something like $20,000
because of some "spotty playing in the cello section." I was much
taken with how the NEA music panelists were able to pin down
this fault, by the professionalism with which they went about the
task of judgment. It seemed to me the way things ought to operate.

But outside certain select programs at the NEA, they seldom
did. By the end of my term, every member on the Council had
been appointed under either the Reagan or the Bush administra-

[2]See Terry Teachout's "Victim Art," *Commentary,* March 1995, for a discussion of the Croce article and the controversy it provoked.

tions—and yet, despite this, the reigning spirit in the room, as among the staff of the Endowment generally, was preponderantly liberal-Left. Time and again, when arguments about standards and quality came up against what was taken to be democratic fairness and sensitivity to minorities, the latter inevitably won the day.

How could it be otherwise? Given our debased standards, how could one hope to make the hard professional judgments about modern painting or sculpture or literature, let alone mixed-media works? The chief problem with "the peer-panel system," as it was reverently called at the NEA—a system in which artists were asked to sit in judgment of other artists in their field—was that the sort of people who served on these panels were the same sort of people who applied for and received grants themselves. Like was giving money to like.

I could not help noticing, too, the special obligation which the people who worked at the NEA felt toward what passed for avant-garde or "cutting-edge" art. The cutting edge, almost invariably, was anticapitalist, anti–middle class, anti–American, the whole-earth catalogue of current antinomianism. What was new was that the artists who wanted to seem cutting edge also wanted the government they despised to pay for the scissors.

Most people at the NEA and on its Council thought this a perfectly workable arrangement. If someone ever suggested that a grant application had all the earmarks of something too obviously political as well as boring beyond excruciation, the air would crackle with potential accusations of censorship and Cassandra-like warnings about slippery slopes heading into McCarthyism.

Those NEA grants that issued in obscenity and horror—Karen Finley smearing her nakedness with chocolate, Robert Mapplethorpe's photographs of men with plumbing and other appurtenances up their rectums, a man spreading his HIV-positive blood on paper towels and then sending them skimming over an audience—have given the Endowment its most serious problems in the press and on Capitol Hill. Yet the NEA's defenders are correct in saying that these comprise only a minuscule proportion of the Endowment's total grants. What they do not say—possibly because they are themselves unaware of it—is how mediocre have been so many of the artists who have received NEA grants.

Mediocrity, the question of what may be called quality control, was rarely discussed during my time at the NEA. It could not be. Most NEA panelists believed in encouraging the putatively disadvantaged more than they believed in art itself, and this made them prey to the grim logic of affirmative action. (Even the panels themselves were put together on an affirmative-action basis.) Add to this the assumption at the NEA that artists themselves were yet another downtrodden minority group, as "entitled" to their grants as other supposed victims. And then toss in plain old-fashioned politics in the form of Congressmen and members of the Council who wanted to make sure that, say, Florida and Colorado got their share of grants. What we had was a fine recipe for spreading artistic mediocrity across the country.

Viewed from the middle distance of a seat on the NEA Council, the grants to individual artists seemed small potatoes. Most were for less than $20,000—an award which generally encouraged self-congratulation and the continued production of unnecessary art. What drained the spectacle of triviality was that the money was not "ours" to give away. No one felt too badly about this, for the NEA budget, generally hovering around $170 million, was, as government spending went, just above the level of walking-around money. Still, the spectacle was more than a little depressing.

The question of what is now to be done about the arts and arts policy in America is not one that admits of easy or persuasive answers. It is made all the more complicated once one concedes how hard it is to explain what, in any society, actually encourages the production of great art.

Traditions help immensely. In 18th- and 19th-century Vienna, the pressure of strong musical traditions along with a system of monarchical patronage played a part in fostering the magnificent music of that era. The splendid efflorescence of painting in 19th- and early-20th-century France can also be partially understood through the role played by French artistic traditions—and the reactions of artists to and against certain of those traditions. But how does one explain Russian literature in the 19th century, except to say that in Pushkin, Gogol, Dostoevsky, Turgenev, Tolstoy, and Chekhov, God chose to create six geniuses who happened to share a geography and a language?

Since genius can never be predicted, one looks to institutions that might encourage art to set out in directions likely to be more rewarding than those of the past few decades. What, today, might such institutions be?

The first that comes to mind is criticism. Critics of the arts have traditionally functioned as gatekeepers, deciding what meets the mark and passes through and what does not and is therefore excluded. Some critics have also taken a much more active hand, preparing the ground for the acceptance of new and difficult art through explication and the main force of their authority. One thinks of Edmund Wilson who in *Axel's Castle* (1931) did just this for modernist literature, and, two decades later, of Clement Greenberg who did something similar for Abstract Expressionism.

Critics of this power are not on the scene today. Nor are there important movements in the arts that require such skills. Today our critics commonly function as doormen—or, more precisely, as cheerleaders. Their job often consists in justifying the trivial, vaunting the vapid. Yet they seem quite happy in their work.

In part this derives from the fact that, like so many of our artists, many of our critics too are not merely university-trained but university-employed. As such they participate in the culture that has dominated academic life over the past few decades: they tend to disbelieve in the possibility of disinterested art; they condone the new multiculturalism and are willing to lower standards to make way for it; they are dubious about judgments of value; and they understand that "criticism" of the work of minority-group members, feminists, or homosexuals must be restricted to praise.

Criticism, then, is not an institution that can be counted on to help revive the arts of our age or in any serious way to arrest their decline—at least not for now. There are a few serious critics on the scene, but the best they can do is continue to remark that the emperor has very few clothes, and wears them badly.

Private foundations, on which many people in the arts depend, are also less than likely to help, for they, too, are hostage to the notion that art ought to be socially useful—that it is most relevant and vibrant when in the service of "social justice." The Lila

Wallace-Reader's Digest Fund is fairly typical in this regard. Consider its program for resident theaters. According to the Fund, money for such theaters should be used

> to expand their marketing efforts, mount new plays, broaden the ethnic make-up of their management, experiment with color-blind casting, increase community-outreach activity, and sponsor a variety of other programs designed to integrate the theaters into their communities.

Other major foundations—Rockefeller, Ford, MacArthur—are not differently disposed. All are committed to art for almost anything but art's sake.

That leaves the institutional linchpin of the arts in the United States, the National Endowment, now under fire from a Republican-controlled Congress. Supporters of the NEA, those who like the system as it now is, talk a good deal about the economic soundness of federal support for the arts. They trot out the following numbers: federal support for the arts costs the taxpayer only 64 cents a year, whereas the figure in Germany is $27 and in France and Canada it is $32. Every dollar awarded by the NEA in grants attracts $11 from state and local arts agencies, corporations, and private parties. There are 1.3 million jobs in the arts; if you add tourism, ticket revenues, and other money-making activities, this creates something like $37 billion in economic activity and brings in $3.4 billion in federal taxes. The arts, the argument goes, are good for the economy. So shut up and eat your arts.

Not only have other nations throughout history supported the arts, NEA publicists maintain, but future generations will judge us by the extent to which we support the arts as "the finest expression of the human condition." (Ah, Mapplethorpe! Ah, humanity!) When, they remind us, Congress established the NEA in 1965, it noted:

> An advanced civilization must not limit its efforts to science and technology alone but must give full value and support to the other

great branches of scholarly and cultural activity in order to achieve
a better understanding of the past, a better analysis of the present,
and a better view of the future.

The arts, therefore, are not only good for the economy, they
serve the purposes of moral uplift. So shut up and eat your arts.

To hear its advocates tell it, the NEA enriches community life,
stimulates local economies, supports the promising young, makes
culture available to the masses, works with "at-risk" youth, satisfies
a deep demand for art among the American people—the NEA is
in fact good for everything but growing hair. The arts are good for
the city, good for the country, good for everyone. So shut up and
eat your arts.

But—aside from all these magnificent side effects—what,
exactly, do the arts *do*? Here we return to the same old litany. Paul
Goldberger, the cultural-news editor of the *New York Times*, a
paper that has a great deal to say about what in contemporary art
gets serious attention, answered the question by writing that "what
art strives to do . . . is not to coddle but to challenge." In other
words, painters who mock your religion, playwrights who blame
you for not doing enough for AIDS, poets who exalt much that
you despise, opera composers who make plain that your politics
are vicious—all this is by definition art, and, whether you like it or
not, it is good for you. So go eat your arts out.

The NEA might have been spared much anguish if someone
truly knowledgeable had been in a position of leadership. But in
its 30-year history, it has never had a chairman with anything
approaching an understanding of the arts. The specialty of Nancy
Hanks, the second chairman (she followed Roger Stevens), was
charming Congressmen to support the agency it had founded in
1965. Her successor, Livingston Biddle, was a platitudinarian, who
to this day likes to expatiate on his slogan that "the arts mean
excellence"; one need only listen to him for 2 minutes to cease
believing in art and excellence both. Biddle was followed by Frank
Hodsoll, an intelligent and capable civil servant who, when it
came to the arts, was clearly learning on the job. John Frohnmayer,
the Bush administration's man, brought to the job enormous
ambition exceeded only by ignorance of the ways of politicians

and artists alike. The current chairman, Jane Alexander, an actress and hence technically an artist herself, has been running a rescue operation; she apparently thinks the way to do this is to talk about her wide travels in which she finds that the people of the United States could not be happier with all the art the federal government has helped to pay for, and to remind everyone that the arts are good for our souls.

One cannot but wonder what it might be like to have someone in a position of leadership who knows what the point of the arts is. But who of any standing would want to take on the job? In the current political climate, he would find himself locked between radical artists shouting censorship and conservative Congressmen crying obscenity. His efforts could only come to grief.

That the future of the National Endowment for the Arts is in peril ought not to be surprising. What people at the NEA and those who accept grants from it have never seemed to realize is that they are sponsoring and producing *official* art, just as surely as the academic painters in France or the socialist-realist novelists in the Soviet Union produced official art. That our official art is against the society that sponsors it does not make it any the less official. But given the obscenity and the mediocrity and the politicization of so much of this art, government sponsorship of it has come to seem intolerable, and there is now talk of closing down the Endowment.

Should that be done? Any serious scrutiny of the NEA must begin with the stipulation that politically motivated art ought not to be underwritten by taxpayer money. (The argument that all art is ultimately political is greatly exaggerated; it is a question of degree, and everyone knows it.) Nor for their part should artists upon receiving a grant be asked to accept any condition that will inhibit them, such as not offending any segment of the population. Since these criteria cannot be satisfied in the case of grants to individual artists, and especially those on the "cutting edge," my own sense is that it would better if all such grants were eliminated: better for the country and, though they are likely to hate it, better, finally, for artists.

In one of his essays the eminent cultural historian Jacques Barzun makes a distinction between "public art" and all other kinds. Individual artists, he believes, should fend for themselves, as artists have always done; I agree with him. But then there is public art, by which Barzun means museums, opera houses, orchestras, theaters, and dance troupes. "If as a nation," he writes, "we hold that high art is a public need, these institutions deserve support on the same footing as police departments and weather bureaus."

William F. Buckley, Jr. has supplied a corroborating argument derived, for conservatives, from the most impressive of all possible sources. It was Adam Smith who, in Buckley's words, "counseled that free societies are obliged to contribute state funds only for the maintenance of justice, for the common defense, and for the preservation of monuments." It is only a small stretch, Buckley suggests, to claim that a great many artistic works qualify as monuments.

I agree with that, too—but only in theory. In a different political-cultural climate—less confrontational and litigious—one could easily imagine a place for a federal presence in the arts. The government could contribute to preserving art: it could help to maintain the costs of museums in financial difficulty and ease the financial strain entailed in the performance and exhibition of established and often difficult art that does not figure to have a wide following. Some valuable art cannot realistically hope to survive in the marketplace, ever, and some of the good things the NEA historically helped to do are not likely to be done by private philanthropy—bringing in art from abroad, underwriting costly exhibition catalogues, helping small but serious local musical and dance groups get under way. There are other things, too, that the federal government would perhaps be in the best position to accomplish, if the political climate were not so deliberately abrasive.

Proponents of the NEA point to the fact that most West European governments do support the arts, without great tumult, for the perfectly legitimate reason that they feel a responsibility to their national cultural heritage and to culture generally. But there would not have been a great tumult in the United States, either, if the NEA's advocates, artists' lobbying groups, and artists themselves had not felt the need to justify the mediocre, the political, and the obscene. These justifications have even extended to the argument that *not* to receive an NEA grant is to be the victim of censorship. When Karen Finley and other performance artists were denied an NEA grant in 1990, they took their case to the courts on this basis, and won. As long as such things go on—and there is no reason to believe that they will not—the federal government would do better to remain outside the arts altogether.

When the abolition of the NEA is currently discussed, many people talk about turning the task over to the states. But the effect of this would most likely be to enlarge state bureaucracies, and art selected for support on the state level is likely to be even more mediocre, and no less political, than that selected on the federal level. The prospect of "devolution" is thus not one that ought to fill anyone with optimism.

It does, however, seem doubtful that, if government divorces itself from the arts, private philanthropy will pick up the whole tab. People who run large artistic institutions—museums, symphony orchestras—seem to agree that the new generations of the wealthy have shown themselves less generous than their forebears: the philanthropic impulse is not, evidently, a genetic one.

This is unfortunate. Although money has its limitations in the arts, there is no question that it also has its distinct uses. In my own time on the NEA Council I sensed that if an art was weak, there was nothing that the injection of money—which was finally all the NEA or any federal program had to offer—could do to strengthen it. If, on other hand, an art was strong, as dance was in the middle 1980's, money could help in small but real ways to support it in its vibrancy. Many dancers, for example, work a 26-week season, or less, and hence are unemployed half the year; and, in a profession that almost guarantees injury, few dance companies are able to offer health insurance. Although nothing was done to rectify either of these situations during even the palmiest days at the NEA, the answer in both instances was fairly simple—money.

Other things that seem eminently justifiable are also not likely to be picked up by private philanthropy. The NEA has sent dance and theatrical and musical groups into rural and backwater parts of the country, so that people, and especially the young, could have an opportunity to see live performance, which, even in a television age, has its own magic. Arts education in the lower grades, which has been gradually yet seriously slipping in recent decades, is something that needs attending to. Private philanthropy is unlikely to step in here, too.

All that having been said, however, it still remains the case that if the Endowment were shut down, the arts would probably for the most part not be drastically affected. In some instances, fresh patrons would step forward to fill the financial gaps; in others, cutbacks in production and exhibition schedules would have to be made; in a minor number of cases, smaller institutions—literary magazines, design projects, local music groups—might go under. But much as the NEA and its advocates would like everyone to think otherwise, the presence of the Endowment is not crucial to the artistic life of this country. This may be a good time to lie low and have no arts policy whatsoever. After all, we had an artistic life—a much richer and more distinguished one—before we had an NEA.

Thanks in part to the NEA, we are now in an age of artistic surfeit. To provide only a single depressing statistic, I read somewhere that there are currently 26,000 registered poets in the United States. Where, it will be asked, do they register? With the Associated Writing Programs, I gather, which are chiefly made up of teachers of writing, who are even now busy producing still more poets, who will go on to teach yet more poets, who will . . . so that in 20 years' time we will have 52,000 registered poets. Degas, more than a century ago, remarked: "We must discourage the arts." What might he say today?

What to Do About

The Schools

CHESTER E. FINN, JR.

Chester E. Finn, Jr., currently on leave from his position as professor of education and public policy at Vanderbilt University, is John M. Olin Fellow at the Hudson Institute. He served as Assistant Secretary of Education in the Reagan administration, and his books on education include *We Must Take Charge: Our Schools and Our Future.*

The Clinton administration crowed in the spring of 1994 about its success in getting Congress to enact an education-reform bill called Goals 2000. "Today will be remembered as the day the United States got serious about education," boasted the Secretary of Education, Richard W. Riley, within hours of Senate passage. Persons acquainted with this measure only through its boosters' rhetoric might suppose that something important had happened, that the country had actually begun solving its persistent education problem.

Yet Goals 2000 is no great advance. It codifies in statute the national-education goals that President George Bush and the 50 governors set 4 years earlier. It creates a new federal council to "certify" education standards. And it offers droplets of federal funds to states and localities that take (federally approved) steps to meet those standards.

In and of itself, this will cause few children to learn to spell, cipher, find Mexico on a world map, or comprehend the difference between phylum and species. More worrying, Goals 2000, particularly in concert with a far larger education bill nearing completion on Capitol Hill, could well make matters worse: chilling state and local innovation; intensifying federal regulation; discouraging testing and accountability measures; stocking the new national-standards council with "experts" and interest-group activists; creating plentiful opportunities for new litigation to redistribute education resources; focusing on school inputs (e.g., spending levels, class size, teacher training, textbooks) rather than pupil achievement; and signaling that Washington—rather than governors, community leaders, principals, parents—is the primary wellspring of change.

That scenario may be too gloomy. After all, past federal-education laws have had only a glancing impact on what is taught and how well it is learned in the nation's 100,000 schools. And because Goals 2000 has even more pig-in-a-poke features than past legislation, its long-term effects cannot be forecast with confidence. But one thing is certain: administration hyperbole notwithstanding, Goals 2000 (and its vast companion measure) will not *solve* the education problem and thus cannot accomplish its primary purpose.

The essence of that problem today, as for at least the past 20 years, is that young Americans are not learning enough for their own or the nation's good. The evidence is so bountiful that I have space for no more than a few examples:

- On a host of international comparisons, the achievement of U.S. youngsters is at the middle (in reading) or bottom (in science, math, geography) of the rankings—test after test, year after year.

- Though nearly all who complete high school acquire rudimentary literacy and numeracy skills, only a fraction has the intellectual candlepower sought by employers, colleges, and policy-makers. In 1993, the National Education Goals Panel reported that "fewer than one out of every five students in Grades 4 and 12 have met the Goals Panel's performance standard in mathematics. One out of every four 8th graders has met the standard."

• Even fewer young Americans acquire an education that could be termed "world class." Thus in 1993, out of every 1,000 high-school juniors and seniors, only 85 took Advanced Placement exams in English, math, science, and history, and only about two-thirds of these received passing scores.

• On a recent (1992) survey of adult literacy, just 11 percent of U.S. high-school graduates could accurately restate in writing the main point of a newspaper article.

• A rising proportion of what universities teach is remedial. Many students spend the first part of college acquiring skills and knowledge they should have gained in high school. (They spent much of high school on what they should have learned in grammar school.)

• Many employers say they cannot find people to hire who have the skills, knowledge, attitudes, and habits needed to do the work; the result is another huge investment in remediation—and the export of skilled jobs.

The main symptom of our education malady, without doubt, is the weak academic achievement revealed by the foregoing facts, even among those who complete formal schooling. To understand the disease itself, however, other elements must be considered, not least because they have much to do with why this ailment has proved so resistant to treatment. I count a dozen such elements:

First, the *equity issue.* Besides millions of middle-class children emerging half-ignorant from suburban schools, our system of education attempts to deal with hundreds of thousands of underclass youngsters whose lives are askew in myriad ways, including (but surely not limited to) the fact that they are not learning much in school—from which many, in any event, drop out. The education debate moves confusedly between these two problems, the solutions to which overlap but are not identical.

Moreover, many remedies for the problem of suburban schools (e.g., higher standards) are opposed because it is feared that they will cause more poor and minority youngsters to fail, even though there is no evidence for this. And the near-meltdown of some schools attended by disadvantaged children, especially urban high schools, is so alarming that it blinds many people to the extent and severity of the middle-class problem. Authors like Jonathan Kozol have won fame, fortune, and the adulation of the education fraternity by getting teary about the former problem while pooh-poohing the latter.

Second, the *schools' limited leverage*. Formal education occupies a surprisingly slender portion of our children's lives. The youngster who faithfully attends class 6 hours a day, 180 days a year, from kindergarten through 12th grade, will, at the age of 18, have spent just 9 percent of his hours on earth under the school roof. The other 91 percent are spent elsewhere.

Under optimal circumstances, quite a lot of science, literature, and geography can be learned in that 9 percent. But such circumstances rarely obtain, and even when they do, the school still lacks the power to prevent AIDS, stop drug abuse, reduce the rate of teen pregnancy, or substitute for family and church. Yet more and more such missions are thrust upon the school every year, sometimes by desperate policy-makers, sometimes by activists keen to enroll malleable youngsters in some cause. ("Environmental education" is big these days; so is "community service," often highly politicized by the likes of Ralph Nader, and recently turned into another new federal program called AmeriCorps.)

Third, the enterprise *lacks clear standards and expectations*, what businessmen call "product specifications." One reason American students do not learn what they ought to is that the education system is so nebulous about what it demands of them. If Goals 2000 does any good at all, it will be by legitimizing some national-achievement standards in core academic subjects. But few states and communities have yet specified the knowledge and skills that their youngsters should possess at the end of schooling, and few parents are clear about what and how much the schools expect their children to learn.

Worse, where states have tried to specify school "outcomes," the list usually turns out to be skimpy on fundamental knowledge and basic skills but lavish in its attention to attitudes, behavior, and interpersonal relations. This has then produced a political backlash against the very notion of standards, even in such "progressive" jurisdictions as Minnesota and Connecticut.

Fourth, we possess *little reliable information about results.* Not only have we had difficulty locating a clear destination for the education vehicle; we also have immense trouble erecting readable mileposts along the journey. The nationwide data are pretty good, but in most communities one cannot obtain timely, intelligible information about how well one's own children are learning, how their school is doing in relation to other schools, and how the community and state are performing in comparison with the rest of the country and the world.

Several factors have caused this data drought: testing is unpopular among educators (and civil-rights and child-advocacy groups, etc.); many of today's tests yield incomplete and misleading information; much of what one would like to know (particularly about the performance of individual children, classrooms, teachers, and schools) is never gathered; what is available rarely lends itself to comparisons; and nobody is responsible for an independent "audit" of educational results. Meanwhile, we are awash in data about spending, class size, and other "input-and-service" gauges beloved by educators.

Fifth, young people see *few real consequences.* Even while lamenting the shoddiness of their applicants' preparation, not many universities and employers discriminate between those who take hard courses, learn a lot, and do well in school, and those who choose the path of least resistance, scrape by with C's, and learn very little. Only a small fraction of young people even applies to the handful of competitive colleges where prior academic performance makes a big difference. For the rest, the "real world" seems not to care much whether they hit the books or play around. (The practice of "social promotion" conveys much the same message to younger pupils.)

Children and adolescents being, in their way, rational creatures, it stands to reason that few see an imperative to study hard. To his credit, Albert Shanker, the president of the American Federation of Teachers (AFT), has tirelessly pointed to the "low-stakes" nature of American education as one of the leading causes of its mediocrity. Yet Goals 2000 bars the use of federal funds for "high-stakes" testing, and the federal Office for Civil Rights is harassing Ohio for tying consequences (receipt of a high-school diploma) to its own state tests.

Sixth, there is *no systemic accountability*. As former Secretary of Education William J. Bennett has noted, there are "greater, more certain, and more immediate penalties in this country for serving up a single rotten hamburger in a restaurant than for repeatedly furnishing a thousand schoolchildren with a rotten education." And as another former Secretary of Education, Lamar Alexander, has observed, "Teaching is the only profession in which you are not paid one extra cent for being good at your job." Those managing the education system slough off all accountability for that system's results, good or bad. No rewards come to the successful, or unpleasantness to those who fail. This is partly because—

Seventh, *power rests with the producers, not the consumers*. One might suppose that "public" education was designed to serve the public interest and to account to the public for its performance. But one would be wrong. Most effective power today resides within the education establishment, an interlocked directorate that includes the two big teachers' unions, the National Education Association (NEA) and the AFT (much the most potent and reactionary forces in U.S. education today); principals and superintendents; a dozen other employee groups; surprisingly docile state and local school boards; textbook and test publishers; and colleges of education. Even groups that we might expect to look after "consumer interests" are coopted. Thus, the PTA serves primarily the interests of educators; business groups entrust responsibility for school reform to establishment fellow-travelers; and many legislative education committees are chaired by present or former educators (whose candidacies were generously assisted by the teachers' unions, etc.).

Eighth, that same school establishment enjoys *near-monopoly control*. In any community, there is but one public-school system, attendance is mandatory, and the particular school a youngster attends is normally assigned by someone downtown. Only the well-to-do can loosen the monopoly's grip by taking up residence in another jurisdiction or paying for their children to attend private schools.

Monopolies, as we know, are seldom responsive to consumer preferences; *government* monopolies are even less so. Nor are they inclined to relent. This is why even such canny reformers as the Wisconsin legislator Polly Williams and Governor John Engler of Michigan have had huge difficulty in extending the principle of school choice. It is also why the education establishment threw millions of dollars against the California voucher referendum in 1993.

Ninth, not surprisingly, *education decision-making is gridlocked*. The monopoly's chief goals are to preserve itself, its clout, and the status quo that it embodies; to increase the resources at its disposal; and to ensure that each constituent part retains its share of power, status, and money. Moreover, the complex layering of local, state, and federal regulations, the bloated, lethargic bureaucracies that run the school system, and the so-called stakeholder groups that must assent before any change is made—all these forces make for inertia, repel reformers, and allow each part of the system to blame others. It is a vast "no-fault" enterprise.

Tenth, we are afflicted by what might be termed *retail complacency*. Most Americans think their own school is fine, even if "the nation is at risk." On the 1994 Gallup education survey, for example, just 22 percent of respondents gave honors grades to "the nation's public schools," while 70 percent conferred high marks on "the school your oldest child attends." This discrepancy arises from many sources, including the falsely positive reports pumped out by local and state education systems, the inability of parents and taxpayers to get reliable outcomes data that they can compare to standards, and, perhaps, a disinclination to alter our own ways. The upshot is that most people seem to think the necessary reforming should happen across town.

Eleventh, our *schools were designed for the 19th century*. Even our "good" schools are not nearly so effective as they should be, because practically all of them follow an archaic formula. This is true of private and public institutions alike. (Private schools do produce somewhat better results, but their margin is surprisingly thin.) We have a school year shaped for the agrarian age; a school day built for the era when most mothers were home at 3 P.M.; primitive instructional technology; obsolete notions of how children learn; dull materials; a bureaucratic management system that prizes uniformity and conformity; and a tendency to judge quality by how many adults are present and what services they provide rather than by what children actually learn. The model itself is woefully antiquated.

Finally, *the education profession is awash in bad ideas*. By and large, educators—at least many of the so-called leaders and experts among them—swear by precepts that have placed us at risk. Among these precepts:

- There is really not much wrong with the schools.

- Whatever may be wrong is the fault of the larger society (parents, TV, Republicans, etc.).

- Competition (among students, schools, states, countries, etc.) is harmful.

- Knowledge is passé; what matters are "cognitive skills."

- A child's sense of "self-esteem" counts more than what he knows.

- What children should learn—and from whom—depends on their race and ethnicity.

- Students should never be grouped for instruction according to their ability or prior achievement.

- Only graduates of teacher-training programs should be permitted in the classroom, and none but products of administrator-training programs should be allowed to lead schools or school systems.

But the main precept by which the education establishment and its friends in high places swear is that the ills of American education, such as they are, can be cured by generous applications of money. One difficulty with this prescription is that it is expensive. Another is that, for the most part, it is wrong.

There is no doubt that some school systems are impoverished. Nor is there any doubt that some teachers are not paid enough. (Some, however, may be overcompensated for the results they produce.) Some schools have leaky roofs, antiquated textbooks, dank gyms, and no Bunsen burners in their chemistry labs. And certainly there are sizable fiscal discrepancies among communities and among states.

Nevertheless, American education, taken as a whole, is spending plenty of money. Per-pupil expenditures in the public schools have tripled *in real terms* since the 1950's, have doubled since the mid-1960's (when, by most gauges, our troubles began), and rose by about a third during the Reagan-Bush years of the 1980's. Teachers' salaries went up 27 percent (in real terms) during that same decade. Meanwhile, class sizes have fallen: the median U.S. elementary classroom had 30 students in 1961, 24 in 1986. The public schools employed 6 adults for every 100 children in 1960, 10 in 1981, and 11 in 1990.

As for international comparisons (a statistical swamp), U.S. public expenditures per pupil for kindergarten-through–12th-grade education surpass those of such allies and competitors as Japan, Germany, Britain, France, and Canada. A study by the Organization for Economic Cooperation and Development found that, in 1991, the United States spent 7 percent of its gross domestic product on public and private education at all levels, exceeded only by Canada. And, at 14.7 percent, we are one of the top three nations in spending on public education as a percentage of total public outlays, tied with Finland and surpassed only by Switzerland.

Yes, some of the changes we may need to make (e.g., a longer school year) are apt to carry a price tag. But the prior questions to ask are why we are not getting a better return on the money we are already spending, and whether, as our education outlays continue to rise (a seemingly ineluctable trend), we will find ourselves plowing the extra money into more of the same. As the economist Eric Hanushek concludes in a forthcoming book: "Strong evidence shows that continuing the policies of the past is extraordinarily expensive and unproductive. Expanding upon them would be worse."

That it is hard to solve this tangled nest of problems is abundantly clear. The politics of education are as intractable as any in the land. To implement change may be even more daunting, considering the vastness, sluggishness, decentralization, and ingrained beliefs of this huge enterprise and the layers of contract, custom, ideology, regulation, and law that envelop it.

Yet it is not difficult to imagine what a radically improved education system would look like. So long as we beware the simplistic "magic potion"—the single treatment that would supposedly fix everything—we can even visualize how the main reforms that need to be made would reinforce each other. As I see it, six of these are key.

POWER

We need major shifts of authority and control over resources from producers to consumers and from experts to civilians. That entails cracking the establishment monopoly, and giving parents, voters, taxpayers, elected officials, and community leaders far greater say over what schools must accomplish, how they will be held accountable for doing this, and how children and schools will be matched to one another. The professionals should retain responsibility—and gain greater authority—for decisions about the *means* of education, but the laity needs to determine its *ends*. And those ends must serve the interests of consumers, not providers.

Such a shift of attitude, priority, and authority is the prerequisite for everything else. It may lead us to new forms of educational governance—for instance, handing control of the education system directly to mayors, city councils, governors, and legislatures rather than the semiautonomous board-and-superintendent structure that prevails in most places. (Most of the boldest reforms in U.S. education today are the work of "outsiders" like Governor William Weld of Massachusetts and Mayor Kurt Schmoke of Baltimore.)

The needed power shift may also mean breaking vast school systems into smaller and more manageable units—and perhaps consolidating some tiny, dysfunctional units. It surely includes allowing individual schools to make many decisions heretofore made by bureaucracies, deeper involvement of parents in school governance, and far greater accountability on the part of managers at each level for quality and efficacy.

Above all, the needed power shift means knocking the props out from under the monopoly; enabling people to select from among alternatives; ending coercive assignment of pupils to schools; rewarding (with students, money, etc.) those schools and educators that do a good enough job to attract "clients"; and ending the disgraceful custom of guaranteeing pupils—and the resources and jobs that accompany them—to bad schools that would sit empty if people could vote with their feet.

STANDARDS

Any well-functioning enterprise begins with clarity about its expectations. Successful institutions can describe with fair precision what they are trying to accomplish, what their markers of quality are, and by what indicators they determine how they are faring. So, too, with education. The quality revolution must start by spelling out what young Americans will know and be able to do if the schools perform their job properly.

At a minimum, this means ambitious high-school-graduation standards that consist not of courses taken or time spent but of demonstrable skills and knowledge. These must be supported by synchronized standards at several checkpoints along the way. The six national education goals set by President Bush and the fifty governors in 1989—including the specification of five core subjects and checkpoints at grades 4, 8, and 12—were a good start down this path. (Regrettably, the mangling—and expanding—that the goals received from Congress this year leaves them rather less satisfactory.)

Current efforts by national professional associations of "subject-matter" experts may help flesh out these expectations, though we ought not expect too much from this process. (Some stress "thinking skills" and downplay knowledge; others tend toward political correctness; and—in addition to the core subjects of English, math, science, history, and geography—these efforts now include such dubious entrants as "social studies" and "teaching English as a second language.")

But *national* standards are not the point. They are not essential. They may even turn out to be harmful. In any case, what is done at the national level matters far less than the goals and standards spelled out by each state and locality. If they are to be enforceable, they must be set by those with real authority over schooling, which again means states and localities. And if community concerns about such touchy matters as values and character are to be resolved in acceptable fashion, it is also at the local level that they must be worked out.

This is an arduous process, to be sure, and one that policymakers dare not hand over to education "experts." Taxi drivers, thoracic surgeons, accountants, and clergymen should have at least as much to say about what the children of their communities need to know and be able to do as curriculum directors, university professors, and teachers' unions. But there is no need to start from scratch. Much good material is at hand—like E.D. Hirsch's grade-by-grade sourcebooks on "cultural literacy"—and more appears daily.

ACCOUNTABILITY

For standards to have a real impact, we need good tests and other assessments of student and school performance vis-à-vis those standards. We need trustworthy information about how we are doing. And we need accountability mechanisms that include real stakes and consequences for everyone involved.

No enterprise that has avoided accountability up to now will welcome its imposition. Countless reasons will be given as to why it is unfair, even cruel, to hold anyone responsible for his own or anybody else's results. The opponents of testing will also raise a thousand objections to the use of any given measuring tool. (The federal intervention in Ohio's graduation test is based on slightly discrepant passing rates by black and white youngsters.) It will take great determination to break through all this.

A true system of accountability has several essentials: exams that mirror the desired goals and standards of the state or community; a blend of teacher-designed assessments (vital for diagnosis and classroom correction) and external tests, prepared and administered—like an independent audit—by people other than the school system's own managers; speed and intelligibility of test results, together with their comparability over time and across jurisdictions; and the employment of other gauges of success, such as attendance, graduation rates, and the incidence of discipline problems.

The purpose is not bean-counting. It is to alter pupil and educator behavior so as to produce better results. Which means that *stakes and consequences* must be tied to those results. This implies, for one thing, that students should be promoted (or graduated) only when they have met specified standards, that universities should adopt explicit (and unvarying) admissions standards, and that employers should do likewise. But consequences should not apply only to the students. Teachers, principals, superintendents, and other responsible adults should also be rewarded for success, penalized for failure, and—ultimately—dismissed if they or their institutions cannot get the job done.

SUPPLY-SIDE PLURALISM

All schools should embrace a common core of skills and knowledge, but they should also be encouraged to vary along other dimensions. Children differ in learning styles, temperament, and personal preference. Families differ in the educational experiences they want for their children (particularly in such domains as values, ethics, and character). Educators differ in philosophy, passion, and expertise. Communities, states, and regions have distinctive traditions, priorities, and concerns. America is too big and diverse a country to expect a single educational model to fit everyone.

Hence, rather than trying to standardize our schools, shackling them with regulations, and punishing them for deviating, we should welcome educational pluralism and the freedom and competition that accompany it. Let schools vie with one another on the basis of their distinctive features; let them do all they can to attract students and families—and to satisfy those they attract.

In addition, we should encourage diverse "proprietors" to create and manage schools. It is time, as the Minnesota analyst Ted

Kolderie says, to "withdraw the exclusive franchise." Instead of supposing that all public schools must be the creatures of large, bureaucratic systems, we should encourage entrepreneurship by teachers and other educators, by various public and private institutions, even by the business sector. And instead of awarding geographic monopolies to particular schools or systems, let them compete on one another's turf. Define a public school not as something administered in uniform fashion by a government agency but, rather, as a school that *serves* the public, that accepts the core standards adopted by its state or community, and that agrees to be accountable for its results.

The appetite for such innovation is vast. Though the Massachusetts legislature—heavily lobbied by teachers' unions, school boards, and administrators—limited to twenty-five the number of "charter" schools[1] that could be started under the Commonwealth's reform law, on the day that charter proposals were due, state Education Secretary Piedad Robertson received sixty-four such requests. More have since flooded in.

Educational diversity also means welcoming the creation of "break-the-mold" schools based on wholly different models of what a first-class education might be. Some of the Massachusetts charter schools promise to incorporate new designs when they open in 1995. So do the nine projects supported by the New American Schools Development Corporation, the Edison Project (with which I have been associated), the Coalition of Essential Schools, and other public and private ventures. A true revolution in education means more than fixing up the schools we already have; it also means creating schools we have never before imagined.

DEMAND-SIDE CHOICE

School choice is no panacea but it *is* the essential lubricant of a reformed education system. Families must be able to select their schools from among all available offerings. They must have the right to leave one school for another if they change their minds.

---

[1]Charter schools are independent public schools, often run by a group of teachers or parents, innovative (or traditional) in content, and free from most regulations and external controls.

And the array of schools from which they may choose should be as broad and variegated as possible.

Myriad details must of course be worked out as education shifts from a monopoly-and-coercion system to one based on pluralism and choice. Nor, given our constitutional history and political sensitivities, is it a simple matter to decide whether all extant private schools, including church-affiliated institutions, should be able to participate in a tax-funded choice system. But it is not difficult to establish some crucial precepts by which educational choice should operate.

Begin by redefining public schools in the manner suggested above, then granting private schools the right to "opt in" so long as they are willing to accept public standards, accountability, and a modicum of regulation. But they must also be free, if they prefer, to remain wholly private, unregulated, and unsubsidized. Parents, too, need the right to educate their children at home if they wish. Whether or not this is wise education policy, home schooling is a needed escape valve for social and political steam.

Regulations for participating schools should be kept to a minimum: health, safety, nondiscrimination, accountability for results, financial probity, and not much more. But any marketplace works best when the customers have ample information about alternatives. In education, it is the public's proper business to ensure that such information is accurate. Especially valuable are "school report cards" that parents can understand. Some families will also benefit from help in analyzing such information and making decisions.

As with testing, the opponents of choice throw up a hundred reasons why it should not even be tried and insist that dozens of conditions be met in advance. A few such conditions are reasonable—working out a transportation arrangement, for example— and advocates should try to meet them. But the critics will never be content. They demand that proponents of new arrangements meet far more exacting standards than ever are laid on the status quo. Reformers should therefore concentrate on establishing the principle of choice—without losing another decade.

PROFESSIONALISM

No school is ultimately better than the people who work in it. Great educators, accordingly, are a precious asset, worth locating, engaging, rewarding, and retaining. They should be treated as professionals, not as hired hands. In return, they must conduct themselves like professionals, which is a long way indeed from the behaviors typically displayed at the collective-bargaining table.

Professionalism involves ceding to individual schools a wide array of decisions historically made "downtown," including matters of instruction, staffing, resource allocation, schedule, school "climate," and discipline. So long as these decisions yield the desired results—and the customers are satisfied—the school's staff should be free to organize itself and its work as it thinks best.

Outstanding educators can be found in many places, not just among graduates of teacher- and administrator-training programs. Multiple paths into the classroom (and principal's office) need to exist, including ready entry for capable but inexperienced individuals who know their subjects, want to teach children, have sound character, and are prepared to learn on the job. The states that have already adopted "alternative certification" schemes have made a start on this.

Once hired, one's compensation should be based on the effectiveness of one's performance, as well as the scarcity of one's specialty, the complexity of one's assignment, the breadth of one's responsibilities, and the difficulty of one's work environment. Uniform salary schedules that treat everyone alike, whether good, bad, or mediocre, have no place in any true profession.

Similarly, professionals need opportunities to remain current in their subjects and up-to-date on broader developments in education. Our institutional arrangements must provide for these, as well as for reasonable vacations, sabbaticals, etc. But professionals must also expect to work year-round and all day—and to take work home with them at night.

Those who falter should have a chance to solve their problem. But if it remains unsolved, they have no right to continue engaging in educational malpractice. This enterprise must run for the benefit of its customers, not its producers. Practices such as lifetime tenure are antithetical to bona fide professionalism.

It is conceivable that the teachers' unions could transform themselves into professional associations that could live with these precepts.[2] But in most places the unions are throwing their considerable might against such changes and therefore must be combated through all available means. What counts is not what Albert Shanker and his NEA counterpart Keith Geiger write in their paid newspaper columns; it is what their hundreds of state and local affiliates do at the statehouse and the bargaining table.

Obvious as these recipes may seem, few are cooking from them today. The entrenched forces of the status quo contend that radical change is unnecessary, even damaging, to "public education as we know it." Furnish them with more time, more money, more leverage, better parents, and a society more committed to education, and whatever may be awry today can—so they tell us—easily be set right tomorrow.

Better still, they would have us believe, the added resources will enable them to broaden the school's responsibilities to include day care, birth control, drug-abuse prevention, health care, and suchlike. That the essential nature of "public education as we know it" is itself a large part of what is amiss is, not surprisingly, quite beyond their ken.

Meanwhile, the Clinton administration and its acolytes murmur that Uncle Sam will take care of everything, so long as everyone does what he says. From time to time, they give a rhetorical boost to ideas like charter schools, even the private management of public schools. (To the astonishment of his staff and the consternation of his union allies, the President personally penned such an endorsement into the 1994 State of the Union address.) But the administration's main education strategy is for the federal government to solve most of what is wrong via something it calls "systemic reform," by which it means an array of spending programs, regulations, and "state plans" subject to approval by the Secretary of Education. Though committed to goals and standards, the administration is also bestowing renewed credibility on inputs and services, and it steadfastly refuses to attach real stakes or consequences to student results.

[2]See my article "Teacher Politics" in the February 1983 *Commentary.*

The giant Elementary and Secondary Education Act (ESEA) reauthorization nearing completion in Congress makes further mischief. In addition to what has already been noted about it above, the version passed by the House of Representatives emasculates the independent, nonpartisan governing board that supervises the "national assessment of educational progress." It turns this sensitive testing program over to political appointees and government careerists disposed to probe deeply for revealing "family-background" data (one way to let schools off the hook) and to adjust test results to compensate for state differences in racial composition.

But Washington is not the only arena where the principles of sound reform are under fierce assault. Nor does the attack come only from the Left. "Silver-bullet" conservatives would have us believe that school vouchers, enabling people to attend private schools at public expense, are both necessary and sufficient to reform U.S. education. In recent months, they have trumpeted that conviction from California to Michigan, from Phoenix to Harrisburg.

Unfortunately, the voucher enthusiasts are only half correct. Wide-ranging choice among schools is indispensable, and—thanks to both the fervor of its advocates and its popularity among parents, especially those trapped in urban school systems—we are going to see more and more of it. But vouchers cannot do the job alone. Not, in any case, so long as there is no parallel supply-side effort to diversify, modernize, and deregulate our essentially uniform schools, private as well as public, and not so long as we have no clear "product specifications," no good consumer information, and no accountability mechanisms other than the marketplace.

Also firing from the Right—and one of the most worrisome developments of the past few years—is a tireless cadre of people who are striving to obliterate the theory and practice of "outcomes-based" education. They are right to be upset, yet their alternative would set back the cause of educational excellence a long way.

There are really only two ways to gauge educational quality and efficacy: in relation to school inputs or in relation to pupil achievement. Either we judge a school by what is learned there, or we inevitably find ourselves evaluating it by how much is spent there—or by kindred measures such as hours devoted, courses taken, and the ratio of teachers to pupils.

It was our decades-long preoccupation with inputs that placed the United States at educational risk and forced belated attention to goals, standards, and results. As elected officials and business leaders came to realize in the mid-1980's that added expenditures were not getting us anywhere, and that clarity about standards and accountability for results were vital ingredients of the reform recipe, they took steps to refocus the debate from inputs to outcomes. The national-education goals adopted by President Bush and the governors (and now enshrined in Goals 2000) are the most conspicuous legacy of this changed way of thinking. But even more important decisions were made at the state level, where one legislature, commissioner of education, or state board of education after another decreed that precise standards would be set forth, that children must study until they met those standards, and that schools and their employees would henceforth be judged by their effectiveness in producing that result. Variants of that policy are now law in South Carolina and Florida, in California and Michigan, in Colorado and Illinois, in Kentucky and Pennsylvania, and in many other jurisdictions.

So far, so good. But the devil lurks in the details. Proclaiming that there shall be standards is not the same as spelling them out, and, more often than not, responsibility for doing that was handed to educators with a radically different conception of what school is for and which results are desirable. Rather than itemizing the basic skills and knowledge that well-educated children should be able to demonstrate in core academic subjects, the lists of outcomes that were actually drafted had more to do with social attitudes, ideological positions, and interpersonal relations. Sometimes this was the product of committees and task forces created within the state; sometimes it came from itinerant vendors of prepackaged "outcomes-based" programs, strategies, and curricula that are heavy on what educators call the "transformational" role of schooling and light on the "three R's" that are what most legislators, parents, and taxpayers have in mind.

This development was bound to alarm many parents, particularly when such dubious outcomes were mandated for all schools and children in the state. It is one thing for a private school or charter school to be forthright about instilling values and attitudes in its students. Nobody is forced to sign up for such a school. But it is another matter altogether when a *state* decrees that nobody can graduate from any of the schools within its borders before acquiring and demonstrating certain values and attitudes.

When the neighborhood school teaches children behaviors or beliefs that parents deem abhorrent, even sacrilegious, those parents can be expected to become forceful in trying to alter the situation, the more so if they have no exit to another school that is closer to their world view. The result, beginning in Pennsylvania but rapidly spreading across the land, has been a storm of protest against outcomes-based education.

The protesters' position has considerable merit. But it must also be noted that, for some people of a fundamentalist orientation, schools err when they teach children to reason independently, think critically, or weigh evidence objectively. While one can share the dismay of parents over a state-sanctioned educational institution teaching doctrines that offend their deepest beliefs, one cannot agree that schools, especially public schools, should forgo all "higher-order" intellectual skills. This conflict poses one of the most vexing dilemmas of contemporary education policy.

Because of these disputes, even the word "outcomes" has become tainted, and most prudent policy-makers and elected officials now eschew it. School inputs are getting a new lease on life, thanks to a wholly unexpected (and surely unintended) marriage of political convenience between fundamentalist parents and an accountability-averse education establishment.

But we will be making a big mistake if we turn away from setting goals and standards or from the principle that students, educators, and schools must account for their performance vis-à-vis those standards. Perhaps the conflict can be modulated by recalling several ingredients of the reform recipe outlined above: "compulsory" outcomes that are confined to a core list of broadly accepted skills and knowledge; families encouraged to choose from an increasingly varied array of schools that approach that core (and other matters) via different routes; and private schools and home-schoolers free to shun even those elements of the academic core that clash with their beliefs.

What has been recommended here is conceptually straightforward, even obvious, but politically it constitutes an immense undertaking. Elected officials and community leaders who seek conscientiously to solve the nation's education problem will have to take on one of the largest and most entrenched sets of interest groups in the land. They will also have to urge a series of changes in attitude and practice that will not prove universally popular among their constituents, particularly those who find their complacency jarred or lives altered by the need to face the education music in their own households and local schools.

There are two reasons why this is worth doing anyway. First, as a matter of politics, it is clear from innumerable surveys that most Americans do agree in principle with the measures suggested here. With the benefit of time, leadership, and accurate information, they are likely to come around in practice as well.

Second, as a matter of public policy, nothing is more fundamental or important than education, save for national defense. In truth, a sound education system can fairly be termed the domestic equivalent of a strong national defense. Getting such a system will take vision, courage, and persistence. But the rewards will be immense.

What to Do About

Health Care

DAVID FRUM

David Frum is a columnist for the *American Spectator* and a
weekly commentator on National Public Radio's *Morning
Edition*. His book, *Dead Right*, was published by Basic Books
in 1994.

In the 1970's, an East German defector to the West was assigned
the task of helping other escapees adjust to life in a free country.
The problem, he remembered years later, was that from kindergarten through college, from the moment the newspaper was
opened in the morning to the moment the radio was turned off at
night, every East German was bombarded by state propaganda
telling him that the West was afflicted by hideous poverty, unemployment, and crime. As a result, East Germans naturally concluded that in the West poverty, unemployment, and crime were
completely unknown.

   In the same way, after two years of hearing President Clinton
insist that health care was the gravest problem the country faced, it
was natural for the President's political opponents to conclude that
health care is one subject they need never think about again. A
consensus has rapidly formed that Clinton's health-care campaign

blighted his presidency. Americans are by and large content with the care they get. They mistrust federal plans to tinker with that care. And other social problems—crime, welfare, immigration—worry them far more. Would it not be wiser to leave the vexed thing alone?

Unfortunately, the mere fact that President Clinton identified health care as an urgent national problem does not automatically prove that it is *not* an urgent national problem. It is, and will remain so.

Yet the persistence and intractability of the health-care problem should not rehabilitate the President's plan. Looking again at this plan, and at the torrent of papers and articles that explicated and defended it, one can only gape at its arrogance and unreality. Apologists insist that it was by no means the socialist document it was represented to be, that it included a dose of market competition. Perhaps so; but this dose of competition was, in a curious sense, the ultimate hubris: the plan's chief architects, Ira Magaziner and Hillary Rodham Clinton, regarded markets not as an infinite series of voluntary exchanges, but as a mechanism, as one more device for state control. They flattered themselves that they could introduce marketlike arrangements where they pleased, bar them where they liked, and generally manipulate them to produce desired results.

Even that, however, does not quite convey the full ambition of the plan Magaziner and Mrs. Clinton wrote for the President. The Clinton plan in the minds of its authors aimed at nothing less than slyly reviving the dying hopes of liberalism. Thus: Health care would displace busing as a means of compelling racial integration, since the plan's compulsory-insurance cachements would group cities and their inner and outer suburbs together. Health care would be the method for snuffing out the independence of university medical and science faculties, as state and federal officials determined which specialties would be taught, to how many students, and from which ethnic backgrounds. Health care would enable Washington to deliver colossal subsidies to favored business interests, by relieving unionized manufacturers of foolishly extended commitments and by offering smaller businesses below-market insurance at rates to be determined by the effectiveness of their lobbying. And health care would revive the Democratic party by proving to an increasingly skeptical middle class that Big Government could once again pay off for them.

Altogether, the Clinton health plan would have amounted to the most ambitious peacetime assertion of state power over civil society since the National Recovery Act of 1935. Its collapse must be reckoned as one of the closest shaves in the history of American democracy.

Good luck cannot, however, always be counted on. If Americans are to ward off future versions of the Clinton plan, or worse, believers in a free economy and free institutions must grapple with the same problem that Ira Magaziner and Mrs. Clinton did. Or, actually, the same five problems.

Health care is, in the first place, a *budgetary* problem. Together, Medicare (which goes to retirees regardless of income) and Medicaid (which goes only to the indigent) cost $55 billion when Ronald Reagan took office. Today they cost nearly 5 times as much. Hence, if the growth of the two biggest federal health-care programs could somehow have been held to the rate of inflation over the past decade and a half, the federal budget would have been sitting comfortably in surplus today. Unless these two programs—and other health-care-driven programs like veterans' benefits and federal employees' retirement benefits—can somehow be brought under control in the future, it is impossible to imagine how the federal budget can be balanced and taxes cut.

Second, health care is an *economic* problem. Americans pay more than 13 percent of the national income for health care—more than any other major industrial nation. And the bills keep mounting at an unbelievable clip. One survey of large employers found that their health costs per employee more than doubled in the 10 years 1984 to 1993, from $1,645 to $3,781. Small employers' costs have mushroomed even more dramatically. True, prices have come off the boil slightly over the past 3 years—but they are still rising faster than inflation and faster than the overall growth in the economy. The exploding costs of benefits are gobbling up money that might otherwise have been paid to employees in cash:

one important reason for the stagnation of wages during the
1980's boom.

Health care is also a *social* problem. The United States is aging
rapidly. While the total population is expected to increase by about
20 percent between 1990 and 2030, the number of Americans
older than 65 is expected to double. When Americans reach age
65, they enter a new country—one characterized by stark dependence on government. The tilting of the demographic balance
toward the old therefore threatens to tilt the country's social balance away from self-reliance and toward welfarism. And even
before they reach retirement, many Americans do indeed suffer
the anxieties that Mrs. Clinton so passionately described during
the debate over her plan: anxieties about losing their insurance if
they lose or change their job, and about insurers or employers
arbitrarily changing the rules of the plans they rely on.

Inevitably, then, health care will again rise as a *political* problem. One thing, at least, Republicans should have learned from the
Bush years—it is not prudent to tell voters who think they have a
problem that they are mistaken. To be sure, most people like the
care they get. A major survey done in 1993 on behalf of Novalis
Corporation—a consultant to the managed-care industry—found
that nearly 80 percent of Americans rated their own personal care
as "good" or "excellent." Only 5.4 percent rated the care they
were receiving as "poor." Startlingly, more than half of the *uninsured* rated *their* care as good or excellent. Even more startlingly,
55 percent of the uninsured reported that they enjoyed the services of a family doctor.

How can this be? For one thing, the typical uninsured American is not the widow Jones and her four hungry children: *she* is on
Medicaid. The typical uninsured American is a high-school graduate looking for his first job, or a recently divorced woman waiting
on tables while she tries to put her life back together. Sixty percent of the uninsured are under 30. Most of them will go without
insurance for only a short time, just as they will go without
employment for a short time: at any given moment, as many as 39
million Americans may lack insurance, but only 4 percent of the
population are without it for as long as 28 months.

Since the uninsured are younger and healthier than average,

and since state regulators have heaped so many minimum requirements onto private health-insurance plans, conventional policies
represent a bad deal for most of these young people. If they could
buy a bare-bones policy for $800 or $1,000, many of them might
do it. But if forced to buy an expensive plan, they will wait until
an employer purchases it on their behalf (not considering that he
will submerge the cost by lowering wages).

Yet while Americans like the care they get, they feel no such
enthusiasm for the national system as a whole. Only 45 percent
rate the health-care system "overall" as excellent or good. Enough
bad news has percolated through the population to persuade a
majority to rate the *nation's* health-care situation, as against their
own personal situation, as fair or poor. Which means that the malfunctioning of the system—its out-of-control costs, and the sense
of powerlessness it inflicts on millions of consumers—will again
sound a political echo.

Fifth, health care represents a *moral* problem for American
democracy. Everywhere one looks, the distorted health-care market
has created incentives for squalid behavior. Because Medicaid reim-
burses hospitals at absurdly low rates, they make up the shortfall by
deliberately inflating the bills of their privately insured patients.
Because Medicaid covers nursing-home care and Medicare does
not, and because Congress in 1988 enacted legislation that prevents
Medicaid from investigating the assets of next-of-kin, old people
can pass their assets intact to their children and then get cared for
by the taxpayer. (This practice has become so routine that Senator
Carol Moseley-Braun of Illinois won her race in 1992 despite the
revelation that she had engaged in just such asset-shifting in order
to qualify her mother for Medicaid.) Because the cost of insurance
is escalating so rapidly, even conscientious employers are pressured
to scale back the coverage they offer. And because welfare recipients are entitled to Medicaid but intact low-income working families generally are not, the failures of the American health-care market add one more temptation to the allurements of the dole.

These are big problems, they are urgent problems, and they are
difficult problems. But anyone who wants to fix them has to begin

by liberating his mind from the illusion the Clinton administration propagated about the American health-care system—the illusion that it is a free-market, private-sector system, and that its faults derive from the brutal appetite for profit.

In fact, health care is the sector of the American economy where government's power weighs most heavily. The vast sums of Medicare and Medicaid money pumped into the health market since 1965 helped to spark the medical-cost inflation of the past 30 years. State regulation effectively outlaws cheap health-insurance plans by specifying a long list of services, from acupuncture to psychiatry, that any employer who decides to set up a plan must provide. But the most important of all the government-created distortions of the health market is the way health benefits are taxed.

Suppose you are given a $100-a-week raise by your employer. If you are a professional or managerial worker, you will be lucky to take home $55 of it after income and payroll taxes. If, however, that same $100 were spent to beef up your health insurance, every dollar of it would be available to you. For anyone whose health is not absolutely perfect, $100 of health insurance is more valuable than $100 in cash.

This distortion has twisted health insurance into strange shapes. Compare health insurance to automobile insurance. When you buy a policy, you pay a price calibrated to the riskiness of the car you drive and your own safety history. Automobile insurance is *insurance*—protection against big losses for which you pay a premium determined by the probability that you will incur such a loss. The policy does not cover new tires, tune-ups, or gasoline.

By contrast, health-insurance premiums are not much influenced by the riskiness of the actual people covered, nor does health insurance pay only against substantial losses. What are conventionally thought of as "good" plans cover eyeglasses, prescription drugs, checkups, and other routine expenses. In other words, health insurance, for most Americans, is not insurance but a disguised form of salary. It is as if the federal government were to decide that money spent by employers to feed lunch to their employees could be deducted from taxes. And it is as if, instead of paying their employees and sending them out to get their own lunch with after-tax dollars, employers would set up lunchrooms and add asparagus and artichokes to the salad bar whenever profits improved.

Making health insurance a perk rather than insurance causes people to divert more of their income toward health care than they would otherwise prefer. If instead of giving me a raise, my employer juices up my health plan so that I can buy a new pair of eyeglasses every year, new eyeglasses are what I will take—even though I would rather have new shoes for the children or books or a little extra money for groceries.

Noninsurance health insurance also teaches people not to care about the price of the medical services they buy. In their remarkable book, *Patient Power*, John Goodman and Gerald Musgrave asked seven different Dallas-area hospitals the price of a complete blood count. The charge varied from $11 to $33. They found the same disparities for big-ticket services, too: the normal delivery of a child could cost anywhere from $1,000 to more than $2,000. The same consumers who would drive across town to save a dollar and a half on a movie ticket neither know nor care what they pay for medical services, because the money they save belongs to their employer, not to them.

Worse, the value of the health-care perk varies not according to your health-care needs, but according to your income. If you are paying a 50-percent marginal tax rate, you would have to earn an extra $6,000 to buy a $3,000 health-insurance policy with after-tax dollars. If you are paying a 25-percent marginal tax rate, you would only need to earn an extra $4,000. Stuart Butler of the Heritage Foundation notes that the nontaxability of health-care fringe benefits amounted to a $48-billion tax expenditure in 1991, most of which was lavished upon the highest-income taxpayers.

Finally, so long as health insurance is thought of as a perk, it will remain a deal not between the consumer and the provider of health services, but between the provider and the consumer's employer. Everywhere else in American society, the past 15 years have humbled giant bureaucracies. Automakers, the phone company, television networks—every corporation that used to hand everyone "take-it-or-leave-it" deals has felt the new power of consumers who enjoy more information and more choices than ever before. But not medicine. There, consumers still approach bureaucracies as dependents and supplicants. Why? Because they do not control the money they are spending.

Whatever the Clinton plan's other evils, it was not illogical. Clinton proposed to eliminate the health market's inconsistencies by proceeding faster in the direction the country had been heading since 1965 toward fully state-controlled medicine. Unless his opponents can reverse course and pull the country back toward a free market in health care, something like the Clinton plan must someday prevail. The choice for America does not lie between the Clinton plan and the status quo. The status quo cannot be sustained. The real choice is between some variant of the Clinton plan and free-market reform.

So far, conservatives have produced three main approaches to health-care reform. In 1983, the Reagan administration sought to cap the increase in Medicare costs by stipulating in advance the amount it would pay to hospitals for 467 distinct procedures. Until then, hospitals had set their own prices more or less as they pleased, and mailed the bills to Washington. The Reagan caps did jolt the hospitals and did produce one-time savings. But as hospitals learned the system, the upward march of prices swiftly resumed.

Worse, while the Reagan caps failed to rein in Medicare, they succeeded in lowering the program's standards of care, by setting reimbursement rates for many simple operations below the hospitals' own costs without creating incentives for hospitals to restructure those costs. As a result, Medicare patients often fail to find hospitals willing to perform simple but important services.

The second conservative approach was the individual-mandate plan designed by Heritage's Butler in 1991. Heritage figured that since everyone in the country was getting some form of health coverage anyway, everyone ought to buy it. But unlike most liberal schemes, the Heritage plan imposed the obligation to buy insurance not on employers but on individuals.

In order to make insurance affordable to poorer people, the Heritage plan would have Washington seize the $48-billion tax subsidy to the private-insurance market and redistribute it. If your employer paid $3,000 a year to buy you health insurance, that $3,000 would now count as "income" on your W–2. What you would get instead would be a tax credit for the purchase of health insurance, ranging from 20 percent if you had a high income to as much as 90 percent if you were very poor.

Thus, an affluent person who bought a $3,000 policy (and he would probably be buying it for himself since the government would no longer be giving his employer a tax subsidy to buy the policy for him) would be able to subtract $600 from his income tax. The remaining $2,400 he would have to pay out of his own pocket with after-tax dollars. That would make him a much more careful shopper. Meanwhile, a low-income person who spent $1,000 on a cheap policy would get a tax credit for as much as $900—and if that $900 exceeded the insured person's income-tax liability, he would get a check for the balance from the IRS.

The Heritage plan would make insurance much more accessible while also inducing Americans to be a little more price-conscious. Upper-income Americans would care about price because they would be paying 80 percent of the cost of their insurance policies themselves with after-tax dollars. Lower-income Americans would care about price because—even though their out-of-pocket costs would nearly vanish—they would be obliged to shop for insurance policies on their own, rather than simply presenting themselves to a doctor who would bill Medicare or Medicaid.

Back in 1992 and early 1993, when some type of socialized medicine hovered ominously close, the Heritage plan looked like a daring free-market reform. As backing for the Clinton plan crumbled, though, the redistributionist features of the Heritage scheme cost it most of its support among Republicans. Libertarian-minded Republicans disliked ordering people to buy insurance, and conservatives generally gagged as they realized that Heritage's system of credits would steepen the progressivity of an already redistributionist tax system—an especially sore point after President Clinton hiked the top federal-tax rate to nearly 40 percent (up from 28 percent just 5 years ago).

Because Medicaid and Medicare would continue to absorb virtually all the health-care costs of the poorest and oldest—in fact, these programs would take on even larger responsibilities—it is doubtful that the Heritage plan would do very much to reduce health care's drain on the federal treasury. Nor would the Heritage plan affect the way Americans react to health costs. From the point of view of the consumer, not much would change: he would go on sending his medical bills to CIGNA or Aetna for reimbursement as he incurred them. All he would notice was that he was paying higher income taxes.

After months of intra-conservative pummeling, Butler surrendered his sword in the winter of 1995. He co-authored an article in the winter issue of *Policy Review*, Heritage's quarterly publication, with one of his severest critics, William Niskanen, retreating from the specifics of the 1991 plan to more general principles that nearly all free-market-minded people would accept.

Niskanen is president of the libertarian Cato Institute, and the principles he and Butler promulgated seem to point more naturally to the approach Cato advocates, and which has been endorsed by nearly 200 Congressmen: the medical-savings (or Medisave) plan devised by John Goodman and Gerald Musgrave of the National Center for Policy Analysis in Dallas. All the technicalities aside, it would work more or less like this:

The tax exemption for contributions by employers to health-insurance plans would be abolished in favor of tax-exempt Medisave accounts. Employees and their employers would make donations to these accounts, out of which individuals would pay for their routine medical expenses. Whatever was left over in the account at year's end would remain the saver's property. Over a number of years, reasonably healthy people would compound tidy nest eggs with which to finance their health costs in old age. In the meantime, they would protect themselves against serious illnesses by purchasing a new type of policy, one made available by the repeal of state and federal regulations controlling what a health-insurance policy must look like.

The new policies would carry very high deductibles—$3,000 a year. Since more than 80 percent of Americans spend less than $3,000 a year on health insurance, the premiums for these policies would be relatively low. Large savings could also be made in administrative expenses. As economists often point out, a $50 claim costs as much to process as a $50,000 claim. Under a Medisave regime, the vast bulk of medical costs would be paid without having to crank up the bureaucratic machinery of the insurance companies.

Over time, these Medisave accounts would eliminate the need for Medicare. As for Medicaid, it could be replaced either by a more modest version of the Heritage Foundation's tax-credit scheme or else by direct payments by the government to Medisave accounts established for low-income people.

The tremendous advantage of the Goodman and Musgrave plan is that it would bring medical-cost inflation screeching to a halt. As people bought medical services for themselves, with real dollars that they could otherwise keep, they would suddenly start to shop as cannily for health care as they do for food and shelter and every other essential of life. There is no inherent reason that health costs must skyrocket: the prices of all other technology-intensive services almost invariably fall.

And the Goodman and Musgrave scheme would accomplish this while protecting the quality of health care: patients would no longer be subject to an insurer's determination—or Medicare's—of what they did or did not need. They could decide for themselves whether or not they required a third day in the hospital after giving birth; they could decide for themselves whether or not they wanted to pay for a policy that covered psychological trauma.

The weakness of the Goodman and Musgrave plan is that it pays comparatively little attention to the problem of insuring America's poorest. Their Cato allies have suggested that the best answer to this problem lies in forming pools of high-risk people whom each state would pay private insurers to take care of. Twenty-eight states have already enacted something very like what Cato recommends. But this remains an inadequate response to the ever-mounting medical ills of America's growing ranks of underclass poor.

★   ★   ★

What, then, to do? The four main goals of health-care reform are:

- To alleviate the burden that spiraling health costs impose on the federal budget.

- To alleviate the burden that spiraling health costs impose on private industry.

- To bring insurance within easier reach of the uninsured.

- To nip in the bud the deterioration in medical quality that has begun to manifest itself as employers and governments control costs with top-down administrative measures instead of competition.

The Goodman and Musgrave Medisave plan goes far toward accomplishing these goals. It ought to be the basic building block of any Republican reform. It does not, however, reach quite far enough. Four additional steps are needed.

First, Medicaid—the most rapidly growing and most abused federal health program—should be reconceived. Instead of being a piece of the health-care puzzle, Medicaid, along with the federal disability program, must be recognized as a piece of the welfare puzzle. Medicaid is already administered by the states, under widely varying rules. Indeed, one man—former New York Governor Mario Cuomo—is almost single-handedly responsible for the explosion of Medicaid costs. New York State, though it contains only 9 percent of the Medicaid population, gobbles up 18 percent of Medicaid spending. Congress should do with Medicaid what it is preparing to do with welfare: cap benefits at their present level, convert the money into block grants to the states, and repeal all rules inhibiting state freedom to experiment.

After all, the tragedies counted among America's most horrific health problems—from premature, underweight babies to AIDS-infected drug addicts to 12-year-old gunshot victims bleeding to death in lackadaisical ambulances—are not really health problems, any more than the plight of the homeless is a housing problem. They are incidents and by-products of the breakdown of social order among the urban underclass.

Thus, for example, the demographer Nicholas Eberstadt has demonstrated that even though ultra-low-birth-weight babies enjoy better odds of survival in America than in any other country, America still suffers a horrific infant-mortality rate because American mothers give birth to so many more low-weight babies than mothers in other countries. Eberstadt has shown that the most important factor in determining birth weight is the mother's own conduct. Mothers who drink, smoke, eat badly, and take drugs during pregnancy will have low-birth-weight babies—and such mothers are highly likely to be unmarried. So long as the welfare system encourages illegitimacy, Medicaid could double its prenatal spending every single year and still fail to make a dent in America's infant-mortality statistics.

Next, Washington must get out of the business of providing health care itself. The Veterans Administration (VA) is the single largest hospital system in the nation—and also a notoriously inefficient and shoddy one. Hospitals are located where long-forgotten Congressmen could profit politically from them. Costs are high, service quality is low. Everybody agrees that veterans have special claims on the public, combat veterans most of all. But those claims could be met, better and more cheaply, if Washington made extra contributions to the Medisave accounts of veterans so that they could buy an insurance policy of their choosing. And then the VA's network of inefficient hospitals could be taken off the nation's books.

As Washington turns Medicaid over to the states and veterans' assistance over to the private sector, the states must likewise limit their own ambitions and abandon their habit of interfering in their medical markets. If an insurance company wants to offer a cheap plan that does not cover acupuncture, chiropractic, or replacement eyeglasses, it should be allowed to do so. If a health maintenance organization (HMO) wants to contract only with a specified list of doctors who agree to follow certain rules, it should be allowed to do that, too—without the state legislature forcing it to deal with "any willing provider." The 39 million uninsured have money to spend. If permitted, the insurance companies would offer policies such people could afford. America has 39 million uninsured people for the same reason that it would have 39 million naked people if the only clothing stores permitted to operate were Bendel's and Saks. We should legalize K-Mart insurance before concluding that the private sector cannot do the job.

Finally, America's most permanent and intractable health problem arises from the most permanent and intractable fact of life: old age. It is expensive to be old even if you are comparatively healthy, and it is very expensive if you are not healthy. Beginning on or about August 15, 2010, the front wedge of the baby boom will turn 65. These people are going to need hearing aids and prescription drugs and pacemakers and hip replacements and all the other wonderful contrivances of modern medical technology. And beginning on or about August 15, 2020, baby-boomer retirees will need nurses and in-home care and, in the end, institutional care.

All that will require money—huge amounts of money. Whose? As things are going, the money will have to come from a penurious government squeezing all it can out of the baby-bust generation. This effectively guarantees that the baby boomers will receive low-grade care in their declining years. If, however, the money paying those nurses and buying the pacemakers is their own, they will enjoy an abundance of choices and eager service in health care, as consumers do in every other sector of a market economy.

In order to ensure that they have the money to spend, though, the baby boomers must begin at once, if they have not done so already, to save like chipmunks anticipating a hard winter. Doing that over the hurdles of a 39-percent top federal tax rate and a 28-percent capital-gains rate will be no easy trick.

Like everything else, then, the health-care problem turns out to be a corollary of the growth of the U.S. economy and the accumulation of private capital. In 1991, the Heritage Foundation convened a conference to discuss whether tax reform was the key to health-care reform. It is, but not in the sense Heritage meant. Low taxes, and especially low taxes on saving, are the key to the health reform that matters most: enabling Americans to sock away the money they will require to buy care when they can no longer care for themselves.

As complicated as the American health-care story is, it can be summed up simply. Through its tax policies, and then through the invention of Medicare and Medicaid, the federal government has twisted the health-care market in ways that threaten the government's own solvency and the profitability of every employer in the nation.

Measured in dollars, health care may present the most gargantuan example of unintended consequences in the whole sorry history of modern welfarism. Probably the harm done can never be fully undone. Still, it is possible to lay down the basic principles of a saner future for American health care: put control over health insurance into the hands of the insured, not their employers, and make the costs of insurance visible; get government at all levels out of the business of providing health care to the nonpoor; and get the federal government out of the business of providing health care to the poor.

If the American health-care system remains in its present form, it will, within 15 more years, bring into existence an enormous voting bloc of retirees utterly dependent on the state for comfort and care in their old age. There is virtually no chance that the era of conservative government promised by the 1994 elections can ensue under those conditions. Hence the health-care argument is more than a technical one, more than an argument about regulations and spending and taxes. If the free-marketeers lose this argument, Medicare and Medicaid will ineluctably bring about a whinier, more dependent culture. If, on the other hand, the free-marketeers win, individual medical savings accounts will not only make for a better health-care system but will also reinforce the thriftiness, self-reliance, and self-confidence of the American people.

What to Do About

The Universities

GERTRUDE HIMMELFARB

Gertrude Himmelfarb is professor emeritus of history at the City University of New York. She is also the author of numerous works of historical scholarship, including *The Idea of Poverty*, *The New History and the Old*, *Poverty and Compassion*, *On Looking Into the Abyss*, and, most recently, *The De-Moralization of Society: From Victorian Virtues to Modern Values* (Knopf).

"There is a great deal of ruin in a nation," Adam Smith informed his readers. And so there is in a university. It is a comforting thought that we might keep in mind as we contemplate the transformation of higher education in recent years and consider what should be done, or undone, about it.[1]

A quarter of a century ago, Robert Nisbet wrote a book that is still the seminal work on the subject, *The Degradation of the Academic Dogma*. To readers fresh from the dramatic events of the

[1] I am using the term *university* generically to include colleges as well, so many of which have been renamed universities so as to make obscure the old distinction between a purely undergraduate institution and one that offers graduate and professional degrees.

1960's—the student "rebellion" at Berkeley in 1964 and the later uprisings in one university after another—Nisbet provided a larger perspective, locating the beginning of the revolution well before that memorable decade and making professors, administrators, and the government complicitous in that revolution.

Until World War II, Nisbet maintained, the university had been sustained by nothing less than a "dogma"—a faith in reason and knowledge, in the rational, dispassionate search for truth, and in the dissemination of knowledge for the sake of knowledge. The objects of knowledge changed in the course of time: the classical curriculum gave way to the modern one, by the addition first of modern history, literature, and languages, then of the sciences and social sciences. But throughout the centuries, the essential dogma, the commitment to reason and knowledge, remained intact.

A corollary of that dogma also remained intact: the hierarchy of knowledge and of the bearers of knowledge. Even in this most democratic of nations, Nisbet found, the university was not a democratic institution. Not all subjects were equal *sub specie universitatis*; not all were worthy of study. Students were not the equals of their instructors, nor administrators of professors, nor junior professors of their seniors.

Nor did the university give equal status, or equal time, to non-Western civilizations. There were courses, to be sure, on Asia, Africa, and India. But they were peripheral to the curriculum and were studied in the spirit and methods of Western scholarship. The university was frankly "ethnocentric" (it is curious to find Nisbet using this word that far back), committed to a "faith in the Western tradition: in the ideas, values, systems, and languages that belong to the tiny part of the world that is the promontory of the Eurasian continent known as Western Europe."

The academic dogma, as Nisbet saw it, was quite different from the democratic dogma. The academy was a community in itself, distinct in its mission, its values, and its structure from the larger society. This was not to say that it was of no social utility. Throughout the centuries it fed into the mainstream of society—into the law, diplomacy, clerisy, polity, civil bureaucracy. It also served as a socializing, civilizing, and even moralizing agent for the students who passed through it (and perhaps as well for the professors ensconced in it). But it did all this indirectly, as a fortunate byproduct of its essential functions, which were the creation, preservation, and transmission of knowledge and culture.

So, at least, it was until after World War II, when the expansion of the university, partly as a result of the GI Bill, brought about a "Reformation" of the university, comparable, in Nisbet's view, to the great religious Reformation of the 16th century.[2] The new reformation was precipitated by money—the influx of funds, first from the government and then from private sources, which generated projects, programs, institutes, and centers that were unrelated either to the teaching function of the university or to the kind of research that had an intimate connection with teaching. The university, already burdened with business and professional schools, was thus transformed into a "multiversity."

The sciences were most obviously affected by these new sources of money, but so were the social sciences, which discovered a new rationale for grant-getting and a new mission for the university: the solving of social problems—poverty, the environment, urban unrest, juvenile delinquency, and whatever other subject might occur to a resourceful professor. If disinterested knowledge was the dogma of the prereformation university, "relevance" was the dogma of the postreformation university.

Having committed itself to solving society's problems, Nisbet observed, the university could hardly ignore the problems of its own students, their emotional needs, egos, sensitivities, and identity crises. The university then assumed the character of a therapeutic institution as well. Since part of the therapy (especially after the uprisings of the 1960's) involved the "empowerment" of the students—their admission to curriculum, governance, even appointment and tenure committees—the result was the conversion of the

[2]Jacques Barzun does not use quite such apocalyptic language, but he, too, dates the transformation of the university from 1945. From his *Teacher in America* (1945), to *The American University* (1968), to a multitude of other books on the subject (most recently *Begin Here*, 1991), Barzun has been one of the most imaginative and incisive commentators on the university.

university, now a multiversity, into something that resembled a "participatory democracy."

From all this, it was only one short step to the politicization of the university. The socially conscious university was, inevitably, a politically conscious one. Professors and students had always had political views and commitments, but they had expressed and exercised them in their extracurricular capacity, as it were—as individuals rather than as professors and students. The 1960's changed that, bringing those views and commitments into the university itself, into classrooms, the curriculum, faculty appoint-ments, and official pronouncements on political affairs.

Nisbet did not suggest that all universities succumbed to these tendencies to the same degree. Some were quite immune to them, remaining liberal-arts colleges rather than multiversities, emphasiz-ing teaching, writing, and research of the old variety, preserving a "core curriculum" that was more than a token "distribution requirement," functioning as genuine educational communities, and resisting the call to social and political "activism."

Nor were all disciplines, even in the large universities, affected in the same way. For history and literature, the 1950's were a period of great fertility and creativity. The sciences flourished in those institutions that managed to resist the distortions produced by government and corporate contracts. And Nisbet's own disci-pline, sociology, was greatly enhanced by the new kinds of student attracted to that relatively new subject. The postwar students, more mature and diverse than the old, had a profound effect on the uni-versity, bringing to it an atmosphere of professionalism and entrepreneurship, and at the same time a more vigorous and fertile intellectual spirit.

A quarter of a century after the publication of Nisbet's book, we may be tempted to speak of a "Second Reformation," much of it prefigured by the first but carried to extremes that even Nisbet could not have anticipated. If the First Reformation enlarged the university by making it accessible, as a result of the GI Bill and a booming economy, to students who could not otherwise have afforded to go to a university or who would not have thought to do so, the Second Reformation has enlarged it in quite another way, by making it accessible, under "open-admissions" and "affir-mative-action" programs, to students who do not meet the regular requirements.

The original, and entirely laudable, purpose of affirmative action was seeking out such students (especially blacks and other minorities), encouraging them to apply, and giving them remedial courses that would enable them to fulfill the requirements and meet the regular standards. In the course of time, however, affir-mative action came to mean the admission of students under a dif-ferent set of standards, with little or no obligation to meet the reg-ular requirements.

Initially confined to students, affirmative action was soon applied to the faculty, so that all universities now find themselves under great pressure to appoint women, blacks, Hispanics, and other "unprivileged" groups. One university recently extended the affirmative-action category to homosexuals, announcing that it would make special efforts to recruit them and promising to give them preferential treatment in appointments; it is to be expected that other universities will follow suit.

A more momentous effect of affirmative action has been on the curriculum itself, especially in the humanities and social sciences. One might say that affirmative action has replaced relevance as the reigning dogma in the university. Women's studies, black studies, and ethnic studies (although not gay studies—this was a later develop-ment) were the product of the First Reformation, initially as indi-vidual courses, then as full-fledged departments. It took the Second Reformation to "mainstream" these subjects into the curriculum, converting some of them from electives into required courses. While most universities have abandoned the Western-civilization requirement (the very idea of Western civilization is anathema in politically correct circles), many have imposed a new requirement, often the only one in the curriculum, of a specified number of courses in African-American, ethnic, or women's studies.

The basic categories of affirmative action—race, ethnicity, and gender (displacing, to the chagrin of Marxists, the older trinity of race, class, and gender)—are being imposed not only on the cur-riculum in general but on individual disciplines and courses. The goal now is to mainstream these categories into every subject, so that a course on the Renaissance may be obliged to give due place (and perhaps more than due place) to the role and status of women, or a course on the novel to include a proper representation (or overrepresentation) of works by women, African-American, and third-world authors.

So far, this goal of mainstreaming has been only sporadically achieved. In some institutions it has been officially prescribed; in others it has been encouraged but not made obligatory. But everywhere there is a considerable amount of social pressure to adhere to it.

It is interesting that gender should have emerged as a far more potent force than race or ethnicity, penetrating into the heart of the disciplines—"transforming" them, as the feminists boast—as the others have not done. Perhaps this is because there are more women students and professors than black or ethnic students and professors, or because the feminists are more ideologically aggressive. Or perhaps the concept of "engenderment" lends itself to bolder, more imaginative uses. The original concept of women's studies—the study of women in particular periods or places—has been transformed into feminist studies—the study of periods and places from the "viewpoint," as is candidly said, of women. To "engender" the French Revolution, for example, is not only to deal with the role and status of women in the Revolution, but to "feminize" the Revolution itself: to interpret it as the struggle of liberty, personified by a female figure, against the patriarchal monarchy (or, as another theory has it, as the struggle of patriarchal republicans against an effeminate monarchy).

The sciences have been more impervious than most disciplines to political pressures and intellectual fashions, but even they are not entirely immune.[3] They are, indeed, the latest converts to engenderment—not in the sense of encouraging more women to become

---

[3] The influence on academic science of postmodernism, environmentalism, multiculturalism, feminism, and other ideologies is documented in the recent book *Higher Superstition: The Academic Left and Its Quarrels with Science*, by Paul R. Gross and Norman Levitt. See the review by Jeffrey Salmon in the June 1994 issue of *Commentary*.

scientists, but in altering the conception of science itself. Some feminists object to the rational, logical, objective structure of science (to say nothing of the language of science—"power," "force," the "big-bang" theory) as inherently "masculinist" and patriarchal, and demand that science be made more compatible with a "feminist perspective" and "female subjectivity." An article, "Toward a Feminist Algebra," complains that conventional mathematics suggests "a woman whose nature desires to be the conquered Other"; and a book, *The Science Question in Feminism*, declares Newton's *Principia* so suffused with "gender symbolism, gender structure, and gender identity" as to be nothing less than a "rape manual."

The effect of this multipronged assault of affirmative action—in student admissions and faculty appointments, in the curriculum and disciplines—has been the Balkanization of the university. The traditional ideal of the university, as a community where professors and students are united in a common enterprise for a common purpose, has been replaced by the idea of a loose, almost amorphous, federation made up of distinct groups pursuing their special interests and agendas (and, often, voluntarily segregating themselves in dorms, dining rooms, and lecture halls).

By the same token, the disciplines have been fragmented, so that they no longer have a common focus and a common body of knowledge. This is the effect of "multiculturalism" as it is now conceived and practiced. Instead of viewing race, class, ethnicity, and gender as parts of a whole, introduced into the narrative of American history, for example, at those points where they are particularly relevant, they are now seen as competing wholes—not as parts of a single story but as quite separate and distinct stories. *E pluribus unum* has been converted into *Ex uno plura*—"from the one many," as the famous gaffe by Vice President Gore has it.

A by-product of Balkanization is the further politicization of the university. The rival groups, recognizing no common mission, are engaged in a continual power struggle, not only about such matters as appointments, tenure, and the like, but about the very substance of education—what should be taught and how it should be taught.

Indeed, knowledge itself, according to a fashionable theory, is nothing but a reflection of the dominant power structure. The older idea of knowledge, implying that there is a truth to be known, is deemed authoritarian and oppressive. Since there is no truth, no objective knowledge, there is only power. "Everything is political," a popular slogan has it. Hence the professor is necessarily an advocate and the classroom a political arena; the only stipulation is that the professor's advocacy be open and clear.

Compared with this ultimate act of politicization—the politicizing of knowledge itself—"political correctness" (PC) may appear to be a lesser evil. Yet PC goes beyond the much-publicized rules governing behavior and speech, beyond even the attempt to govern thought by means of "sensitivity" and "consciousness-raising" sessions. It goes to the heart of the academic enterprise. It may seem benign to neuterize language, disallowing *he* in a generic sense (although even that can wreak havoc with the study of Shakespeare or of historical documents). But to be made sensitive to the sexual connotations of such words as *force* or *penetrating* (as in a preceding paragraph of this essay), or to the racial implication of a phrase like "black thoughts," is distracting and inhibiting. Far more serious, of course, is the suppression of research on intelligence, for example, on the ground that the subject itself is suspect and that the conclusions might be politically incorrect.

In the light of all these problems, it may seem carping to complain of the trivialization of study and research—courses on comic books and popular films, dissertations on deservedly obscure writers merely because they are "unprivileged," distribution requirements fulfilled by ludicrously inappropriate and undemanding courses (a course in interior design to satisfy the humanities requirement, or on "Lifetime Fitness" for the social-science requirement). Combined with the absence of any structured program of study, such trivia contribute to a further fragmentation of the university and the dissipation of any sense of educational coherence.

What makes it worse is that these are not "gut" courses devised by pandering instructors and sanctioned by a lax administration. Some are seriously intended and defended by professors flaunting their defiance of traditional standards—or, indeed, of any standards. The well-known professor of literature Houston Baker says that choosing between Pearl Buck and Virginia Woolf is "no different from choosing between a hoagy and a pizza," and proudly declares that he himself is "dedicated to the day when we have a disappearance of those standards."

That these are not isolated cases is demonstrated by a survey conducted by the National Endowment for the Humanities a few years ago, which found that students could graduate from:

- 78 percent of the nation's colleges and universities without ever taking a course in the history of Western civilization

- 38 percent without any history at all

- 45 percent without a course in American or English literature

- 77 percent without a course in a foreign language

- 41 percent without a course in mathematics

- 33 percent without a course in the sciences.

Another survey conducted by the Gallup Organization showed that:

- 25 percent of college seniors could not locate Columbus's voyage within the correct half-century

- 25 percent could not distinguish Churchill's words from Stalin's, or Karl Marx's ideas from those of the U.S. Constitution

- 40 percent did not know when the Civil War occurred

- most could not identify the authors of works by Plato, Dante, Shakespeare, and Milton.

So much for the bad news. The good news is that it is not all bad. What I have been describing is real enough and prevalent enough, but it is not the only reality and it is not universal. It is a tribute to human nature that some students succeed in acquiring a decent education, and some professors manage to think and teach and write as if there is such a thing as knowledge and as if truth can still be aspired to, however difficult it is to achieve.

These students and professors are not innocents. They know the pressures they have to resist and the price they have to pay. The author of a dissertation on the political philosophy of John Adams does not expect to receive the kinds of job offers (especially if he is a white male) as the author of a dissertation on the sexual politics of Alice Walker (especially if she is a black female).

There is, then, a saving remnant in the university—and perhaps more than a remnant, perhaps even a large, if silent, minority of professors and students who would prefer a more traditional mode of teaching and scholarship but who do not have the intellectual resources or, in some cases, the moral courage to speak out openly. (Tenure, we have discovered, is a security against unemployment, not against timidity.)

Some professors try to avoid confrontations with their students and colleagues by making minimal concessions to the prevailing fashions in the classroom (putting the obligatory number of books by women and blacks on the reading list), while continuing, in their own research and writing, to "do their thing." One can sympathize with them. They disapprove of the politicization of the university and do not want to spend their own time and energy in political disputation. They want only to teach and work. But inevitably the pressure to conform intensifies and finally becomes intolerable.

It is these professors and students, openly or covertly disaffected, who give us cause for hope. And it is upon them that we may usefully direct our attention.

I am painfully aware of the anticlimactic nature of this approach. It would be gratifying to launch a counterreformation to undo the damage done by the two massive reformations that the university has experienced in the past half century. And it is not difficult to think of ways of bringing about such a counterreformation:

- Restore a core curriculum, a structured course of studies such as was common only a few decades ago, not only at Harvard, Columbia, and Chicago but at most colleges and universities throughout the country.

- Spin off the institutes, centers, and special projects that clutter up the university and distract it from its main purposes. And while we are about it, spin off, too, the professional schools: business, medicine, law, social work, the performing arts, even the advanced scientific research that might better be conducted in specialized institutions.

- Reduce the number of departments, courses, programs, administrators. A massive retrenchment policy would concentrate the mind admirably upon what is important and what is not (as well as having the incidentally salutary effect of making the university more solvent and less dependent on government subsidies).

- Reverse the process by which liberal-arts colleges are transformed into universities. There are still a number of colleges that have resisted the lure of graduate programs, but far too many that have not. (Recently all the state colleges in Pennsylvania declared themselves universities. Hence we now have Slippery Rock University of Pennsylvania—not, as one might think, a branch of the University of Pennsylvania, but a separate, state-supported institution.)

- Eliminate the category of Teaching Assistants (TA's), the graduate students who currently bear much of the burden of undergraduate teaching in many eminent universities, and who are themselves only barely more knowledgeable than the students they presume to teach.

- Reinstitute the old prohibitions against indoctrination in the classroom.

- Restore the original meaning of affirmative action.

One can think of other reasonable measures of reform. But all of this, in my opinion, is an exercise in futility. The reformations

have gone too far to be undone. There are too many vested interests in and outside the university, too many professors committed,
intellectually as well as politically, to the new programs and policies, too many recent graduates (and future professors) who know
no other mode of scholarship and teaching, too many timid spirits
who cannot envision any radical departure from the present conception of the university, and too many cynical ones who want
only to enjoy their comfortable sinecures. There have been very
few successful counterreformations in history, and this, I am afraid,
would not be one of them.

I return, then, to the idea of a saving remnant, those dissidents,
open and covert, who currently keep the spirit of education alive.
I can only offer some modest proposals designed to support and
embolden them.

The first proposal, befitting an educational institution, is to
engage in an educational campaign, reminding people, in and outside the university, of the proper mission of the university and
showing how far the university has departed from it.

That mission should be defined broadly. Even in the prereformation days, there was no single model of a university, no standard
curriculum that would fit all sizes and shapes of institutions and
students. There was, in fact, a good deal of diversity—perhaps
more than we have today when that word has become the code
name for a new kind of uniformity.

What we then had, in addition to a wide range of programs of
study, was a common denominator of subjects deemed to be the
minimal requirements of a liberal education, a common assumption about reason and objectivity governing both the classroom
and research (not always attained but always aspired to), a common
view of a scholarly community that brought together professors
and students, however different in all other respects, in a common
enterprise for a common purpose.

The first task of the educational reformer, then, is education
itself—education about what a university was, what it has become,
and what it might be. Even for those who have lived through the
reformations of our time, it is all too easy to be seduced by present

preoccupations and passions—to forget the difference, for example, between the original meaning of affirmative action and the current one, or between women's studies and feminist studies, or between black studies and Afrocentric studies, or between pluralism (in the sense of "from the many one") and multiculturalism (in the sense of "from the one many").

The blurring of these differences has been facilitated by the kind of obfuscation that only academics are capable of, and that the present generation of academics, trained in the arcane language of postmodernism, is more adept at than most. Only by recalling ourselves to first principles and comparing them with present practices can we appreciate the gravity of the situation and the need for reform.

The most heartening experience of recent years is the public exposure of PC and the resulting widespread revulsion against it. The first reaction on the part of the guardians of PC was to belittle the evidence as "anecdotal" and "impressionistic": the cases cited, it was said, were probably not true, and if true, they were isolated incidents of no significance. That argument is now rarely heard, as the evidence has mounted and as the supporters of PC have been forced into the open to defend what most people sensibly regard as indefensible.

If the public were similarly alerted to other practices—the "advocacy teaching," for example, that transforms the classroom into a propaganda and proselytizing forum—and if it heard professors blatantly supporting that practice, it would be similarly dismayed, not only at the particular views (political, sexual, moral) that are being conveyed, but at the idea that teachers (and, even more presumptuously, TA's) should feel free to impose those views upon their students.

The second proposal is a corollary of the first. Even a saving remnant needs saving. The most strong-minded dissidents need to know that they are not entirely isolated, that others share their principles and, at the very least, are aware of their existence.

Here we may be encouraged by the example of the National Association of Scholars (NAS), an organization of professors dedicated to a more traditional view of the university and expressing that view through conferences, publications, and other activities. Professors who formerly felt too beleaguered to make public their disaffection now feel freer to do so, secure in the knowledge that they are not alone, not hopeless eccentrics or mavericks. (It is also helpful to know that if their institutions try to penalize them, others will come to their support.)

The existence of such an organization has the additional virtue of making it impossible for the dominant forces in the academy to pretend that there is no opposition to their policies, that everyone agrees with them. For many this is not a pretense. Like the film critic who said that she could not understand how Richard Nixon got elected because she knew no one who had voted for him, so those who are caught up in the prevailing fashions are often genuinely unaware that any enlightened person can differ with them. My own measure of the success of the NAS is the remark I sometimes hear, by those hostile to the organization, that they are astonished to find so many reputable scholars associated with it. A more objective measure of its success is the formation of not one but two rival organizations to counteract it.

If some professors have been moved to protest against the current tendencies in their universities, alumni and trustees may be encouraged to do so as well. A national association of alumni and trustees would keep its members informed of problems that are not regularly reported in the press (the accreditation, for example, of universities based upon affirmative-action criteria), and of measures that might be taken to forestall or combat undesirable policies. It would thus serve as a clearinghouse for alumni and trustees who are often ignorant of what is happening even in their own institutions, let alone in the academy at large.[4] More important,

---

[4]A recent case that merits more attention than it has received is the experience of Georgia Institute of Technology. Five years ago, it scrapped its ineffectual remedial program and started a much more rigorous 5-week summer course for minority students. Required to achieve a higher standard, the students did just that, so that they are now outperforming white students at that college and producing a significant number of qualified engineers. If alumni and trustees in other institutions knew of this program, they would be in a better position to urge their own colleges to pursue a similar policy—affirmative action in its best sense.

such an organization would suggest to alumni and trustees that they have not only the power but the duty to take a more active part in the institutions with which they are identified, to which they are contributing in time and money, and for which they are assuming moral and, in the case of trustees, legal responsibility.

Finally, there are the students. During the turbulent 1960's, when the students were putting forward their claim to "empowerment," the professors put forward a counterclaim. "We are the university," they announced. (Some of us, reminded of Pogo's famous remark, "The enemy is us," irreverently translated the faculty's slogan as "The university is us.") The present generation of professors—made up of the students of the 1960's, now released from all the institutional and moral inhibitions that once restrained the professoriate—are more than ever acting on that dictum. In reaction, some dissident students—dissidents from the Right rather than the Left—are expressing their dissatisfaction, not by demanding (as their predecessors did) a larger role in the governance of the university, but by publicizing their grievances in the "alternative" student newspapers that have been cropping up in one university after another.

It is surprising that there has been no serious effort to create an "alternative" national-student organization, in the manner of the Students for a Democratic Society (SDS) in the 1960's, or the American Students Union (ASU) in the 1930's. I am loath even to raise the idea: students have all too little time to get an education, without the distractions of such activities. Yet dissident students, like dissident professors, need the satisfaction of knowing that there are like-minded souls elsewhere. They require the sense of legitimacy that comes from being part of a community with shared values. I sincerely hope that if such an organization were founded (and I am not sure I am recommending it), it would confine itself, unlike both of its predecessors, to university affairs rather than national politics, and that it would resist the very politicization that would be one of its chief grievances.

If little can be done about the university at large, something can be done about the enclaves within the university where the saving remnant is found, the oases where traditional study, teaching, and research are still being conducted. In some universities, they consist of nothing more than individual courses given by specific teachers (known to other students by word of mouth); in others, of a subfield within a department (the history of philosophy in the philosophy department); or of a one- or two-year concentration (on "Western Civilization," perhaps); or of a separate liberal-arts or humanities division (focusing on "great books").

Here we can exploit one of the vices of the modern university: greed. The university today is even more avaricious than it was in the 1950's and 1960's. As it has assumed the burden of more and more extracurricular activities, as its administration has proliferated (each new program spawning its own complement of deans, associate deans, assistant deans, administrative assistants, and secretaries), and as it has been obliged to grant more generous scholarships to students and higher salaries to professors to fill its affirmative-action quotas (as well as offering above-scale salaries and minimal teaching assignments to attract the "academic superstars" in the fashionable fields), so it has also found itself, in this economy-minded era, with reduced funds from the government. Alumni and foundation support has therefore become more coveted than ever.

This is yet another reason to form "alternative" alumni organizations, which can put financial, as well as intellectual, pressure upon the university. And it is also the reason that "alternative," as it were, foundations can exert an influence disproportionate to the funds actually expended.

The older, exceedingly well-endowed foundations (most notably, Ford and MacArthur) have long been active in financing "innovative" programs that have transformed the university. In response, smaller, more traditional-minded foundations have begun to support the programs of their liking. By a judicious use of their resources, these foundations can cultivate those oases where traditional study and teaching still flourish. (In more affluent days, universities were reluctant to accept outside support for restricted purposes; today they are more willing to do so.)

This proposal carries with it a strong caveat. Constant vigilance is required to make sure that the purpose of such grants is not subverted. My own experience on the council of the National Endowment for the Humanities is instructive. At a time when the Endowment was swamped with applications for Marxist, neo-Marxist, feminist, deconstructionist, and other modish projects, the chairman and staff devised a new program that would concentrate on the traditional works of philosophy, literature, and history. High-school teachers would be invited to apply to one of a number of summer courses, each led by a distinguished scholar and each devoted to the reading and study of a single great work— Plato's *Phaedo*, perhaps, or Dostoevsky's *The Brothers Karamazov*, or John Stuart Mill's *On Liberty*.

It seemed a wonderful idea. Imagine how intellectually stimulating and spiritually refreshing it would be for a high-school teacher to return to the fount of wisdom after coping for years with teenagers and textbooks. The first round of seminars did exactly what we had hoped for and we were elated. The second year was something of a letdown; the books chosen by the instructors were not all of the highest quality and the approach to them was less rigorous. By the third summer, it was obvious that this program was going the way of all the others: the books were being Marxized, feminized, deconstructed, and politicized. High-school teachers, far from being exposed to "the best which has been thought and said in the world," were being indoctrinated in the prevailing dogmas of academia. With the best of intentions, the Endowment was disseminating—and, worse, legitimating—the very tendencies it was trying to counteract.

Michael Joyce, president of the Bradley Foundation, the wise man of the foundation world, taught me the lesson of this experience. When a garden consists of weeds rather than flowers, he said, the more one waters and fertilizes the garden, the more weeds one will get. So too, when the dominant culture of the university is degraded, everything that comes within its province (as the Endowment programs do, since they are dependent upon peer review by academics) will be susceptible of degradation.

This is a good argument against a publicly funded Endowment. But it is also an argument for private foundations that have a clear conception of what they want to do and how they can best do it: by making grants not to the university, not even to a department, division, center, or institute, but to a particular individual or group for a specified purpose and for a limited time.

This "oasis" theory of reform is a very modest approach to a massive problem. It does not promise much, but what it promises, it can deliver. If watering and fertilizing a garden full of weeds has the effect of producing still more weeds, the watering and fertilizing of a flower bed in that garden will surely produce more flowers, and in time the flower bed itself will expand and displace some of those weeds. More important, the existence of those oases reminds us that there is a difference between flowers and weeds—a distinction that the prevalent relativism of our culture tends to obscure.

In offering nothing more than the most modest proposals for reform, I do not mean to belittle the gravity of the problem. For it is not only higher education that is at stake; it is all of education and the whole of the culture. Again, a personal experience may be illuminating.

Ten years ago, when the "new history"—social history, the history of ordinary people in their ordinary lives—was all the rage, I wrote an article deploring, not social history itself, but the dominance given to it, the claim that it was the most important mode of history, even the only proper mode, to the denigration or exclusion of political, diplomatic, even economic history.

To those who contended that I exaggerated the importance of social history, that it was confined to a few elite graduate schools, and that it did not affect the study of history in general, I cited some recent Advanced Placement examinations taken by high-school seniors. In one the main essay was, "How and why did the lives and status of Northern middle-class women change between 1776 and 1876?"; this was described in the bulletin of the American Historical Association as a "mainline topic." Another examination required the student to discuss methods of child-rearing in England between the 16th and 18th centuries. (These are high-school students who are barely familiar with the English Revolution, let alone with methods of child-rearing at that time—a subject that many a professor of English history, including the author of the present article, would hardly presume to comment on.)

Within a matter of years, this kind of history had filtered down from graduate schools to high schools, and had become "mainline" in all. It even penetrated the elementary schools. In my daughter's school, an ambitious young teacher (an ABD—All-But-Dissertation—from Harvard) devised a course for 6th-graders, their first in European history, on "the nature of revolutions," which had so little regard for chronology that at the end of the semester the students had no idea, as my daughter put it, "which came first," the French, Russian, or Industrial Revolution.

A more familiar example today is multiculturalism, which has permeated all educational institutions down to the very first grades. Arthur Schlesinger, Jr., in his aptly titled book *The Disuniting of America*, cites the New York State curriculum for "global studies," which calls for equal time to be devoted to seven specified regions of the world—this for students who are notoriously ignorant of the most elementary facts about their own country. (An official commission has recently criticized this program for its "European-American monocultural perspective.")

"Filtering down" is to education what "trickling down" is to economics. It is often said that the university is a microcosm of society and necessarily assumes the social obligations and political characteristics of society at large. A traditional view of the university rejects that theory, insisting upon the unique nature and function of the university. But if the university is not, and should not be, a microcosm of society, it is a microcosm of education. What happens in the university is apt to be replicated, and in a remarkably short time, at all levels—from graduate to undergraduate school and from high school to elementary school; from elite universities to state universities to small colleges; from the most avant-garde institutions to the most conventional ones.

This is hardly surprising. Teachers, after all, at all levels, come from the university, and they naturally bring to their jobs what they have learned, or imbibed by osmosis, from the university. (Professors in the smallest colleges are often most eager, as evidence of their professional credentials, to emulate and even surpass their colleagues in their enthusiasm for the latest intellectual fashion.)

The university is also a microcosm of culture—popular culture as well as high culture. Writers, journalists, movie makers, and television producers have also spent their formative years in the university. For their part, academics, having blurred the line between popular culture and high culture (or between popular culture and higher education), find it easy to import into the university the ideas, values, and the very subjects of popular culture. Films and television are respectable courses of study in most universities, and soap operas, comic strips, and advertising jingles are the solemn subjects of doctoral dissertations. It is a reciprocal process of legitimation that is taking place: the university legitimates the popular culture, and the popular culture legitimates the university that is so well disposed to it.

Lionel Trilling once expressed his misgivings at offering a course in modern literature (Joyce, Proust, Kafka, Lawrence, Mann, Gide) on the grounds that these writers were best read outside the university and that it was not the job of the university to make the students "at home in, and in control of, the modern world." Parents today might wonder if it is the job of the university to make their children even more at home than they already are in the world of television, the movies, videos, and comic books.

The popular culture does, however, suggest one final source of hope. Just as even the most successful TV serials have a life span of only a few seasons, and the best-sellers of one year are relegated to the remainder tables the following year, so the intellectual and political fashions that prevail in the university today may suffer the fate of all fashions.

Robert Nisbet, who alerted us to the "degradation of the academic dogma," has written a short piece that may suggest to us (although it did not to him) a possible saving grace. His essay on "Boredom" opens: "Among the forces that have shaped human behavior, boredom is one of the most insistent and universal." Boredom—nothing so pretentious as "ennui," or "anomie," or even "apathy," but simple boredom. For Nisbet, boredom is an affliction, with no redeeming virtue. In our present condition, we may take a kindlier view of it.

Boredom has already overtaken some of yesterday's enthusiasms. In the age of deconstruction, who remembers existentialism? Deconstruction itself is already self-destructing in this country, as it did earlier in France. It takes only a few years for the "cutting edge" of a discipline to move to the center, lose its edge, and become dull.

Bright young academics, eager to make their mark, will seek new theories, new methods, new themes to assert their individuality and originality. They will even come to see their own mentors, the radicals of an earlier generation, as an establishment ripe for disestablishing. They may find, however, that the road to power is not as easy as they think. Establishments, especially those that have come to power with all the fervor and self-righteousness of radicals, do not readily relinquish power. It is many generations now since the disciples of John Dewey captured schools of education throughout the country. There have been serious efforts to discredit and dislodge their ideology, but by adapting to changing fashions (abandoning pluralism in favor of multiculturalism, for example), they have retained power even though pragmatism has long since become one of the most boring philosophies of our time.

Those committed to a traditional view of education can take small comfort in the volatility of fashions—not only because there are vested interests and institutional rigidities that make those fashions more enduring than they might otherwise be, but because there is no assurance that the succeeding ones will be any better than the old ones. (Deconstruction has all the defects of existentialism, and more.)

Nevertheless, this volatility does provide a window of opportunity for reform. Bored with trivia, with a specious relevance, with a smorgasbord of courses, with the politicization of all subjects and the fragmentation of all disciplines, professors and students might welcome a return to a serious, structured curriculum and to a university that is an intellectual and educational, not a political or therapeutic, community.

One can envision the sense of liberation that would be experienced by women and blacks released from the shackles of gender and race, free to participate in a culture that transcends the mundane conditions of their lives, that elevates and dignifies them because it is itself elevated and dignified. This is not a romantic or utopian suggestion. It is exactly what an earlier generation of students from poor, immigrant, and, often, culturally impoverished backgrounds felt when they gained admission to the university and discovered a new world, a world not bound or blinkered by their class or ethnic origins.

That was the old mission of the university. Today it is a new, bold, challenging mission, one that might well appeal to a new generation of enterprising, idealistic academics.

What to Do About

Foreign Policy

ROBERT KAGAN

Robert Kagan, who served in the State Department from 1984 to 1988, has recently completed *A Twilight Struggle: American Power and Nicaragua, 1977–1990* (Free Press). Mr. Kagan's article prompted a round of responses from foreign-policy experts and former government officials; their comments—and Mr. Kagan's reply—follow the text of his article.

Future historians will record—perhaps in astonishment—that the demise of the Soviet Union ushered in an era of American worldwide engagement and armed intervention unprecedented in scope and frequency. Despite a widespread conviction that, in a post-cold-war world, the American role would diminish, in a brief 4 years the United States has launched a massive counteroffensive against the world's fourth largest army in the Middle East; invaded, occupied, and supervised elections in a Latin American country; intervened with force to provide food to starving peoples in Africa; and conducted punitive bombing raids in the Balkans.

Nor is this all. The United States has sent troops on another humanitarian mission in Africa, and volunteered troops to serve as peacekeeping forces in the Middle East and in the former Yugoslavia.

It has worked in the UN Security Council to enact punitive sanctions against at least a half-dozen international scofflaws. It has seriously considered extending military protection to several important
nations of Eastern Europe that have never before been part of an
alliance with the United States. And it has interceded in disputes
among the former republics of the Soviet Union.

How is this increased activity to be explained? The answer is
rather easily found in the new relations of power in the post-cold-
war world. The fall of the Soviet Union removed restraints on foreign leaders unhappy with the order imposed by the cold war and
unleashed new struggles for power in areas hitherto under the former superpower's thumb. Some would-be challengers of the old
order were encouraged by the belief that the United States would
not step in. The United States, however, itself freed from the
restraints of the cold war, began to fill the gap left by the absence
of Soviet global power and continued a historical tradition of
using its influence to promote a world order consistent with its
material needs and philosophical predilections.

But if the course America has followed has been natural
enough, to many American strategists, policy-makers, and politicians it seems also to have been unexpected—and unwelcome.
Today, a scant 2 years after the intervention in Somalia, 3 years
after the Gulf war, and 4 years since the invasion of Panama, foreign-policy theorists continue to write of the need for a "global
retrenchment" of American power. Before and after each venture
abroad, they have argued that such high levels of American
engagement cannot be sustained, politically or economically, and
that a failure to be more selective in the application of American
power will either bankrupt the country or drive the American
public further toward the isolationism into which, they warn, it is
already beginning to slip.

This political judgment has found intellectual buttressing in
the so-called realist approach to foreign policy, which asserts that
the United States should limit itself to defending its "core"
national interests and abandon costly and unpopular efforts to
solve the many problems on the "periphery."[1] During the cold

---

[1]See, for example, "The Core vs. the Periphery," by Fareed Zakaria in the
December 1993 *Commentary*.

war, realists fought against efforts by Presidents from Truman to Kennedy to Reagan to equate American interests with the advancement of a democratic world order. In the post-cold-war era, they have gained new prominence by again recommending a retreat from such ambitions and the definition of a far more limited set of foreign-policy goals.

Yet the realist view remains inadequate, both as a description, precisely, of reality—of the way the world really works—and as a recommendation for defending America's interests, either on the "periphery" or at the "core." When Americans have exercised their power in pursuit of a broad definition of interests—in pursuit, that is, of a more decent world order—they have succeeded in defending their "vital" interests as well. When they have sought to evade the dangers of global involvement, they have found themselves unexpectedly in a fight for national survival.

Throughout this century, the United States has faced the problem of its expanding power—and has responded with ambivalence. Americans are perhaps more suspicious of power than most people on earth, but just like others they have nonetheless sought it, guarded it, and enjoyed its benefits. As products of a modern, nonmartial republic, Americans have always tended to cherish the lives of their young more than the glories to be won on the battlefield; yet they have sacrificed their young for the sake of honor, interest, and principle as frequently as any nation in the world over the past 200 years. Again, as the products of a revolution against an imperial master, Americans have always abhorred imperialism; yet where their power was preponderant, they have assumed hegemony and have been unwilling to relinquish it.

The common view of American foreign policy as endlessly vacillating between isolationism and interventionism is wrong: Americans in this century have never ceased expanding their sphere of interests across the globe, but they have tried to evade the responsibility of defending those interests, until they had no choice but to fight a war for which they were unprepared. The American conception of interest, moreover, has always gone beyond narrow security concerns to include the promotion of a world order consistent with American economic, political, and ideological aspirations.

It was Theodore Roosevelt, paradoxically a President admired by realists for his shrewd understanding of power politics, who first grafted principled ends to the exercise of power. Roosevelt insisted that it was America's duty to "assume an attitude of protection and regulation in regard to all these little states" in the Western hemisphere, to help them acquire the "capacity for self-government," to assist their progress "up out of the discord and turmoil of continual revolution into a general public sense of justice and determination to maintain order."

For Roosevelt, American stewardship in the Western hemisphere was more than a defensive response to European meddling there; it was proof that the United States had arrived as a world power, with responsibilities to shape a decent order in its own region. When Woodrow Wilson, the quintessential "utopian" President, took office later, his policies in the hemisphere were little more than a variation on Roosevelt's theme.

The same mix of motives followed the United States as it reached out into the wider world, especially Europe and Asia. Growing power expanded American interests, but also expanded the risks of protecting them against the ambitions of others. After the 1880's, America's navy grew from a size comparable to Chile's to become one of the three great navies of the world. That increase in power alone made America a potential arbiter of overseas conflicts in a way it had never been in the 18th and 19th centuries. Greater power meant that if a general European war broke out, the United States would no longer have to sit back and accept dictation of its trade routes. It also meant, however, that the United States could not sit back without accepting a diminished role in world affairs.

Nor could Americans escape choosing sides. Although German- and Irish-Americans disagreed, most Americans in the 1910's preferred the British-run world order with which they were familiar to a prospective German one. Wilson's pro-British neutrality made conflict with Germany almost inevitable, and America's new great-power status made it equally inevitable that when the German challenge came, the United States would not back down.

It was the growth of American power, not Wilsonian idealism and not national interest narrowly conceived, that led the United States into its first European war. A weak 19th-century America could not have conceived of intervening in Europe; a strong 20th-century America, because it could intervene, found that it had an interest in doing so.

After World War I, Americans recoiled from the new responsibilities and dangers which their power had brought. But they did not really abandon their new, broader conception of the national interest. Throughout the "isolationist" years, the United States still sought, however half-heartedly and ineffectually, to preserve its expanded influence and the world order it had fought for.

Although they refused to assume military obligations, Presidents from Harding to Franklin Roosevelt tried to maintain balance and order in Europe and in Asia through economic and political agreements. In Central America and the Caribbean, the Republican Presidents found themselves endlessly intervening, occupying, and supervising elections only so that they might eventually withdraw. (Only FDR decided that the best way to be a "good neighbor" in the hemisphere was to allow dictatorship to flourish.)

Americans, then, did not shun international involvement in the interwar years. Rather, they tried to enjoy the benefits of such involvement while hoping to avoid its inevitable costs. They resisted Japanese attempts to swallow China, but they did not believe the national interest required them to fight in Asia. They were unwilling to see France and England defeated by an increasingly dangerous Germany, but they did not see an interest in risking American lives in Europe. Through arms control and the theoretical banning of war, the United States sought ever more utopian mechanisms for pursuing its interests without risk. In the end, of course, this refusal to acknowledge the need to defend its expanded interests helped make war inevitable. Americans allowed the world order to collapse only to realize that this was a result they could not afford.

But if World War II marked the destruction of the old world

now-hallowed doctrine of containment was denounced as dangerous and impossibly ambitious by clear-headed "realists" of the time. (Walter Lippmann, for example, called containment a "strategic monstrosity" because it seemed to require an American response to every conceivable Soviet thrust anywhere in the world.)

There were, as it happens, few certainties in the cold war. The gray areas in which the hardest decisions had to be made were much like the gray areas of today. The two major American wars of that era were fought in regions and involved conflicts—Korea and Vietnam—where the direct interests of the United States were at least debatable. Throughout the cold war, indeed, fighting took place almost entirely on the "periphery," and was often conducted in the name of universal ideals that transcended the strategic importance of the plot of ground being contested.

The end of the cold war has required the United States once again to face the old dilemmas. As in the aftermath of World War II, the areas of the world where America exerts influence have expanded, not contracted. So, too, have the burdens of promoting and sustaining a world order that serves American material and spiritual needs.

The demise of the Soviet Union has not eliminated the threat to that order; it has only changed its form. Instead of arising from a single, large adversary, the threat has devolved into a large number of smaller but collectively serious challenges. As in the past, many experts have come forward to argue that resources are lacking for a globally active policy designed to meet those challenges, that the American public would be unwilling to support it, and even that American power is declining.

The evidence does not support these claims.

The percentage of the American economy devoted to military spending has dropped to the small digits. This is too low to allow the United States to carry out the many new tasks it will face in the post-cold-war era, but the increases that will be necessary will hardly bankrupt the country.

Nor is the assumption warranted that the American public

order, it also extended the reach of American power beyond
Theodore Roosevelt's capacity to imagine. And it offered American leaders another chance to confront the new responsibilities
which the expansion of power had created.

We often forget that the plan for world order devised by
American leaders in the last years of the war was not intended to
contain the Soviet Union. Their purpose was to build a more stable international system than that which had exploded in 1939.
They hoped that the new system, embodied in the United
Nations, would eventually become a self-regulating mechanism,
protecting American interests without requiring the constant exercise of American power. But they also understood that American
power had become the keystone in the arch of any world order.

The threat to the new system which soon emerged in the
form of the Soviet Union quickly changed Americans' sense of
what the United States was trying to accomplish. The original
goal of promoting and defending a decent world order became
conflated with the goal of meeting the challenge of Soviet
power—and in the minds of many people it remains so to this day.

Thus, all the policies that the United States would have continued to pursue without the existence of a Soviet Union—seeking a stable international economic system, exercising dominant
influence in the Western hemisphere, insisting on an ever-increasing
role in Europe, Asia, and the Middle East, demanding adherence
to international agreements, preferring dictatorship to disorder but
also preferring democracy to dictatorship—became associated
with the strategy of containment. This had the effect, unfortunate
in retrospect, of obscuring the essential continuities in American
foreign policy since the beginning of the century.

The fact is that America was simultaneously pursuing two
goals during the cold war—promotion of a world order and
defense against the biggest threat to it. Characteristically, each of
them was beset by ambivalence. There is a common presumption
today that the choices of that era were somehow easier, that there
was a broad consensus about at least a few basic certainties. Nostal-
gia for these alleged "certainties" obscures from memory the long,
bitter debates over the proper definition of American interests
during the cold war. But it is worth remembering that even the

does not support the overseas commitments and interventions undertaken in these past 4 years, or opposes further commitments today. Americans have rarely been enthusiastic about extensive overseas involvements, but the public has clearly been more willing to support them in the 1990's than it was in the 1970's and 1980's, as is demonstrated by the popularity of successful actions in such places as the Persian Gulf and Panama. Even in Bosnia and Somalia, ordinary Americans have complained not about action, but about confused and half-hearted policies and weak and incompetent execution.

We have also learned that the use of force need not be tied to unmistakable and narrowly defined security interests in order to win public support. A Latin American dictator cancels elections and helps Colombian drug dealers sell cocaine; a Middle Eastern despot invades a tiny neighboring country in order to control its oil wells; an African country dissolves into civil war and chaos, and famine threatens millions with starvation; one ethnic group tries to drive another ethnic group off its land and commits atrocities; an unfriendly Asian power develops nuclear weapons in violation of international agreements. Among these various events, only the Iraqi invasion of Kuwait qualified as a direct threat to American economic interests. In general, the issues that have invited an American response—aggression, political illegitimacy, genocide, mass starvation, nuclear proliferation, violations of international agreements—are all matters that fall under the general heading of threats to the kind of world order Americans value.

Can we sustain a policy of active response? Henry Kissinger has recently argued that, contrary to appearances, American power is actually in decline relative to other nations. While he admits that it "will remain unrivaled for the foreseeable future," nevertheless, because all power in the world has become more "diffuse," America's ability "to shape the rest of the world has actually decreased."

But surely the same level of American power applied to a world where opposing power is more diffuse should be more, not less, effective. America's problem today is not that its power is in relative decline but, on the contrary, that the places where it can exert potentially decisive influence have increased in number, and so have the choices we must confront.

Do "losses" on the periphery matter? Indeed, can there even be American "losses" on the periphery if America does not choose to become involved? Should America resist all those who oppose its view of world order? Or should the United States keep its powder dry for the really serious threats to its existence—the dominance of Europe or Asia, for instance, by a single power? Such is the nature of the questions Americans have faced throughout this century, and have answered in two different and historically instructive ways.

It would seem to make sense to heed the realists' assertion that a nation may become distracted, or exhaust itself by lesser endeavors, and thus fail to guard that which is most important. But this in fact is the path the United States followed in the 1930's, and lived to regret. First it failed to respond to the peripheral Italian invasion of Ethiopia, the peripheral Spanish Civil War, and the peripheral Japanese conquest of Manchuria, and then it failed to respond as well when the big threat to "core" interests did finally emerge in the figure of Hitler's Germany. The big threats and vital interests, as it turned out, were no less debatable than the small threats and lesser interests.

American policy during the cold war provides an interesting contrast. Despite a terrible debacle on the periphery, the United States did not lose sight of the core. On the contrary, concern about the core and concern about the periphery seem to have been mutually reinforcing. The "lesson of Munich," which dominated cold-war thinking until its temporary replacement by the "lesson of Vietnam," taught that a failure of will on small matters eventually led to a failure of will on more vital matters as well. This proved to be a sound strategy for defending American interests, both large and small, and it was this strategy that made possible a peaceful victory in the cold war.

There is no certainty that we can correctly distinguish between high-stakes issues and small-stakes issues in time to sound the alarm. In the past we did not know for sure whether an invasion of Ethiopia was merely the whim of an Italian despot in an irrelevant part of Africa or the harbinger of fascist aggression in

Europe, whether a North Vietnamese victory was a signal of national reunification or the prelude to a hostile takeover of Southeast Asia. So today we do not know whether Serbian aggression is "ethnic turmoil" or the first step in the breakdown of European order.

But the way one handles the small threats is likely to determine the way one handles the larger threats. It does not take much imagination to envision what those larger threats may be: the rise of militant anti-American Muslim fundamentalism in North Africa and the Middle East, a rearmed Germany in a chaotic Europe, a revitalized Russia, a rearmed Japan in a scramble for power with China in a volatile East Asia. If the goal is a United States capable of meeting these more serious threats when they do arise, then the best policy is one that seeks involvement rather than shuns it. Once appeasing adversaries and wishing away problems becomes a habit, it becomes a hard habit to break.

While America's realists claim to await confrontation with the next Nazi Germany or Soviet empire, the tests of American strength, character, and endurance, essential to the preservation of a more stable world order, will continue to come in such unlikely places as Bosnia, Haiti, Somalia, and Korea. If we cannot plug every breach in the world order, we also cannot allow potential challengers of that order to act in the confidence that the United States will stand aside.

The post-cold-war era is a time of readjustment. Relationships of power change constantly, but how Americans respond to crises, even small ones, in this time of transition will affect the nature of the changes yet to come. Only if it is ready to engage its power when and as needed can the United States hope to shape the character and direction of the forces of change rather than be overwhelmed by them.

Finally, a political question that needs to be asked: who among us, Democrat or Republican, is prepared to rise to the challenge and follow the demanding (if in the long run safer) course of global activism?

On the Democratic side, even those Clinton-administration officials who appear willing to assert American leadership find it hard to overcome the instinctive aversion to the use of power which still burdens them 20 years after Vietnam. They seek the fruits of American intervention, yet seem incapable of doing what is necessary to secure them. Democrats today are paying the price for their years of opposition to Republican assertions of American strength abroad.

Since the Vietnam war, indeed, only the Republican party has had the understanding and the confidence to use American power in defense of the nation's interests. Yet the Republican party itself is now teetering on the edge of a historic transformation. Increasing numbers of Republican politicians, policy-makers, and intellectuals agree with Newt Gingrich's judgment that the United States is now "overextended around the world." There are fewer Republican calls for increases in the defense budget, and more Republican calls for decreases in overseas commitments. The Republican party is less and less recognizable as the party of Ronald Reagan or the George Bush who sent troops to Panama and the Persian Gulf.

In the same way, 75 years ago the Republicans transformed themselves from the party of the internationalist Theodore Roosevelt into the party of the isolationist Senator William Borah. In defeating Woodrow Wilson's brand of utopian internationalism, Republicans also killed the more practical internationalism of men like Henry Cabot Lodge, who believed American power had a critical role to play in preventing another war in Europe. When that disaster finally loomed, it was not Lodge but Borah who spoke for the party.

Victory in the cold war came when Republicans vehemently rejected the idea that the United States had to accept a diminished capacity to shape the world and adjust to the increasing power of its strategic and ideological adversaries. Such a prescription is as disastrous today as it was then, and shows the same lack of faith in the American people and their acceptance of responsibility. It took confidence and determination to take the United States safely through the end of the cold war. It will take no less confidence and determination to move America through this next, dangerous phase of history.

Critics Respond to Robert Kagan

Elliott Abrams

> Elliott Abrams served as Assistant Secretary of State
> for Inter-American Affairs from 1985 to 1989. He is
> currently with the Hudson Institute.

Robert Kagan's excellent survey of 20th-century American
foreign policy presents an accurate picture of the dangers the
country will face if it now attempts to withdraw from world politics. Mr. Kagan, however, underestimates the significance of one
phenomenon whose role he does mention. "Americans did not
shun international involvement in the interwar years," he writes.
"Rather, they tried to enjoy the benefits of such involvement
while hoping to avoid its inevitable costs."

I would suggest that this effort to avoid paying the "inevitable
costs" of intervention, which started long before the cold war, has
been especially visible since it began. Thus did the electorate
throw the Democrats out of the White House when the Republican candidate in 1952 promised to end the Korean war, and when
the Republican in 1968 promised to end American involvement
in the war in Vietnam. Thus did the "Nixon Doctrine" suggest
that with proxies like the Shah of Iran American security could be
protected without sending any more boys overseas, and the "Reagan Doctrine" tried to do the job with proxy guerrilla armies.

Why did these internationalist Presidents feel the need to
avoid American casualties? Because they understood that the
American people were willing to go along with an interventionist
foreign policy only so long as the cost was low. Several of Mr.
Kagan's examples—Panama and Grenada are the most striking—
demonstrate only that any military action will gain public support
if it is announced when it is, in essence, over. Public reaction to
the deaths of American Marines in Lebanon and Rangers later in
Somalia suggests that the Presidents who postulated a low public
tolerance for the shedding of American blood were not far off the
mark.

Or, to be more precise, they were not far off the mark when it
came to American casualties incurred in actions apparently

peripheral to the national interest. I believe there would have been considerable tolerance for casualties in the Gulf war, for most Americans came to be persuaded that that battle involved key American political and economic interests.

Here there are two points worth remembering. First, American interests in each potential intervention need to be explained and people need to be persuaded. This calls for presidential leadership, and strong leadership can expand the public's willingness to intervene overseas. An administration that cannot seem to make up its mind what America's interests are, and where they require military action, will never persuade a reluctant public to support action that may cause American deaths.

Second, while Mr. Kagan is right to argue for American "confidence and determination" and to defend the proposition that early action will often prevent much more bloodshed later, some matters are truly peripheral to American national-security interests. Acting to prevent nuclear proliferation is one thing; sending troops on "nation-building" missions whenever there is a humanitarian crisis is another. Intervention in the Caribbean, where American interests have been clear since this country was founded, is a lot easier to defend than intervention in areas where American economic and political interests are nonexistent.

Mr. Kagan is right to push the pendulum back now toward American involvement in world affairs. He should, however, acknowledge that it can swing too far in that direction. Intervention when American national interests are not at stake—when United Nations resolutions become a substitute for the careful calculation of where tangible and intangible U.S. interests lie—will eventually undercut the willingness of Americans to meet even essential national responsibilities.

Angelo M. Codevilla

> Angelo M. Codevilla, formerly a professional staff member of the Senate Intelligence Committee, is a fellow of the Hoover Institution.

Robert Kagan tries to make the case not for intervening here rather than there, in this or that circumstance, to do this or that, but for intervening as opposed to not doing so. Mission: impossible. The core of his argument is that refusal to exercise power anywhere becomes habitual, and debilitates the country's capacity for self-defense even in the most obvious cases. In fact, however, leaders who commit lives and treasure unwisely debilitate the country's capacity for self-defense even more directly. So the case for any action must be made in terms relevant to that action. Mr. Kagan's argument has two corollaries: "The big threats and vital interests" are "no less debatable than the small and lesser interests," and it is not really necessary to tie the use of force to narrowly defined security interests. It is difficult to imagine a more direct incitement to irresponsibility.

Mr. Kagan is correct that great power and widespread interests imply much responsibility. But because his reading of history turns up no case of unwise intervention or wise restraint, he does not help us distinguish worthwhile actions from errors. That reading of history is debatable, at the very least.

Mr. Kagan says that the United States had to enter World War I to preserve a benign British-dominated world order against the possibility of a German-dominated one. But in 1917 the world's order was not at stake, because neither side could have won a lopsided victory. Such a victory became possible only when the United States entered the war. The results of World War I are indefensible. If the United States had not intervened, the seeds of World War II would not have been sown, and the American people would have faced later developments without the burden of their understandable reaction to 126,000 lives having been thrown away.

The very concept of "intervention" beclouds the real questions: For what purpose should we kill and die? Is *this* purpose worthy? What do we have to do to achieve it? Will the results be worth the effort? Are we willing and able to do what it takes? Mr. Kagan discounts the necessity of clear objectives clearly related to the means to be employed. But the concatenation of ends and means is the very essence of policy. Our intervention in Vietnam was the very negation of policy. In the name of noble purposes, the U.S. government disrupted tens of millions of lives, and spent hundreds of billions of dollars. But our leaders thought that the enemies were hunger and disease, and were full of contempt for the idea of victory. By similar lights, the U.S. government dispatched Marines to Beirut in 1982 and a variety of troops to Somalia in 1992. These troops had no enemy to defeat—only blood to shed. By contrast, consider the common sense of Douglas MacArthur's paraphrase of Aristotle: in war there is no substitute for victory.

Consider also that, willy-nilly, to use force is to assume responsibility for the outcome. The U.S. government decided to intervene against Iraq to remove Iraq as a threat to the Gulf states. But since Iraq is an empire, to break the power of the regime is to dismember the country. The U.S. government seemed to realize this only when the defeated Iraqi army's disarray was making it happen. Unwilling to take responsibility for victory, the U.S. government then acted to ensure the survival of Saddam's regime. Now America's bolt is shot, and Saddam's power looms over the region. So, because blather about a new world order helped U.S. officials forget the fundamentals, our mighty war machine killed tens of thousands of people whose death made no difference, while sparing a few whose death would have accomplished our long-range purposes.

The real lesson of history is that any attempt to establish a "world order" is chimerical. The best we can do is to follow the example of the Founding Fathers, pay attention to the fundamentals, and let the world order take care of itself. The Monroe Doctrine, which puts friendly borders at the top of our priorities, makes as much sense today as it did 170 years ago. As ever, our location amid oceans is a source either of security or insecurity depending on the capacity of our Navy to control them. To the extent that any mission weakens our Navy's supremacy in midocean, it is a potentially fatal diversion. Equally important in our time is defense of the air and space approaches to our country against aircraft and missiles.

It is very important to us that the Western Pacific Rim and Atlantic Europe be friendly, or at least not under the influence of major enemies of ours. But guaranteeing that was, is, and always will be beyond us. Control of the ocean and of space is the one factor bearing on such friendship that we can come closest to guaranteeing. Our air and ground forces can never make more than a contribution to big battles in Europe or Asia. Because we cannot make a future for ourselves on the land mass of Eurasia, only lose it, we should never try to substitute ourselves for shaky allies. Which country may be willing to do what for us depends primarily on our power. Hence it behooves U.S. officials to husband that power.

Lest we cease to be ourselves, we must always and everywhere be on the side of those who believe that "all men are created equal, and that they are endowed by their Creator with certain inalienable rights. . . ." But prudence rather than principle must dictate what, if anything, we do about it. Who among us is willing to impose civilization on the Somalis or Rwandans? Are we willing to police the streets of Sarajevo? On the other hand, there is every reason to call the Milosevics of this world the names they deserve. One might make a case for putting cruise missiles into their bedrooms. A case can be made for guaranteeing Poland *et al.* against eventual Russian aggression. The case for making war to destroy North Korea's nuclear arsenal and regime—and thus to preserve the current orientation of Japan—is clear enough to me. But remember, if the U.S. government does any of these things, all of us who must bear the consequences must decide. The Constitution specifies how: Congress must vote on a declaration of war. The debate should clarify the relationship between ends and means.

Mr. Kagan asks, "Who among us . . . is prepared to rise to the challenge of global activism?" I would ask in turn: who among those who pretend to lead the United States in the world is prepared to serve in the armed forces and submit his body to the blood tax? Today only one-third of Congressmen and fewer than a tenth of executive appointees, professors, journalists, and executives of major corporations have ever served in the armed forces. Nor do their families serve. Nor, by and large, are they personally acquainted with those who do. There is a great and growing gap between those sectors of society that contribute to the armed forces and those whose personal remoteness emboldens them to play global chess.

Finally, leadership requires a little humility. Mr. Kagan writes that "Victory in the cold war came when Republicans. . . ." I wish! In fact, it came with the declaration of independence by the Baltic Republics on August 25, 1991, just 3 weeks after George Bush, culminating a long and increasingly lonely effort to help Gorbachev save the Soviet Union, told the Ukrainian people to be good little Soviet citizens. Today, U.S. global activism means, in part, giving smoke-and-mirrors guarantees to the Ukrainians to induce them to render themselves naked to Russian nuclear black-mail. It means helping to weaken the northern border of Israel, and then guaranteeing it. And it means a lot of other silly things, like invading Haiti.

In sum, it is easy to make the case for going to war where we should, for worthy purposes, in well-calculated ways, and under wise leadership. And it is just as easy to make the case against the wrong wars in the wrong places, for the wrong purposes, badly waged. The trick is to tell the difference.

Aaron L. Friedberg

> Aaron L. Friedberg is director of the research pro-
> gram in international security at the Center of Inter-
> national Studies, Princeton University.

Like the realists with whom he takes issue in his thoughtful and provocative essay, Robert Kagan seeks to ensure that, in the wake of the cold war, the United States will continue to play the part of a world power. But, where the realists urge modesty in the selection of ends and caution and discrimination in the application of means, Mr. Kagan prefers boldness and "global activism." As it has done throughout this century, he argues, the United States must use "its influence to promote a world order consistent with its material needs and philosophical predilections."

Mr. Kagan is surely right that an excessively narrow definition of the nation's interests, and undue timidity in the application of its power, will increase the likelihood of paralysis, disengagement, and the eventual emergence of fundamental new threats. Given the nature of its domestic regime, America cannot be concerned only with the preservation of its physical security; if it tries to be a "traditional" power, it will end up by not being much of a power at all. Moreover, as Mr. Kagan reminds us, great-power status is a state of mind as well as the product of a mere accumulation of material resources. Once unlearned, the habits of engagement and action may not be so easy to reacquire. Having defeated its long-time foe, the United States should therefore set itself appropriately ambitious goals and act in ways intended to achieve them. But there are serious difficulties and dangers with the course that Mr. Kagan appears to be proposing.

To begin with, he is overly optimistic (and, yes, unrealistic) in his assessment of American power. One need not accept the notion that the United States is in a state of terminal decline to recognize that, despite our continuing preponderance in most important measures of capability, our relative power *has* diminished in recent decades and is likely to decline still further in the years immediately ahead. The margin of U.S. economic, technological, and, in some respects (such as the more widespread possession of nuclear weapons), military advantage over all other nations will not be as great at the end of this century as it was at its midpoint. Not surprisingly, our capacity to remake the world in our own image will also be diminished. Whether or not God truly does look after "children, drunkards, and the United States," for most of the past century the rising curve of American power has helped to compensate for a multitude of strategic sins and blunders. In the 21st century the diffusion of capabilities will impose greater burdens on our collective capacity for strategic thought and action.

Even if the U.S. share of world-power resources were to remain unchanged, the character of many of the situations that matter most to our future security will make them highly resistant to our influence (or to any other outsider's for that matter). Whether militant Islamic fundamentalism spreads and becomes more virulent, for example, or Russia and China become more liberal and democratic (and presumably peaceful) are matters of enormous importance, but they are also beyond our capacity for direct control. These observations should not be taken as an argument for fatalism or passivity. There is every reason for the United States to try to propagate its values and to do what it can to mold the post-cold-war international order; but good reason, too, for being restrained in our expectations of what we can achieve.

Regarding means: Mr. Kagan places a great deal of emphasis on the use of American military power. Indeed, at times, his "global activism" appears to consist of little more than a willingness to intervene in a series of what realists are inclined to regard as "peripheral" conflicts. Although armed force will surely remain an important tool of American foreign policy, it would be a mistake to concentrate every ounce of analytical energy on only one of the instruments at our disposal. With the end of the cold war, the utility of everything from foreign aid to covert operations needs to be reexamined.

Moreover, if only because the number of potential trouble spots is likely to increase, while the old constraints on American action remain low, the need for discrimination in the future will be even greater than in the past. Saying, in effect, that we ought to be willing to "bear any burden and oppose any foe" does not get us very far in sorting out the costs, benefits, and risks of military action, or inaction, in Bosnia, Somalia, Rwanda, Haiti, Cuba, the Persian Gulf, the South China Sea, the Baltic, and so on.

What we need are not ironclad rules ("avoid the periphery" or "intervene everywhere"), but better and clearer ways of analyzing and debating each new situation as it arises. Every conflict on the periphery may not be peripheral to American national interests properly understood, but some conflicts will surely be more important (and some will, in any case, be more promising candidates for military intervention) than others.

The problem with departing from a strict "clear and present danger" test for intervention is, of course, that looser guidelines risk becoming formulas for overextension and exhaustion. The American people may, indeed, be appalled by evidence of "aggression, political illegitimacy, genocide, mass starvation, nuclear proliferation, [and] violations of international agreements." But this does not mean that they are willing to expend American lives to deal with these problems wherever and whenever they occur, nor should they be. The early returns on patterns of post-cold-war public support for intervention are far more mixed, and the future trends much less certain, than Mr. Kagan lets on. Hesitation regarding the use of force in Bosnia (and, for that matter, the Persian Gulf) and the strong reaction to the loss of a comparatively small number of

American lives in Somalia suggest that popular enthusiasm for foreign military adventures is limited and potentially fragile.

To date we have been extraordinarily lucky. It would be doubly tragic if a future military debacle (or even a string of more costly successes) were to undermine support, not only for intervention but also for the less dramatic forms of American activism. Especially in an era when direct security threats will seem remote, public support for continued engagement is a resource to be husbanded.

Mr. Kagan's article closes with what is, in effect, a Republican call to arms. If Republicans do not advocate "global activism," he suggests, then no one else will. Whether or not this is the case, there is no question that, as the cold war fades, renewed partisan divisions could distort and eventually cripple American foreign policy. Because of the way power is divided and distributed within it, our system works best when there is debate but also, ultimately, a considerable degree of consensus. Agreement on the broad outlines of the strategy of containment did not emerge immediately in the years after World War II, but, once it had, it held for nearly a half-century. We should hope that the new debate in which we are engaged, and to which Mr. Kagan has made an important and valuable contribution, leads to a consensus as solid and a policy as successful.

Francis Fukuyama

> Francis Fukuyama, the author of *The End of History and The Last Man,* served as deputy director of the State Department's Policy Planning Staff in 1989.

There is a great deal I find appealing about Robert Kagan's argument. I believe that the United States should be unafraid to apply its power in the world, and that there is need for a kind of world order which only a militarily dominant great power can provide. I am not a hard-core realist and do not believe that the United States should construe its interests narrowly: support for ideological and moral causes is also important to America's sense of itself as a democracy. Furthermore, I do not believe that we are nearly as constrained economically as many argue: the country has never been richer or more productive, and despite the budget deficit, resources remain much more a matter of will than of fiscal constraints.

Nevertheless, I find I like the "Kagan Doctrine" much more in the abstract than when I try to apply it to any present-day, real-world foreign-policy problems. Apart from purely humanitarian cases, it is hard to be enthusiastic about intervention in Bosnia, Haiti, Somalia, or any of the myriad ethnic conflicts in the former Communist world. These kinds of civil wars are inherently intractable, and do not easily submit to influence by outside powers. In the absence of a larger great-power rivalry, their outcome is in virtually all cases not important to U.S. strategic or ideological interests.

As Mr. Kagan himself acknowledges, there are a number of serious foreign-policy challenges looming on the horizon, such as a revived Russia and an ambitious China. He is quite correct in asserting that the chief task of foreign policy at the present moment is to keep alive the practice of and capability for activism until such time as it becomes truly criticial to core U.S. interests. He is of the "use-it-or-lose-it" school, as are many former NATO specialists who have been searching desperately for something useful for that institution to do.

In my opinion, the much greater danger at present is "use-it-*and*-lose it," that is, intervening for secondary and poorly thought out objectives, and therefore wasting the political capital we have for large interventions later. For while our financial capital is enormous, the political capital available for international involvement at this point in our national history is small and relatively inelastic. The most important issue we are going to face down the road is NATO expansion to include the new democracies of Eastern Europe, though there can be tactical differences on the speed and manner with which this is to be done. NATO would be far more endangered were it to try to solve ethnic conflicts like Bosnia, which it cannot properly do, than were it simply "freeze-dried" and reconstituted later if and when a real threat from Russia emerges. Like instant coffee, a reconstituted NATO won't look or taste as good as the original, but it will be better than nothing at all.

In my view, Americans should be prepared, when the time comes, to have their young people die for Poland. I think they will be less inclined to make the proper decision then if their young people have been dying on behalf of unfamiliar causes in places like Sarajevo and Kigali along the way. If the political vision and leadership to make the right case for a big commitment later are not forthcoming, then we will have a serious problem. But we cannot sneak in this kind of decision under the guise of doing something less ambitious, nor can we work our way up to it by swatting flies in anticipation.

In a larger sense, I do not think it is inappropriate for the United States to concentrate on domestic problems right now when the foreign environment is relatively benign. There is a genuine crisis in American civil society today, from the family to public education to crime, race, and a variety of related problems which, if not thought through, will undermine our position abroad surely but steadily in the long run. Bill Clinton's election was a manifestation that many Americans feel this way as well. Though Clinton's solutions are not the right ones, there is a certain wisdom in that emphasis. In this respect, an activist foreign policy in the absence of real foreign-policy problems will only be a distraction.

Fred Charles Iklé

> Fred Charles Iklé was director of the Arms Control and Disarmament Agency from 1973 to 1977 and Under Secretary of Defense for Policy from 1981 to 1988. He is now at the Center for Strategic and International Studies (CSIS).

To promote democracy, human rights, market economies, and peace throughout the world makes good sense for the United States—as it does for Germany, Canada, Sweden. Yet, for all these worthy goals, the United States will not, cannot, and should not pay any price, bear any burden. Global activism, as advocated by Robert Kagan, recalls Napoleon's grand strategy: "*on s'engage et puis on voit*"; first "one becomes engaged" (in Egypt, Spain, Russia) "and then one shall see" (at Waterloo). To be sure, American global activism has many lasting achievements to its credit. So did Napoleon Bonaparte with his enduring improvements of administration and laws, not only for France but for much of continental Europe.

Mr. Kagan criticizes those who express concern about an American "Waterloo." In a revealing aside, he writes that the American intervention in World War I was not due to "national interest narrowly conceived," but that the United States had an interest in intervening because it had the power to intervene.

My point is not that Mr. Kagan's interpretation here is wrong. On the contrary, he is right in a larger sense than he spells out. The United States had the power to intervene yet used its power unwisely. A credible case can be made that the United States should have used all its influence to end World War I in 1916 (as many leading Europeans advocated at that time). If successful, such a compromise peace might have led to a gradual democratization of Imperial Germany and a gradual breakup of the Hapsburg empire, a sequel that would have prevented many of the disasters that are now cited (by Mr. Kagan and others) as reasons why the United States should engage in global activism.

To intervene *just because we have the power to do so* is not a strategy that will build a world order consistent with our "economic, political, and ideological aspirations." It did not work in World War I. And recently, it did not work in Somalia. Even the 1989 intervention in Panama produced rather dubious results. The drug trafficking through Panama has not been greatly reduced, and the legal implications of dragging Noriega into U.S. courts may yet come to haunt us. The U.S. Justice Department's global activism might be imitated—say, by Iran kidnapping "blasphemers" in the United States and bringing them to "justice" in Teheran.

In choosing among different foreign policies we should not mislead ourselves by using obsolete labels. Isolationism is not an option today, since U.S. territory is no longer isolated by geography from devastating attacks. At the other extreme, a policy of Manifest Destiny—that is to say, establishing U.S. dominion over foreign lands—is also no longer an option; even though in some cases it might make a lot more sense than current versions of interventionism. The significant, hard choices today are between tilting in favor of intervention or tilting in favor of staying disengaged when the pros and cons are nearly balanced—as they usually are.

Contrary to the global activists, I believe a strong case can be made today for tilting in favor of staying disengaged in nearly all those instances where the need for intervention is not overwhelmingly compelling. My reasons are both military and political.

To clarify matters, let us first set aside interventions for charity.

Charity has its own transcendental reasons and need not be justified in strategic terms. About charity it can be said: it is better to
have tried and failed than not to have tried at all. About strategy,
the opposite normally holds true. Sentiments of charity may even
be mixed with patriotic pride. We feel good seeing our military
forces, with their splendid dedication and efficiency, provide
humanitarian assistance in Rwanda, Somalia, Bangladesh. Although
the American people know that charity begins at home, they support charity abroad. Up to a point.

In my view, the main reason for a noninterventionist tilt today
is the new asymmetry in the tools of intervention. The dreadful
truth is that for many of the contingencies now mentioned by the
pundits, our potential enemy could marshal more effective tools
than we could. Of course, this is something every American
wishes to see corrected—in theory. In practice, political disagreements at home make it well-nigh impossible to correct these
asymmetries. Clearly, the problem would not be fixed by merely
adding 10 or 30 percent to the U.S. defense budget (even if that
were as easy as Mr. Kagan intimates).

For example, if American forces in the Caribbean were doubled, the U.S. government would not gain the tools to depose Fidel
Castro or to clean up the mess in Haiti. Or, when North Korea
brandishes a nuclear capability that could destroy South Korean or
Japanese cities, we will not keep Seoul or Tokyo from propitiating
North Korea merely by a 30-percent increase in the present types
of U.S. forces in the Pacific. Or, if U.S. intelligence suspected that
Iran was acquiring an enormously potent biological-warfare capability, the asymmetry in threats and counterthreats between the
United States and a fanatical Iranian leadership could not be reme-
died without major structural changes in our intervention capabilities. In sum, for contingencies where the potential enemy is willing
to run the highest risks and accept massive losses, the U.S. ability to
intervene has been greatly weakened over the last few decades.

Two developments account for this deterioration, whose profound impact many American experts (including, it seems, Mr.
Kagan) fail to appreciate. One is the appalling increase in the vulnerability of the United States to but a single weapon of mass
destruction. Much is being written about the fact that access to such

weapons is spreading. What has been less noticed is the increased vulnerability of our economy: delicate computer networks, fragile power grids, total dependence on computers and electricity for most commercial activities, and porous borders plus almost no air defenses (not to mention the absence of any missile defenses).

The second of these developments is the political hobbling of a whole range of nonmilitary (paramilitary) means that the U.S. government in the past could use to intervene against a dangerous enemy. Prior to the 1970's, U.S. national-security policy could use military-assistance programs in ways that are now precluded. It could mount covert actions far more freely than today. It could generously allocate foreign "assistance" to buy friends and weaken enemies. It could rely on a worldwide support system, now largely dismantled, that comprised hundreds of military bases, several global airlines and communications carriers totally responsive to official requests, a worldwide oil production and distribution system largely United States-controlled, and easy options to deploy America's then-dominant financial power. Last but not least, the President could count on a sense of discipline throughout the government bureaucracy that today would be regarded as authoritarian.

We may not regret the loss of these policy tools; many Americans, in fact, welcome the change as some kind of moral cleansing. But in arguing for global activism, it behooves us to keep in mind that the President today cannot use the tools—even if he wanted to—that Franklin D. Roosevelt, Truman, Eisenhower, and Kennedy could so easily employ to intervene abroad.

Joshua Muravchik

> Joshua Muravchik, a resident scholar at the American Enterprise Institute, is the author of *Exporting Democracy: Fulfilling America's Destiny*.

I salute Robert Kagan for the core of his argument but not its periphery. I agree that it is usually foolish to ignore small problems on the grounds of husbanding energies for larger ones. First, small problems, unattended, may feed or grow into big ones. Second, a nation's ability to respond effectively to paramount challenges may depend on habits and character developed in confronting less decisive ones. Third, a nation's pattern of behavior will shape the anticipations of others. This does not mean, however, that all small problems are equal. Some are threats to the peace, while others are tragedies confined within the borders of a single state. Bosnia and Korea are examples of the former; Haiti and Somalia, the latter. Yet Mr. Kagan lumps all four together.

I also find strained and unconvincing Mr. Kagan's claim that American policy since the cold war has been dramatically internationalist. He goes on to argue that America's behavior in the 1920's and 1930's should not properly be called "isolationalist." Well, by that standard, perhaps today's policy currents are not "isolationist," either. Whatever you want to call them, however, they smack of flight from burdens. Mr. Kagan offers U.S. efforts in Somalia, Bosnia, and Rwanda as evidence of "worldwide engagement and armed intervention unprecedented in scope." But if our flight from Somalia, abdication in Bosnia, and fly-by of Rwanda constitute robust internationalism, then many of our realist/isolationists will rest easy. The real point is that since America stumbled into the unprecedented status of sole superpower, it has engaged the world only in a patchwork and irresolute way, concentrating instead (to no good effect) on domestic issues.

I fear that Mr. Kagan is trying to turn back on the realists their own stratagem of conflating the *is* and the *ought*. Nations necessarily behave "realistically," they say; therefore, America must do so too—ignoring the obvious point that if the first clause is true, the second is superfluous. Mr. Kagan seems to be on his way to saying that America should be internationalist because it is bound to be internationalist. Alas, it is not so easy.

Peter W. Rodman

> Peter W. Rodman served as deputy assistant to the President for National Security Affairs (1987–89) and director of the Policy Planning Staff, State Department (1984–86). He is now director of National Security Programs at the Nixon Center for Peace and Freedom in Washington, D.C.

Robert Kagan's case for activism is compelling in many ways, and tempting, but in the end his approach is no substitute for a more sober strategic judgment.

It is healthy that this discussion could take place at all. Two decades ago, the United States was mired in a Vietnam-era funk and was disarming unilaterally. We have recovered; the West's triumph in the cold war has vindicated American internationalism. The country's willingness to engage in a series of interventions—most particularly Desert Storm—is the mark of a body politic that is capable of sustaining a significant international role.

While Mr. Kagan thus probably exaggerates the continuity in postwar American policy, he is certainly right that the current domestic support for our international leadership is a refutation of the theories of American decline. He also makes the correct observation that, in the absence of serious rivals, the pivotal U.S. role in many international issues is more decisive than before. All this is to the good.

None of it, however, obviates the need for strategy. No country is omnipotent. Our goals may be expansive—and there are many humanitarian goals now open to us—but some principle of selectivity is unavoidable. There are, believe it or not, a few recent upheavals we have kept our forces out of (Liberia, Sudan, Algeria) and others we have been hesitant to plunge more deeply into (Bosnia). Rightly or wrongly, explicitly or implicitly, we choose where we go. But what are our criteria? What priorities are guiding us?

Mr. Kagan makes another important point: that abdication is a bad habit to get into and that credibility can be lost (or won) in the little conflicts as well as in the big ones. (Every President needs some air-traffic controllers on whom to prove his mettle early in his term.) This has been a big part of Bill Clinton's problem. The string of mishaps in 1993 in Haiti, Somalia, and Bosnia undermined the U.S. position generally. No doubt the North Koreans and other big-leaguers were watching and drawing their conclusions.

Now, some of this was just a question of competence in execution. In the real world there is a premium on well-thought-out military plans that aim at a decisive result. Interventions cannot be sustained by good intentions alone, and the new era of limited interventions has revived some (I thought) discredited notions about incremental uses of force.

But beyond this question of tactics, some principle of strategic selection is also needed, for two reasons. One is that the body politic cannot be strained without limit. Whatever the fundamental health of our society, the quality of our political leadership is still a contingent variable. On the Democratic side, there is good news and bad news: the good news is the apparent end of the recent liberal taboo against any use of force; the bad news is that this liberal epiphany is still divorced from rigorous analysis of strategic and military realities. Some on the liberal side (Anthony Lewis *et al.*) will almost certainly revert to their anti-interventionism in any case where the goals are not purely humanitarian. On the Republican side, we have seen in the past year how politically tempting it has been to revive the whole war-powers case against presidential authority as botched interventions have multiplied. The congressional war-powers apparatus is by definition an antiinterventionist cause.

In the post-cold-war era, the public's judgments (as well as those of our political elite) are clearly still unformed; the President's margin for error is not all that great. As Somalia and Rwanda together demonstrate, the American people gladly support humanitarian engagements if the costs are not high; once the casualties mount, then the public's tolerance does not seem to be sustainable if no showing of a more concrete national interest can be made.

Second, a sensible national strategy for the United States has to give priority attention—inescapably—to maintaining the basic *structure* of international order. This means maintaining the balance of power in Europe and the Far East; it means keeping the newly powerful Germany and Japan firmly anchored to the international-security structure; it means shielding the world community against what Charles Krauthammer calls the Radical Weapons States (Iran, North Korea, Iraq). How can these not be the fundamental tasks of our national-security policy? The more exalted humanitarian goals are fine—so long as the military forces will still be available to meet the strategic tasks when a threat comes.

The gutting of our defense capabilities must, of course, be reversed. One of the extraordinary anomalies of our current national debate is, indeed, how the proliferation of missions for

our troops grows while our capabilities are rapidly shrinking. The
timidity so far of both Democratic and Republican leaders on the
question of the necessary rearmament is not only a national dis-
grace; it is also an obvious weakness of any doctrine or aspiration
of global activism such as the one Mr. Kagan espouses.

His enthusiasm, to repeat, is the sign of a healthy America. But
someone still has to be around to ask the tough questions, case by
case, about strategic necessities and military realities.

Helmut Sonnenfeldt

> Helmut Sonnenfeldt, now at the Brookings Institu-
> tion, served in the State Department from 1952 to
> 1977 in a variety of positions, including director of
> the Office of Research and Analysis for the USSR
> and Eastern Europe, and counselor.

As the single most powerful and influential power to emerge
from the cold war, the United States cannot avoid involvements
around the globe even if that were the preference of large portions
of the American public. In that sense, Robert Kagan's plea for
"global activism" is a case for the obvious.

There are, of course, voices among us that call for retrenchment. There are those who worry about overextension. There are
those who would like to use—and have to some extent succeeded
in using—the defense budget as a cash cow for a host of other
purposes. There are efforts to establish "core" or "vital" interests as
the only ones warranting the use of military force and the loss of
American lives. But even among these groups there are few who
would contend that the United States should or could now return
to its continental shell.

I am in substantial sympathy with Mr. Kagan's essential argument. But as he himself notes, in a "world where opposing power
is more diffuse," the choices we must confront have increased in
number. Moreover, it is not only power in its various forms that is
more diffuse. Without the disciplining effects of large-scale hot
and cold wars, the international system as a whole is more complex and diffuse. American power to influence the shape of an
eventual new world order is enormous. But it does have limits.

And so does America's wisdom and skill in wielding that power. And even American power and determination cannot repeal the effects of the law of unintended consequences.

So I would hope that our debate about the American role in the post-cold-war world will not degenerate into one between minimalists and maximalists or, even worse, between those who see America tending toward either impotence or omnipotence.

We do need to come to grips with choices, especially where the use of military power is involved. (Vocabulary, incidentally, is not trivial. Activism should not be confused with interventionism. Involvement and engagement are not synonymous with commitment. Leadership does not, or at least not necessarily, mean unilateralism.)

Mr. Kagan generally tends to address the issue of choice as if it were settled. Yet he also says: "Only if [the United States] is ready to engage its power *when and as needed* [emphasis added] can the United States hope to shape the character and direction of the forces of change rather than be overwhelmed by them." But the "when and as needed" is precisely what serious debate turns on and what, ultimately, affects not only the amount but the content of the defense budget.

Intellectual or even political debate cannot be expected to settle this issue definitively. The Clinton administration almost certainly had no intention on January 20, 1993, of finding itself 18 months later militarily engaged in the Caribbean, central Africa, the Balkans, the Middle East, and, potentially, Korea. And it seems unlikely that the highly professional leadership of the Clinton Pentagon expected that its Bottom-Up Review, promulgating defense programs to cope with two major regional crises and providing for advanced-technology equipment for the decades ahead, would quickly become financially insupportable.

Mr. Kagan compliments Theodore Roosevelt for being the first to graft "principled ends to the exercise of power." But Roosevelt also sensed the dangers of extravagant interventionism. "We would interfere" with countries in the Caribbean, he said in his annual message to Congress in December 1904, "only in the last resort, and then only if it became evident that their inability or unwillingness to do justice at home and abroad had violated the rights of the United States or had invited foreign aggression to the detriment of the entire body of American nations."

I would guess that many internationalists who opposed invading Haiti might have supported doing so if the present administration came closer to Roosevelt in the precision of its purpose. Even then, it is worth recalling that the admonition of Woodrow Wilson's Secretary of State, Robert Lansing, that the United States should "aid the people of the [Caribbean Republics] in establishing and maintaining honest and responsible governments *to such extent as may be necessary in each particular case*" [emphasis added] did not prevent a bloody and ultimately ineffectual U.S. occupation of Haiti that lasted 19 years.

It is not clear where Mr. Kagan would have come out on the issue of invading Haiti in order to dislodge the illegal military regime and restore and maintain the democratically elected—but not notably democratically inclined—Jean-Bertrand Aristide. The administration, of course, compounded the problem by its demonstrative assembly of naval and ground forces around Haiti, thereby raising serious questions about the credibility of its threats if no invasion had taken place despite the continued sway of the military regime.

Mr. Kagan is silent about the use of American ground forces to help bring order, justice, and a civilized society (to use Theodore Roosevelt's terminology) to Bosnia. Nor does he address the vexing question of how long and at what level of effort the United States should have continued its humanitarian operations in Rwanda, since their termination without the establishment of a reasonably stable and humane government could well lead to renewed catastrophe. How many Somalias, in short, would Mr. Kagan accept? Would he extend NATO (i.e., U.S.) commitments eastward and with what kind of force?

This is not meant to criticize Mr. Kagan for lack of specifics in his relatively brief article. It is, rather, to point out that his "when and as needed" criterion for the use of U.S. power is the beginning of the debate, not its end.

Mr. Kagan's point that American defense spending has become "too low to allow the United States to carry out the many new tasks it will face in the post-cold-war era" is incontestable. So is the proposition that "the increases that will be necessary will hardly bankrupt the country." But where does this leave us?

If the numbers and types of military operations already undertaken by an administration whose officials "find it hard to overcome the instinctive aversion to the use of power" are anywhere near the norm for the years ahead, would he make any trade-offs with the other capabilities needed to "move America through this next, dangerous phase of history"?

In sum, Mr. Kagan's next article should start where his last one left off.

Paul Wolfowitz

Paul Wolfowitz, dean of Johns Hopkins's Paul H. Nitze School of Advanced International Studies, was Under Secretary of Defense for Policy, 1989–93, and United States Ambassador to Indonesia, 1986–89.

Robert Kagan correctly emphasizes the difficulty of making any simple distinctions between core interests and peripheral ones. The Sudetenland (or, more precisely, stopping Hitler from dismembering Czechoslovakia) turned out to be a core interest of the Western powers in 1938, although it was peripheral geographically and its importance was not seen clearly at the time.

To be fair, the so-called realists do not deny that small threats can eventually become large ones. That consummate realist, Henry Kissinger, has often commented on the dilemma that frequently confronts statesmen—when problems are easiest to handle, the need to act is usually less obvious; by the time the urgency is clear, the range of options available is much narrower. Serious realists thus acknowledge the difficulty of distinguishing core interests from peripheral ones.

However, true realism also must come to terms with another point that Mr. Kagan emphasizes: the distinction between core interests and peripheral ones must ultimately be the result of a political process, rather than the conclusion of some splendid Metternichian calculation. For the United States that political process will necessarily reflect the peculiar strengths and weaknesses of American democracy, so that the determination of our core interests cannot realistically be based solely on hard-headed calculation, divorced from the characteristic American insistence on an idealistic basis for international action. Paradoxically, hard-headed realism is finally unrealistic.

Mr. Kagan is also right in saying that the real limitations on America's role in this historical moment are limitations of will rather than of power. The collapse of the Soviet Union has left us with no powerful enemies, with the world's strongest economic powers as our allies. The problem is not that the relative power of the United States has declined but more nearly the opposite: there appears to be so little power opposing us that there are possibilities of getting involved almost everywhere.

Mr. Kagan seems to feel that this is not a problem. The best way to counter threats to our national existence, he asserts, is not by keeping our "powder dry for the really serious threats," but instead by resisting "all those who oppose America's view of world order." Mr. Kagan argues that the way we handle small threats will determine the way we handle the larger ones, because "once appeasing adversaries and wishing away problems becomes a habit, it will be a hard habit to break." While acknowledging that "we cannot plug every breach in the world order," he seems to propose doing almost exactly that: even Haiti and Somalia appear as tests of American will that we cannot afford to fail.

But the choice is not so starkly between either responding to all threats to "world order" or responding only to threats to our national existence. There really is no way to escape the need for some degree of selectivity about where we intervene, particularly if it is a question of intervening with American force.

The need for selectivity arises less from the limitations on American power—although that power is *not* unlimited—than from the same concern about America's long-term willpower that Mr. Kagan proposes to deal with by making intervention a habit. While it is true, as he says, that the use of force need not be tied to "unmistakable and narrowly defined security interests" in order to gain public support, support for the use of force is not likely to last long—particularly not in the face of American casualties—if it is based solely on an appeal to American idealism, and all the less if such an appeal is itself based on the abstraction of a commitment to "world order."

During my visits with troops preceding the Persian Gulf war, what impressed me about the young men and women who were prepared to face death for their country was that they seemed to be moved by the thought that "if we don't do it now, some other Americans will have to do it later, at much higher cost." Is this an appeal to American self-interest or to our idealism—or both?

If Americans need both a sense of interest and a sense of duty to sustain the use of force, they also need two other things which Mr. Kagan's argument tends to neglect. They need to believe that others are doing their share; and they don't like failure (the damage to American will, as well as credibility, from Vietnam and Lebanon are reminders of the price that failure can extract). All of this argues for much greater caution than Mr. Kagan advocates when it comes to putting American servicemen and women in harm's way in a place, such as Haiti, that is peripheral to American interests and where the chances of success are problematic.

Fareed Zakaria

Fareed Zakaria is managing editor of Foreign Affairs.

Robert Kagan and I agree that America should exercise its power "in pursuit of a broad definition of interests—in pursuit, that is, of a more decent world order." We disagree on two counts: first, whether my agenda for the United States—securing its core interests—is skimpy; and second, whether instability in peripheral areas of the world matters much.

In my article "The Core vs. the Periphery" (*Commentary*, December 1993), I argued that American foreign policy during the cold war helped create peace and prosperity among most of the major powers of the world. American leadership, I wrote, "created an open world economy that, more than any other single factor, explains the extraordinary progress toward peace, democracy, and civilized conduct in the industrial nations over the last half-century."

This represents a massive accomplishment for America's interests and ideals. It is also a fragile one. If strains in the central balances of power in Europe and East Asia were to deepen, if mercantilist pressures among the great industrial states were to increase, the consequences could be catastrophic.

Power imbalances—specifically the decline of British power and the failure of the United States to take its place—and economic crises were important ingredients in the collapse of the international system during the 1930's. Hence I proposed a foreign policy that is highly internationalist and expansive; one that commits the United States to secure its achievements during the cold war and to consolidate the benefits gained by the collapse of the Soviet Union. Such a policy requires the Unites States aggressively to consolidate free trade, capitalism, and constitutional government abroad, providing political and economic assistance to friendly governments and groups. It commits America to be actively engaged in—in many cases formally committed to defend—several major countries in Asia, Europe, the Middle East, and Central and Latin America. It requires a formidable military capability, some of which will need to be permanently stationed in Europe, the Middle East, and Asia. This is an agenda worthy of the Roman empire at its peak. It is not enough for Robert Kagan.

He wishes that the United States involve itself in peripheral areas of the world, taking up the old imperial quest for order. He points out that during the cold war the United States intervened in the periphery many times, even fought a war in Vietnam, where American interests were "debatable." Precisely. What did the United States gain from that noble but unwise course? Nothing: the loss of Vietnam was supposed to make all the dominoes of Southeast Asia fall; instead, those countries allied ever more closely with the United States. What did Britain gain from acquiring millions of square miles in the hinterlands of Africa and Asia? What did France gain from its ruinous defense of Algeria? What did the Soviet Union gain from its bloody efforts in Afghanistan?

Mr. Kagan does not seem to deny that crises on the periphery are "low-stakes issues." His rationale for universal activism is different: since we really cannot distinguish between important and peripheral interests, we should intervene everywhere. This startling assertion would seem to preclude the need for any strategic analysis whatsoever. It is true that international relations is not an exact science and serious people can, have, and will disagree over what constitutes an important American interest—Bosnia is an example of a country that is "on the cusp" in such debates—but surely the answer is not to throw up one's hands and intervene everywhere just to be safe.

In fact, Mr. Kagan himself seems quite able to distinguish between "high-stakes" and "small-stakes" issues; almost all the potential problems he lists as worrisome—which would, I agree, require an American response—involve a resurgent threat from a great power: Russia, China, Japan, and Germany. On the other hand, almost all the current crises he lists—Somalia, Haiti, Serbia—involve small, dysfunctional countries that can cause trouble, even bloodshed, in their neighborhoods, but do not pose a serious threat to the broader region. There will always be points of instability in the world; to see all of them, indiscriminately, as "tests of American strength, character, and endurance essential to the preservation of a more stable world order" is to invite the United States to engage in the limitless and futile business of ordering the world. This is a task for world federalism, not American foreign policy.

Finally, Mr. Kagan asserts that his vision of the world should find a natural home in the Republican party. History suggests otherwise. From Versailles to Haiti, the Republican party has always been the party of prudence in foreign policy. Theodore Roosevelt, whom Mr. Kagan cites approvingly, was once asked what he thought of Woodrow Wilson's belief that America should be willing to intervene in Europe if rules of "world order" were violated. He scornfully inquired whether this meant that the United States should go to war "every time a Jugoslav wishes to slap a Czechoslav in the face." TR believed in, and spoke the language of, spheres of influence and national interests, rather than world order and global activism. With the end of the cold war—in which ideological and strategic lines criss-crossed—the Republican party will return to its internationalist, but realist, roots.

William F. Buckley, Jr., once said that the defining element of conservatism is realism: realism about the limits of state power, the malleability of human beings and societies, the intractable nature of a world of nation-states. Mr. Kagan has a Wilsonian vision that sees governmental power as omnipotent, rejects the need to set priorities, advocates the social engineering of complex and ancient societies, and expects that these good intentions coupled with state power can transform the world. Sounds like a job for the liberals.

Robert Kagan Replies

My goal in making a case for global activism was, as Elliott Abrams notes, to push against what seemed to me an increasing drift, especially among conservatives and Republicans, away from what over the last 20 years had been an expansive view of America's role in the world. My main point was that the end of the cold war, and the collapse of our long-time foe, had neither ended the requirement for an active, vigilant foreign and defense policy nor deprived the American people of an important goal in foreign affairs: the maintenance of a decent world order conducive to American material and philosophical interests. I thus argued against the idea that only vital, core interests were worth engaging our attention and our power, and I questioned whether the divide between core and periphery was as clear and determinative as some have claimed.

Helmut Sonnenfeldt says I have made a case for the obvious. I agree. Most of those who have been kind enough to respond to my article share the conviction, as Francis Fukuyama eloquently puts it, "that the United States should be unafraid to apply its power in the world, and that there is need for a kind of world order which only a militarily dominant great power can provide." But I am less sure than Mr. Sonnenfeldt that such an expansive view of America's role dominates the current discussion.

The case for a more limited set of goals—tied to the defense of identifiable vital interests—has been powerfully made by leading conservative foreign-policy theorists from Owen Harries to Henry Kissinger to Jeane Kirkpatrick. Neither isolationists nor neo-isolationists, they have simply opposed shouldering the burden of promoting an American-style world order except against those threats which rather directly imperil American security. The very idea of the United States as "the sole remaining superpower," Harries has recently written, is an anachronism in the post-cold-war era. The United States has ceased to be such a power "because its circumstances and its interests no longer require or permit it to be one." Kissinger advises us, as he did in the 1970's, to "learn the limits of our capacities." Jeane Kirkpatrick has suggested that "with 'normal' times, we can again become a normal nation."

Such arguments have force and appeal. The difference between their view and mine is not the difference between isolationism and crusading idealism, but, as Aaron L. Friedberg points out, between two different perspectives on what it means to be a world power. I think most of my respondents agree with Mr. Friedberg and Peter W. Rodman that this is a debate worth having, even if they do not fully share my perspective.

Some of my respondents have criticized me for apparently advocating constant intervention everywhere and at all times. I did not intend to suggest any such thing, but I obviously erred in not making it clear that a policy of global activism can and should be conducted with as much prudence as any other kind of policy. Let me now say what I had thought it unnecessary to have to say in my article. I, too, believe the United States cannot intervene any time and any place a problem arises. I, too, believe judgment must be exercised, prudence must be shown, resources must be matched to commitments, priorities must be balanced, and recklessness, carelessness, insobriety, foolishness, and irrationality must be avoided. Such requirements exist whether one advocates greater or lesser activism in international affairs.

Let me also acknowledge that I did not set forth what Mr. Rodman calls a "principle of selectivity" for judging where to intervene and where to stand aloof. But this was not an oversight. I doubt that such a priori principles can be set forth, unless one is willing to restrict American policy to the defense of strategic choke points, sea lines of communication, commercial markets, and other of the more measurable interests. Henry Kissinger, on the antepenultimate page of his most recent book, Diplomacy, writes that "not every evil can be combated by America . . . [but] some monsters need to be, if not slain, at least resisted. What is most needed are criteria for selectivity." But in the remaining two pages of his book, he does not even suggest what those criteria might be. I do not blame him.

Those who find my argument lacking in this way have a hard

time explaining precisely what should and should not prompt an American response. They certainly do not agree among themselves. Elliott Abrams correctly writes that intervention in the Caribbean, "where American interests have been clear since this country was founded," is easier to defend than intervention elsewhere. But Mr. Abrams has also taken the perfectly defensible position that the United States has no interest in intervening in Haiti. Fareed Zakaria lists "Central and Latin America" as part of America's "core" interests, but by omission consigns the Caribbean, where Haitians live, to the "periphery." Europe is also part of Mr. Zakaria's "core," but the part of Europe where war currently rages is on the "periphery." (As Paul Wolfowitz rightly notes, there was a time when the Sudetenland also looked to many like the "periphery.") Most of my respondents would omit Somalia from any list of areas where America should intervene, but Mr. Wolfowitz has elsewhere ably defended at least the Bush administration's version of the humanitarian mission in Somalia (see *Foreign Affairs*, January/February 1994).

This is not to find fault with any of these judgments. It is only to say that the demand for a doctrine which spells out precisely where and under what circumstances the United States should intervene is impossible. Unless one is prepared to oppose all the actual and potential interventions of the post-cold-war era—in Panama, in Iraq, in Somalia, in Haiti, in Bosnia—then one will be hard-pressed, I believe, to set forth "criteria of selectivity" that would explain why we should, for instance, intervene in Panama to depose a military dictator, but not in Haiti.[2]

---

[2] It will not do to argue that the United States moved against Manuel Noriega because he sold drugs, or threatened the Canal, or harmed Americans in Panama. Efforts to oust Noriega began when he refused to turn over power to elected democratic presidents in the early and mid–1980's. The indictment against Noriega for narcotics trafficking actually worked against efforts to remove him in 1988—as Elliott Abrams knows better than anyone. As for the Canal, Noriega consistently went out of his way to declare that he would not threaten it, which was one reason the American military, especially in Panama, opposed any efforts to remove him. The harming of Americans in Panama came only after the United States had launched a campaign to force Noriega from power.

Perhaps those who believe it was a mistake to use U.S. military power to restore President Aristide are right, although so far it would not appear so. But would they construct an entire doctrine around that judgment? As for Somalia, those who argue that the original mission of the Bush administration was correct, but that the Clinton administration's expansion of that mission was a mistake, may also be right. But is there a doctrine that will unerringly guide us through situations like the one in Somalia? Would we want to promise, for instance, to abide by a "Somalia Doctrine" (i.e., that the United States should *never* get involved in the internal politics of a nation where we have intervened for humanitarian purposes)? Or will there not be some occasions when such involvement might be proper and necessary? The "no nation-building" doctrine heavily influenced American policy at the end of the Gulf war. But some might reasonably ask, in retrospect, whether we would have been wiser to remove Saddam Hussein when we had the power to do so directly, even if that meant shouldering the burden of "nation-building" in Iraq.

No general approach to foreign policy can provide the kinds of answers some of my critics are seeking. Whether we tilt toward or away from engagement and intervention, choices will have to be made on the basis of the unique circumstances of each situation. The most successful doctrine of our time, the doctrine of containment, could not have satisfied the requirement for "criteria of selectivity." And indeed, as the events in Vietnam attest, it was a doctrine capable of leading the United States into misjudgment and failure. But neither the errors nor the failures discredited the overall approach.

Today, a policy of global activism in pursuit of a more decent world order must also suffer its share of misjudgments and failures. In my opinion, however, a policy of retrenchment, a policy of defending only "core" and "vital" interests, a policy of behaving not like the global superpower we are, but like the "normal" power we are not, is fraught with many, greater dangers.

Some of my respondents, while generally supporting a more activist approach to world affairs, still worry that the demanding course I advocate will overtax American capabilities, depleting both our material and spiritual reserves. The popular mood may, as

Messrs. Friedberg, Abrams, Fukuyama, and Wolfowitz suggest, be unwilling to expend lives for the defense of "world order" in Kigali, Sarajevo, or Port-au-Prince. I tend to believe public attitudes have been influenced by the rather lackluster debate between a Republican party warning against "quagmires" and a Democratic President unable to articulate, much less consistently carry out, a strong and active foreign policy.

But public hostility to overseas involvement is hardly a new phenomenon. In the 1930's a much better case could have been made that the public was unwilling to intervene in Europe and that American resources, in the short term, were lacking. In the 1970's, Richard Nixon and Henry Kissinger founded the policy of détente, in part, on their assumption that the United States lacked the will and the capacity to engage in an all-out competition with the Soviet Union. Kissinger argued then, as he does now, that a "new era" had arrived which required scaling back American ambitions and accepting the limits of a "new equilibrium." Then, too, the United States was to have difficulty "bringing [its] great power to bear on the issues most likely to arise." Then, too, there had been a "global diffusion of political power" in a world of "turbulence and complexity." And Kissinger had recommended then as he does now that Americans had to "learn the limits of our capacities."

It is worth considering the likely state of the world today had America heeded Kissinger's advice to accommodate itself to Soviet power in the 1970's. Today, if there is a need for the United States to engage itself actively in international affairs—and most of my critics agree that there is—then the responsibility lies upon us to make the issues plain to our fellow Americans. Political leadership was essential to overcome material and spiritual weaknesses in the 1930's and 1970's; it is no less essential in the 1990's.

Overextension and overconfidence are errors to be avoided. I believe the problems confronting the United States today, however, have more to do with lack of confidence and underachievement. The pendulum, to borrow Mr. Abrams's metaphor, has not swung too far in the direction of engagement in world affairs.

A reluctance to act is often praised as prudence, while a willingness to act can be labeled rashness. The history of the 20th century ought to have upset these misguided assumptions. Even today, however, an intelligent student of American foreign policy like Mr. Zakaria can praise the "prudence" of the Republican party in the years after Versailles. Mr. Wolfowitz, by contrast, writing in *Foreign Affairs* earlier this year, described those Republican policies as "based on illusions—illusions that helped to produce the debacle of the 1930's." I am hopeful that we will not succumb to some of the reigning illusions of our own time.

What to Do About

Welfare

CHARLES MURRAY

Charles Murray is Bradley Fellow at the American Enterprise Institute. In addition to *The Bell Curve*, he is the author of *Losing Ground* and *In Pursuit*.

Mr. Murray writes: "This article was to have been done jointly with the late Richard J. Herrnstein, but his illness prevented him from working on it. Parts of the discussion are drawn from the book we wrote together, *The Bell Curve*, and all of it is suffused with Richard Herrnstein's influence on my thinking."

In the 1992 campaign, Bill Clinton's television ad promising to "end welfare as we know it" was one of his best vote-getters, so effective that it was the first choice for a heavy media buy in closely contested states at the end of the campaign. This should come as no surprise. No American social program has been so unpopular, so consistently, so long, as welfare. But why? What is wrong with welfare that evokes such a widespread urge to "do something about it"?

One obvious candidate is size and cost. Bill Clinton campaigned during a surging increase in the welfare rolls. By the end of his first year in office, more than fourteen million people would be enrolled in Aid to Families with Dependent Children (AFDC), representing more than 7 percent of American families and two million more recipients than had been on the rolls in 1989.

With so many working-aged people being supported by government, the amounts of money involved have mounted accordingly. But, as with so many other questions involving welfare, there is no uncontroversial answer as to exactly how much, because few can agree about where the definition of "welfare" begins and ends.

In 1990, before the most recent increase in the rolls had gotten well under way, figures cited by various parties in the welfare debate ranged from $21 billion to $210 billion. The lower figure, used by those who claim that welfare is really a piddling part of the budget, represents just AFDC. But no serious student of the issue denies that Medicaid, food stamps, and public housing are also part of welfare. That brings the total to $129 billion. But this number covers only part of the array of programs for low-income families. The upper-end figure of $210 billion is the bottom line for the Congressional Research Service's report of state and federal expenditures on "cash and noncash benefits for persons with limited income" in 1990. Of that, $152 billion came from the federal government.

Two hundred and ten billion dollars works out to $6,270 for every man, woman, and child under the poverty line in 1990, only a few hundred dollars less than the official poverty threshold ($6,652 for a single unrelated individual in 1990). Statements such as "We could eliminate poverty tomorrow if we just gave the money we're already spending directly to poor people" may be oversimplified, but they are not so far off the mark, either.

One approach to the topic of "what to do about welfare" could thus reasonably involve ways to reduce expenditures. Yet, though complaints about wasting money on welfare loafers are commonly heard, and though the country truly does spend a lot of money on welfare, it is not obvious that money is really the problem. Suppose that for $210 billion we were buying peaceful neighborhoods and happy, healthy children in our low-income neighborhoods. Who would say that the nation could not afford it? Money may well become a decisive issue as the dependent population continues to grow, but it has not yet.

Instead, I will proceed from the assumption that the main source of the nationwide desire to do something about welfare is grounded in concerns about what welfare is doing to the health of the society. Judging from all that can be found in the press, on talk shows, and in the technical literature, an unusually broad consensus embracing just about everyone except the hard-core Left now accepts that something has gone drastically wrong with the family, that the breakdown is disproportionately found in poor neighborhoods, and that the welfare system is deeply implicated.

Different people put different emphases on just what has gone wrong. There are so many choices. In many welfare families, no one has ever held a regular job. This is bad for the taxpayer who supports such families, bad for the women who are trapped into poverty, and, most portentously in the long run, bad for children who need to be socialized to the world of work. In many welfare families, the mother works, but only sporadically and surreptitiously in the illegal economy. The welfare system becomes an instrument for teaching her children all the wrong lessons about how to get along in life.

In the vast majority of welfare homes, there is no biological father in the house. In many, there has never been a father. The male figure in the home is instead likely to consist of a series of boyfriends who do not act as fathers but as abusive interlopers.

These circumstances are damaging to children in so many ways that to list them individually would be to trivialize them. On this issue, the intellectual conventional wisdom has changed remarkably in just the last few years. The visible turning point was Barbara Dafoe Whitehead's 1993 *Atlantic* article, "Dan Quayle Was Right," but the groundwork had been laid in the technical journals in preceding years, as more and more scholars concluded that single parenthood was bad for children independently of poverty and other markers of socioeconomic disadvantage.

Statistically, measures of child well-being tend to order families by their structure: conditions are best for children in intact families, next best for children of divorce (it does not seem to help if the custodial parent remarries), and worst for children born out of wedlock (even if the woman later marries another man). This ordering applies to a wide variety of outcomes, from emotional development to school performance to delinquency to family formation in the next generation.

But the evidence accumulated so far tells only part of the story. Families that have been on welfare for long periods of time are overwhelmingly concentrated in communities where many other welfare families live. While it is unfortunate when a child must grow up in a family without a father, it is a disaster when a generation of children—especially male children—grows up in a neighborhood without fathers. The proof of this is before our eyes in the black inner city, where the young men reaching 20 in 1994 came of age in neighborhoods in which about half the children were born out of wedlock. Social science is only beginning to calibrate the extent and nature of the "neighborhood effects" that compound the problems associated with illegitimacy.

If these results were confined to the inner cities of our major cities, the effects on American society would still be grim enough. A look at the national mood about crime shows how a problem that is still localized (as the most severe crime rates still are, impressions notwithstanding) can nonetheless impinge on American life as a whole. But there is no reason to think that the effects will remain within the black inner city. The white illegitimacy ratio, which stood at 22 percent for all whites in 1991, is approaching the 50-percent mark in a number of working-class American cities. There is no good reason to assume that white communities with extremely high illegitimacy ratios will escape the effects of an unsocialized new generation.

These observations have led me to conclude that illegitimacy is the central social problem of our time, and that its spread threatens the underpinning of a free society. We cannot have a free society, by this reasoning, unless the great majority of young people come of age having internalized norms of self-restraint, self-reliance, and commitment to a civic order, and receive an upbringing that prepares them to transmit these same values to their children. We cannot achieve that kind of socialization without fathers playing a father's role in the great majority of homes where children grow up.

For those who accept this pessimistic reasoning, extreme measures to change the welfare system are justified; for those who still
consider illegitimacy to be one problem among many, more incremental reforms seem called for. Put broadly, four types of welfare
reform are being considered in various combinations: workfare;
the substitution of work for welfare; penalties for fathers; and the
complete abolition of welfare.

Workfare refers to a variety of reforms that would make welfare
beneficiaries show up at some sort of job, usually a public-service
one, or lose their benefits. Softer versions of workfare call upon
welfare recipients to attend job-training programs or risk losing
their benefits. Offshoots include such things as "learnfare," in
which mothers lose part or all of their benefits if their children
drop out of school.

The rationale for workfare that resonates with the voters is,
roughly, "make them do something for the money we're giving
them." Many also hope that the prospect of having to work for
benefits will either deter young women from having babies in the
first place or induce them to find real jobs on their own and leave
welfare.

An additional intellectual rationale has been advanced by
Lawrence Mead, a political scientist at New York University, who
argues that what welfare recipients really lack is the ability to cope
with the routines of ordinary life. Surveys show that they share the
same aspirations as people in mainstream society, Mead says, but
their lives are so chaotic and their discipline so ill-formed that the
government must provide the framework that has been missing in
their own lives.

Workfare is not an untried idea. Local attempts to force
women to work for welfare have been made off and on in scattered jurisdictions for decades. The 1988 welfare-reform bill put
the federal government's imprimatur on such programs. The evaluation reports now add up to a fair-sized library, and they tell a
consistent story. Participants in training and work programs usually
have higher mean earnings than persons in the control groups. But
these mean differences amount to hundreds of dollars per year, not

thousands. The effects on long-term employment are small. The most successful programs tend to be located in small cities and rural areas rather than large cities.

A few exceptions to these generalizations are noteworthy. A program in Riverside, California, showed dramatic early results, apparently because of an energetic, decisive administrator who was given extraordinary freedom to define work rules, replace staff who did not perform, and enforce sanctions against welfare recipients who did not cooperate. If anyone can figure out how to duplicate these conditions nationwide, workfare might be able to produce much larger effects than shown in the typical evaluation.

As far as I know, no one has ever documented a deterrent effect for workfare. But evidence indicates that many welfare recipients, sometimes a significant portion of the total caseload, will drop out of a welfare program if a strictly enforced work requirement is installed.

In 1986, the social critic Mickey Kaus proposed an alternative to workfare that would scrap the existing welfare system and replace it with public-service jobs at the minimum wage. The government would provide medical care and child care for preschool children, but otherwise the woman would be on her own. If she showed up at one of the local job sites and worked, she would get a paycheck at the end of the week. If she chose not to work, that would be her business.

Kaus's proposal, which he subsequently elaborated in his book *The End of Equality*,[1] has much to recommend it. Workfare programs break down because of built-in contradictions. Welfare bureaucracies do not function well as employers. They have no incentives to reduce their caseloads and no incentives to make welfare recipients behave like real employees. Trying to enforce sanctions against uncooperative cases tends to become a long and tedious process. The Kaus system asks only that the government recreate a WPA-style agency for administering public-service jobs—something that the government did successfully in the 1930's.

[1] See the review by Michael Horowitz in the December 1992 *Commentary*.

Whether the government could do as much again is open to question. The typical WPA male worker in the 1930's came to the program with a set of motivations much different from those of the typical AFDC mother in the 1990's. Yet it seems plausible to me that the Kaus system would not only achieve substantial effects on work behavior among AFDC mothers but also have a substantial deterrent effect.

The program's cost, which Kaus himself set at $43 billion to $59 billion for national implementation, might not be as large as expected. Since we know that large proportions of the caseload have taken themselves off the rolls when a strict work requirement was imposed, we could expect a similarly large drop if the Kaus plan were implemented. And while it is difficult to imagine the federal government adopting a scrap-welfare-for-work proposal with the pristine purity necessary to make it succeed, it is possible to imagine a state doing so, if states were given the option of folding all the money currently spent on AFDC, food stamps, and public housing into a public-service jobs program.

Enforcement of child support among unmarried fathers is one of the most popular reforms under consideration, not least because it gives people a chance to say the right things about the responsibilities of the male. Like workfare, enforcement of child support is an old idea. Toughly worded laws are already on the books requiring child support, and the federal government is spending about $2 billion a year on the Child Support Enforcement program originated in 1975.

Despite these efforts, paternity is not established for about two-thirds of illegitimate births. The failure rate is so high partly because of poor enforcement, but mainly because the law asks so little of the unwed mother. The government has leverage only when she wants to qualify for AFDC benefits. For this, she is required merely to cooperate in identifying the father, a condition that can be satisfied by giving the name of a man whose whereabouts are unknown or even by her earnest statement that she does not know who the father is.

The proposed reform with the most teeth is to withhold all

AFDC benefits unless the father is actually identified and located. Would such a threat help control the behavior of males? Perhaps—if the father had a job in the aboveground economy, if the state had in place methods of garnisheeing his wages, and if the state were able summarily to jail fathers who failed to meet their obligations.

Yet to list these conditions is to expose the reasons not to expect much from reforms of child support. Many unwed fathers have no visible means of support, and an even higher proportion will flee into that category, or disappear entirely, if child-support enforcement is tightened.

Would such measures nonetheless "send the right signals" about the responsibilities of men for their children? Many think so; I am a holdout. The alternative "right signal" is to tell young women from the outset—from childhood—that they had better choose the father of their babies very carefully, because it is next to impossible for anyone, including the state, to force a man to take on the responsibilities of fatherhood.

This brings us to the fourth option, scrapping welfare altogether, a proposal with which I have been associated for some years. I am under no illusions that Congress is about to pass such a plan nationally. But, as with the Kaus plan, a state can do what the federal government cannot. And it is conceivable that Congress will pass reforms permitting the states wide discretion in restructuring the way they spend their welfare budgets.

The main reason for scrapping welfare is to reduce the number of babies born to single women. The secondary reason is to maximize the chance that children born to single women are raised by mature adults who are able and willing to provide a loving, stable, nurturing environment—a result that will ensue because more children will be given up for adoption at birth, and because single mothers who choose to keep their babies in a no-welfare society will be self-selected and thus their number will be limited to those who have the most resources for caring for children.

These goals presume that ending welfare will have a drastic

effect on behavior. One must ask whether there is good reason to believe that it will.

One way of approaching the question is to ask whether welfare causes illegitimacy in the first place. I have written two reviews of this debate in the past 2 years—one long and technical, the other shorter and nontechnical[2]—and will not try to cover all of the ground here. These are the highlights plus a few new points:

Academics have focused almost exclusively on comparisons of illegitimacy based on the differences in welfare payments across states. It is now generally if reluctantly acknowledged by these scholars that the generosity of welfare benefits has a relationship to extramarital fertility among whites. More recent work is showing that a relationship exists among blacks as well. The size of the effect for whites seems to be in the region of a 5-percent change in extramarital fertility for a 10-percent change in benefits, with some of the estimates substantially larger than that.

This effect is called small by those unhappy to admit that welfare has any relationship at all to extramarital fertility. I treat the fact that any effect has been found as I would treat favorable testimony from a hostile witness—the analyses have generally consisted of regression equations with a multitude of independent variables, making it as hard as possible to show an independent effect for AFDC.

A broader observation about these studies is that trying to analyze the relationship of welfare to illegitimacy by examining cross-state variation in AFDC benefits has a number of serious methodological problems that are bound to limit the magnitude of the effect that AFDC is permitted to show. I have been pointing to such problems in print for many years. So far as I know, none of the analyses using cross-state benefits has even acknowledged the existence of these technical problems, much less tried to deal with them.

Last summer, seventy-six social scientists signed a statement saying that the relationship of welfare to illegitimacy was small.

[2]"Welfare and the Family: The American Experience," *Journal of Labor Economics,* January 1993, and "Does Welfare Bring More Babies?," *Public Interest,* Spring 1994.

When I replied that the very studies they had in mind were consistent with something in the neighborhood of a 50-percent drop in white illegitimacy if welfare were eliminated, there were cries of outrage—but not because my statement was technically inaccurate. It was a straightforward extrapolation of the 5-percent (or more) change in white fertility per 10-percent change in welfare benefits that has been found in recent research.

I should add that I do not place much faith in such linear extrapolations in this case. Indeed, I argue from other evidence that the effects would most likely steepen as the reductions in welfare approached 100 percent. But this is speculative—no one has any empirical way to estimate how the curve might be shaped.

Meanwhile, two characteristics of illegitimate births imply a stronger relationship to welfare than that indicated by the cross-state analyses.

The first of these characteristics is that the illegitimate birth rate has been increasing while the legitimate birth rate has been decreasing. The *rate* in this case refers to the production of babies per unit of population, in contrast to the more commonly used statistic, the illegitimacy *ratio*, representing the proportion of live births that are extramarital.

The logic goes like this: birth rates are driven by broad historic forces that are so powerful and so consistent that they have applied everywhere in the West. Put simply, birth rates fall wherever women have an option to do something besides have babies. The options are brought about by better medical care (so more babies survive to adulthood), increased wealth and educational opportunities, and the opening of careers to women. Improved technology for birth control and access to abortion facilitate the effects of these forces.

Thanks to all this, among both blacks and whites in America, the number of legitimate babies per unit of population has been falling steeply. But during this same period, concentrated in the post–1960's, the number of illegitimate babies per unit of population has been rising. In other words, something is increasing the production of one kind of baby (that born to single women) at the same time that the production of the other kind of baby (that born to married women) is dropping.

The scholars who say that welfare cannot be an important cause of the breakdown of marriage and the encouragement of illegitimacy have yet to offer an explanation of what this mysterious something might be. The existence of a welfare system that pays single women to have babies meets the test of parsimony.

Perhaps, however, the "mysterious something" is the lack of these new options for disadvantaged women. But why specify *single* disadvantaged women? That brings us to one of the most provocative features of illegitimacy, its relationship to poverty— not poverty after the baby is born, but before. It is one of the stronger reasons for believing that the welfare system is implicated in the production of illegitimate babies.

Begin with young single women from affluent families or women in high-paying jobs. For them, the welfare system is obviously irrelevant. They are restrained from having babies out of wedlock by moral considerations, by fear of the social penalties (both of which still exist, though weakened, in middle-class circles), by a concern that the child have a father around the house, and because having a baby would interfere with their plans for the future.

In most of the poorest communities, having a baby out of wedlock is no longer subject to social stigma, nor do moral considerations still appear to carry much weight. But the welfare system is very much part of the picture. For a poor young woman, the welfare system is highly relevant to her future if she has a child, easing the short-term economic penalties that might ordinarily restrain her childbearing. The poorer she is, the more attractive the welfare package, and the more likely that she will think herself enabled by it to have a baby.

The implication of this logic is that illegitimate births will be concentrated among poor young women—and they are. This may be inferred from the information about family income from the Bureau of the Census data, showing that in 1992 women with incomes of less than $20,000 contributed 73 percent of all illegitimate babies, while women with incomes above $75,000 contributed just 2 percent.

But these data are imprecise, because income may have fallen after the baby was born (and the woman had to quit work, for example). The logic linking welfare to illegitimacy specifically refers to women who are poor before the baby is born. For data on this point, I turn to one of the best available bases, the National Longitudinal Survey of Youth (NLSY)[3], and ask: of women of all races who were below the poverty line in the year prior to giving birth, how many of their children were born out of wedlock? The answer is 56 percent. Among women who were anywhere above the poverty line, only 11 percent of babies were born out of wedlock.

Why should illegitimate births be so much more likely to occur among women who are already poor? The common argument that young women with few prospects "want something to love" may be true, but it has no answer to the obvious rejoinder, that single poor young women in the years before the welfare system began probably wanted something to love as well, and yet the vast majority of them nonetheless made sure they were married before bearing a child. Other things being equal, poor single young women face the most daunting prospects if they have a baby without a man to help take care of it, and that reality used to govern the behavior of such young women. Of course the sexual revolution has changed the behavior of young women at all levels of society, but why has it produced babies predominantly in just one economic class?

Once again, an answer based on a welfare system that offers incentives only to poor women meets the test of parsimony. Once again, the scholarly literature has yet to offer an alternative explanation, or even to acknowledge that an alternative explanation is called for.

There is one additional characteristic of women who are at most risk of giving birth to children out of wedlock: they gener-

[3]The NLSY is a very large (originally 12,686 persons), nationally representative sample of American youths who were aged 14 to 22 in 1979, when the study began, and have been followed ever since.

ally have low intelligence. This point is new to the welfare debate. Richard Herrnstein and I discuss it at length in *The Bell Curve*, again using the National Longitudinal Survey of Youth, which administered a high-quality cognitive test to its subjects when the study began. The chances that a poor young woman's baby would be born out of wedlock were 68 percent if she had an IQ of 85, but only 26 percent if she had an IQ of 115.

Lest it be thought that this result is conflated with racial complications, it should be noted that the relationship held among whites as powerfully as among the population as a whole. Lest it be thought that the result is conflated with the opportunity that smart women have to go to college, it should also be noted that the relationship holds as powerfully among women who never got beyond high school as it does for the population as a whole. Lest it be thought that this is a reflection of socioeconomic background, the independent importance of IQ is still great after holding socioeconomic status constant. Conversely, the independent importance of socioeconomic background after holding the effects of IQ constant is severely attenuated.

Summarizing the overall picture: women in the NLSY (in their mid-20's to early 30's when this observation applies) who remained childless or had babies within marriage had a mean IQ of 102. Those who had an illegitimate baby but never went on welfare had a mean IQ of 93. Those who went on welfare but did not become chronically dependent on welfare had a mean IQ of 89. Those who became chronic welfare recipients had a mean IQ of 85.

Now back to the first and most crucial goal of welfare reform, that it drastically reduce the number of children conceived by unmarried women. In trying to develop methods for accomplishing this goal, we know from the outset that both sex and the cuddliness of babies are going to continue to exert their powerful attractions. We know that decisions about whether to have sex and whether to use birth control are not usually made in moments of calm reflection.

Therefore, any reform must somehow generate a situation in

which a young woman, despite not being calm and reflective, and often despite not being very bright, is so scared at the prospect of getting pregnant that she will not have intercourse, or will take care not to get pregnant if she does.

This means that the welfare reform will have accomplished one of two things. Either the change has been so big, so immediate, and so punishing that even a young, poor, and not very smart girl has been affected by it; or else the change has directly motivated people around that young woman to take an active role in urging her not to have the baby.

Bill Clinton's program, based on the threat of "2 years and out, if you've had a reasonable chance at job training and a reasonable chance to find a job," is not calculated to meet this criterion. Two years is an eternity to a young girl. The neighborhood is filled with single women who have been on welfare for ages and have not gotten thrown off. Is a 16-year-old going to believe that she will really be cut off welfare 2 years down the road, or will she believe the daily evidence around her?

Other commonly urged recommendations—sex education, counseling, and the like—are going to be just as futile. A major change in the behavior of young women and the adults in their lives will occur only when the prospect of having a child out of wedlock is once again so immediately, tangibly punishing that it overrides everything else—the importuning of the male, the desire for sex, the thoughtlessness of the moment, the anticipated cuddliness of the baby. Such a change will take place only when young people have had it drummed into their heads from their earliest memories that having a baby without a husband entails awful consequences. Subtle moral reasoning is not the response that works. "My father would kill me" is the kind of response that works.

From time immemorial, fathers and mothers raised the vast majority of their daughters, bright ones and dull ones, to understand these lessons. Somehow, in the last half-century, they began to lose their capacity to do so—curiously, just as social-welfare benefits for single women expanded. I want to press the argument that the overriding threat, short-term and tangible, which once sustained low illegitimacy ratios was the economic burden that the single woman presented to her parents and to the community. I do not mean to deny the many ways in which noneconomic social stigma played a role or to minimize the importance of religious belief, but I would argue that much of their force was underwritten by economics.

At this point, we reach a question that cannot be answered by more social-science research but only by experience: if welfare were to be abolished in the late 20th century, would a revival of the economic threat be enough to drive down illegitimacy? Or do we need a contemporaneous revival of the moral sanctions against illegitimacy to make the economic penalties work? The good news is that the two forces can be counted on to work together, because of a built-in safety mechanism of American democracy. Welfare will not be abolished until the moral sanctions against illegitimacy have also gained great strength. There will not be enough votes until that mood is broad and deep.

It is only because of the sea change in the conventional wisdom about the deficiencies of single-parent families that proposals to end welfare are now being taken seriously. So far, that change has been couched in utilitarian terms. The next step, already well under way, is for language to change. Now, the elites are willing to say, "Having a baby if you are young and single is ill-advised." It seems to me that the truer way to put the issue is this: bringing a new life into the world is one of the most profoundly important moral acts of a person's life. To bring a child into the world knowing that you are not intellectually, emotionally, or materially ready to care for that child is wrong.

When the elites are broadly willing to accept that formulation, and not before, welfare will be ended. And at that stage, we can also be confident that the financial penalties of single parenthood that ending welfare would reimpose are going to be reinforced by moral suasion.

Different parts of the country will reach this state of affairs sooner than others. In Utah, for example, with its low illegitimacy ratio plus the moral force of the Church of Latter Day Saints and that church's elaborate system of social welfare, one may be confident that if the entire federal welfare system disappeared tomorrow, the result would be overwhelmingly positive, with only the most minor new problems. But if the same legislation were to apply to

Harlem, where more than 80 percent of children have been born out of wedlock for a decade and nongovernmental social-welfare institutions are scattered and in disarray, one may be equally confident that the short-term result would be chaos on a massive scale.

Drawing these strands together, here are the characteristics of legislation that might have a chance of passing in the next several years:

• *The centerpiece of the legislation should be freedom for the states to experiment.* Congress knows beyond doubt that the welfare system it currently mandates for the entire country is a failure. The next thing for Congress to learn is that it does not have a one-size-fits-all answer to amend that failure. The solution is to permit the states to adopt a wide variety of plans.

Thus, Congress should develop a simple formula whereby states can take the money that would otherwise flow into them in the form of AFDC payments, food stamps, and housing benefits (and as many other means-tested programs as possible) and use it for other ways of dealing with the needs of children currently supported by the welfare system.

One example of a simple formula is to base the amount of the allocation on the budgets for those programs in the last year before the federal legislation is passed. States should also be permitted to end those programs altogether and forgo federal funds completely, though it is doubtful whether any state would choose to go that route.

Initially, most states would probably opt for modest reforms along the lines Congress is contemplating—more workfare, more job training, perhaps soft time limits. But a few brave states are likely to try something more ambitious. Probably one or two will adopt much more aggressive workfare or time limits than the ones in the Clinton plan. Perhaps a state somewhere will choose to adopt a version of the Kaus plan, funding public-service jobs in lieu of welfare benefits. My hope is that some state will also end welfare. If a state should consider doing so, here are some guidelines that I would recommend:

• *Grandfather everyone now on the system, letting them retain their existing package of benefits under the existing rules.* The reasons for grandfathering are both ethical and pragmatic. For many women, welfare has turned out to be a Faustian bargain in which the government plays the role of the devil. Having made this bargain, many of the women on welfare are so mired in the habits of dependency and so bereft of job skills that it is unethical for the government now to demand that they pull themselves together. Pragmatically, grandfathering is probably a prerequisite for getting any such plan through a state legislature.

I should add that some grace period is also necessary between the passage of the legislation and the time it takes effect. Nine months and one day is the symbolically correct period. Practically, a year seems about right: long enough to allow the word to spread, abrupt enough to preserve the shock value that is an essential part of changing behavior.

• *Limit the reform to unmarried women.* This step is primarily to facilitate building a political coalition that can get the legislation passed, but it also can be taken without jeopardizing the desired result. Divorced and abandoned women are not at the heart of the welfare problem. On the contrary, most of them treat welfare as it was originally intended: as a temporary bridge. When you read statistics such as "half of all women get off welfare within 2 years," it is divorced women who have brought down the average.

It may be objected that to limit the reform to unmarried women provides an incentive for pregnant girls to enter into a marriage of convenience. This may well be true, but it is a good result, not a bad one. Men who sign a marriage certificate are much more easily held to account for support of the child than men who do not.

Is not limiting the reform to unmarried women discriminatory? Yes, that is one of the main points of doing anything about welfare. I am not enthusiastic about using government policy positively to reward marriage, but it is another thing to end government policy that undermines marriage—as welfare for single women undeniably does.

• *"Ending welfare" should mean at a minimum cutting off all payments which are contingent on or augmented by having a baby.* The core benefit to be ended altogether is AFDC. Medicaid benefits for the child should be left in place, because the existence of Medicaid has gutted the alternative ways in which medical care could be made reliably available to poor children (whereas there remain many alternative ways of providing children with food, shelter, and nurturing).

What about housing and food stamps? I doubt if it is possible to end them altogether. If a woman is poor enough to qualify for housing benefits and food stamps without a child, it seems unlikely that the courts would allow those benefits to be cut off because a child has been born.

Instead, a state that adopts the "end-welfare" option should simply become neutral with regard to births out of wedlock. In principle, the best way for the state to become neutral is the approach advocated by Milton Friedman: dismantle the entire social-welfare structure with its multiplicity of benefits and bureaucracies, replace it with a cash floor using the mechanism of the negative-income tax, and make that cash floor invariant regardless of the number of children. But I cannot imagine Congress giving states the option of converting all federal-subsidy programs into a negative-income tax (though it is certainly an intriguing idea). Some steps short of that need to be worked out.

One attractive possibility is to return to the original intention of the 1935 act that created welfare. AFDC would continue to be available for widows with young children and for divorced or abandoned women with young children, with a higher cash payment to compensate for the cuts in housing and food benefits. Unemployment benefits would also remain available for men and women alike, with or without children. I favor broadening and strengthening the unemployment-insurance system as part of this approach.

• *Limit the initial legislation to teenagers.* It is widely assumed that if welfare is ended, some other mechanisms will be required to replace it. Most of these options (I will describe some presently) involve extensive interventions *in loco parentis*. Limiting the initial legislation to teenagers has two merits. First, it is much better to let the government act *in loco parentis* for minors than for adults.

Second, a political consensus already exists about single teenage girls having babies that has not yet consolidated about single adult women having babies.

If a state ends welfare in the ways I have just described, a large behavioral impact may be expected—somewhere in the region of a 50-percent reduction in illegitimate births among whites (and probably among blacks as well) if the cross-state analyses are taken seriously.

Other effects are hard to predict. Some people assume that large numbers of pregnant women will move across the border to the next state, others predict a surge in abortions. The type and size of the effects will also depend on the nature of a state's caseload. The effects in a mostly rural plains or mountain state are likely to play out much differently than the effects in states with large cities. In any case, a substantial number of single women will continue to get pregnant. What happens to them and their children? These measures should be considered:

• *Actively support adoption at birth.* Today, the welfare system and its satellite social-work agencies typically discourage adoption. The pregnant single woman who wants to give up her child for adoption is more likely to be encouraged to keep the baby than to be praised. This is perverse. In America, the pool of mature, caring adoptive parents is deep, not just for perfect white babies but for children of all races and for children with physical and mental handicaps, if—the proviso is crucial—the child can be adopted at birth. Any comparison of what is known about child abuse and neglect, emotional development, or educational success suggests that the child of a never-married teenager has a better chance in an adoptive home.

If welfare has been ended, many more pregnant women will be looking at adoption, and the state can do much to help. Changes in laws can encourage a larger pool of adoptive parents by reinforcing the rights of the adoptive parents and by strictly limiting the rights of the biological parents. Adoption agencies can facilitate the adoption of black children by ending restrictions on transracial adoption.

• *Offer group living for pregnant women.* For a pregnant young woman from a functioning family and a functioning community, the best support network consists of friends and relatives. One of the chief reasons for ending welfare is to revitalize those networks. But one of the saddest aspects of today's burgeoning illegitimacy is that many pregnant young women have no friends and relatives who are competent to provide advice and nurturing during the pregnancy, let alone to help think through what will happen after the baby is born. This will continue to be true when welfare is ended.

States that end welfare should therefore look carefully at the experience of the homes for pregnant single women that dotted the country earlier in the century, most notably the Florence Crittendon homes. In a modern version of such a home, the young woman would receive the kind of prenatal care and diet—meaning, among other things, no drugs, alcohol, and tobacco—that would help children of unwed mothers get off to a better physiological start. Group homes of this sort can also be excellent places to help young women come to grips with their problems and prepare for their futures.

• *Offer group living for teenage single mothers.* Another intriguing suggestion is to extend the Florence Crittendon concept to the period after birth. The mother who keeps her baby is no longer given welfare services, but she is given the option to live in a group home. She and her child receive food and shelter; the mother receives training in parenting and job skills; and the child is in an environment where at least some of the adults understand the needs of infants and small children.

• *Maintain a clear bright line short of coercion.* Adoption services or group homes must be purely optional; no young woman should be required to use these services. This bears on a broader point. Having a baby you are not prepared to care for is wrong, but this does not mean that the state has the right to prevent you from doing it—a nice distinction between immoral acts and the state's power to regulate them that could easily be ignored once the Left decides that illegitimacy is a bad thing.

An idea gaining favor—requiring welfare recipients to use Norplant—illustrates the danger. From a legal standpoint, I find nothing objectionable about the idea. Welfare is not a right but largesse, and the state may legitimately place conditions upon dispensing largesse. But once the government requires any use of birth control, a barrier has been broken that has frightening possibilities.

For the same reason, the government must be passive regarding the encouragement of abortion. If enough people think that low-income women should have easier access to abortions, let the subsidies come from the philanthropies that private citizens choose to support. The process of ending welfare must unambiguously represent a withdrawal of the state from personal decisions, not new intrusions.

• *Enforce the existing laws on child neglect.* One of the most common questions about ending welfare is, "What happens to the woman who keeps her baby anyway?" The answer is that some women will indeed choose to keep their babies. As I have already suggested, the self-selection process imposed by the end of welfare also means that such women are likely to be those who have the greatest commitment to their children. They are likely to be the ones who have done the best job of lining up support from relatives and friends, or the ones who have well-paying jobs.

But the main point is that single women who keep their babies will be in exactly the same situation as every other parent who takes a baby home from the hospital: that child is now the parent's responsibility. There is no need to keep a special watch on how a single mother does; rather, she falls under the same laws regarding child neglect and abuse as everyone else, to be enforced in the same way.

And that, finally, should be the overriding theme of what we do about welfare: treating the human drama of "having a child" as the deeply solemn, responsibility-laden act that it is, and treating all parents the same in their obligation to be good parents. The government does not have the right to prescribe how people shall live or to prevent women from having babies. It should not have the right even to encourage certain women to have babies through the granting of favors. But for 60 years the government has been granting those favors, and thereby intervening in a process that human communities know how to regulate much better than governments do. Welfare for single mothers has been destructive beyond measure, and should stop forthwith.

What to Do About

The CIA

RICHARD PIPES

Richard Pipes, Baird Professor of History at Harvard, served in 1981–82 on the National Security Council as Director, East European and Soviet Affairs. In 1976 he chaired Team B, a panel of outside experts who successfully challenged the CIA's interpretation of the Soviet military buildup. His books include *Russia Under the Old Regime*, *The Russian Revolution*, and *Russia Under the Bolshevik Regime*.

For the second time since it came into being in 1947, the Central Intelligence Agency is fighting for its life. Twenty years ago, following revelations by the Church (Senate) and Pike (House) committees of the Agency's involvement in illegal activities on U.S. territory, such as spying on American citizens opposed to the Vietnam war, there was a clamor for its abolition. The KGB added fuel to this fire by supporting and financing disinformation purporting to show that the CIA, a painful thorn in its side, was a threat to American democracy. The Agency managed to weather the assault, only to face today an even more daunting challenge to its existence.

The current movement is inspired not by alleged illegal activities, which have not recurred since the mid–1970's, but by the charge that the CIA has consistently provided the government with faulty assessments and tolerated inexcusable security breaches in its ranks. The main argument against it, however, is that with the collapse of the USSR the Agency has become redundant.

The CIA was indeed founded at the onset of the cold war for the specific purpose of coping with the Communist threat to the United States and forestalling another Pearl Harbor, which, especially after the Soviet Union had exploded an atomic device in August 1949, would present the prospect of an incomparably more damaging surprise attack. President Truman created a *central* intelligence organization to collect and analyze information obtained by the government's separate intelligence services. He did so despite protests that he was setting up an "American Gestapo," because inquiries into the Pearl Harbor disaster revealed that in 1941 the United States had had at its disposal enough indications of a pending Japanese strike to anticipate and prevent it, but had taken no action because it lacked an organization capable of collating the diffuse bits and pieces of intelligence information.

Before proceeding with an assessment of the CIA, a few facts need to be established. The CIA is neither the only nor the largest intelligence branch of the U.S. government. The United States has approximately a dozen intelligence organizations, some attached to the civilian branches (from the Departments of Defense and State to that of Agriculture), others to the military services. By far the largest recipient of intelligence appropriations is the Department of Defense, which, in addition to maintaining its own intelligence bureau (the Defense Intelligence Agency, or DIA), manages both satellite surveillance and communications intercepts. Recent leaks from Congress indicate that of the $28 billion budgeted annually for intelligence, the CIA receives only $3 billion. Thus, even if the CIA were abolished, a huge and costly intelligence apparatus would remain: lost would be an organ capable of bringing together the evidence obtained by the different services. We would find ourselves in the same position as before Pearl Harbor.

The second fact to bear in mind is that the CIA is only in a limited sense a "spying" organization, in that *spying* in the precise sense of the word (involving deliberate disguise and deception) constitutes only a small part of the CIA's activities, whether measured in terms of personnel or of budgets. The Agency has two principal divisions: the Directorate of Operations, which carries out clandestine work, including espionage, and the Directorate of Intelligence, which collects and analyzes data that flow from diverse sources. According to knowledgeable persons, clandestine operations currently absorb less than 5 percent of the Agency's budget, and possibly as little as 1 percent. Much covert work consists of small and peaceful operations such as sponsoring publications and funding trade unions.

The principal business of the Agency is analysis and estimation: the CIA resembles far less the world inhabited by James Bond and the heroes of John le Carré's novels than a gigantic think tank, staffed with people who have nothing to do with spying (even if they benefit from covertly obtained information) and who in their training and duties resemble academic researchers.

Triumphs and Fiascos

The opponents of the CIA stress its recurrent intelligence failures as an argument for its liquidation. And undeniably, the Agency has had more fiascos than the law of averages would suggest. It misjudged from the outset both the pace and the magnitude of the Soviet nuclear effort, its main responsibility: its 1966 projection of Soviet ICBMs for 1970, for instance, was half of what they turned out, in fact, to be.[1] It minimized or ignored Soviet defensive measures, such as dispersal, hardening, and redundancy of command-and-control systems, as well as shelter provisions for the leadership—measures which told a great deal about Soviet strategic intentions. Year after year, it depicted the Soviet economy as healthier than it actually was and Soviet defense expenditures as considerably lower than they actually were. On President Kennedy's accession in 1961, the CIA provided projections of Soviet economic growth, based on Moscow's statistics, from which it emerged that by the year 2000 the USSR would have a gross national product (GNP) three times that of the United States![2] At

[1] John Prados, *The Soviet Estimate,* Princeton University Press, 1982, pp. 183–96.
[2] Richard Reeves, *President Kennedy: Profile in Power,* Simon & Schuster, 1993, p. 54.

the same time, the Agency consistently underestimated the Soviet defense budget, placing it originally at 6 to 8 percent of GNP and then, in February 1976, inexplicably doubling that figure to 10 to 15 percent.[3] As has become known since, the true figure was close to double even the doubled figure.

The reasons for these misjudgments will be spelled out in due course. Here, suffice it to say that such absurd miscalculations had serious political consequences. For by depicting the Soviet Union as both stronger and less menacing than previously thought, they pushed the United States toward accommodation with it in the form of détente and an obsession with arms-control negotiations.

The Agency's record of predictions is hardly better than its estimates. In 1950, it failed first to anticipate North Korea's invasion of South Korea and then the intervention of China. In 1962, it denied that Russia intended to install missiles in Cuba up to the very moment when photographic imagery proved beyond the shadow of a doubt that the missiles were being deployed. It anticipated neither the Warsaw Pact aggression against Czechoslovakia in 1968, nor the fall of the Shah of Iran in 1979, nor the Soviet invasion of Afghanistan later that same year, nor even Iraq's assault on Kuwait in 1990. It was surprised by the crushing of Solidarity in Poland in 1981. Such instances of failure can be multiplied.

Less often mentioned are the CIA's successes. It has done an excellent job of tracking Soviet weapons developments. In the 1950's, it correctly downplayed the prospect of a Soviet attack on the United States which had many Washington politicians and generals worried. It set in motion a variety of programs to counter Communist propaganda, one of which, Radio Free Europe/Radio Liberty, contributed powerfully to keeping alive dissent inside the Communist bloc. In the 1980's, under President Reagan and his Director of Central Intelligence (DCI), William Casey, it helped, by various covert economic, military, and political operations, to undermine Soviet authority in Poland and Afghanistan.

Many of the Agency's intelligence failures can be attributed to identifiable and remediable flaws of methodology. But even the best-functioning intelligence service cannot be counted upon reli-

---

[3]John Ranelagh, *The Agency: The Rise and Decline of the CIA,* Simon & Schuster, 1987, pp. 621–22.

ably to predict the actions of foreign powers: divining political intentions is far and away the most difficult aspect of intelligence work. This holds especially true of dictatorial regimes, with which U.S. intelligence is particularly concerned, because their decisions are in the hands of unstable and impulsive individuals subject to few if any external controls. It is hard to predict the behavior of unpredictable personalities.

To place the CIA's performance in proper perspective, it helps to look at the record of other intelligence organizations. In the 1930's, the vaunted British secret service, notwithstanding excellent contacts in Germany, persistently misjudged Hitler's military capabilities as well as his intentions, having convinced itself that the Nazi rearmament program was purely defensive. After Hitler had gone to war in September 1939, British intelligence believed that economic exigencies would make it increasingly difficult for Germany to continue fighting beyond the spring of 1941.[4] British intelligence, which at the time, like its U.S. counterpart, lacked a center to collate secret data, firmly rejected the possibility of a Nazi-Soviet rapprochement, a German invasion of Norway, or a Wehrmacht assault on France by way of the (allegedly) impassable Ardennes Forest.[5]

Japanese intelligence, for its part, managed to persuade its superiors that once the American Pacific fleet had been crippled, the Americans, being prudent businessmen, would sue for peace rather than fight an unprofitable war. The German secret service assured Hitler that as soon as the Nazi-Soviet nonaggression pact of 1939 became public, Britain would renege on its pledge to defend Poland and abandon that country to its fate. Both misjudgments had catastrophic results for the countries concerned.

[4]Christopher Andrew, *Her Majesty's Secret Service,* Viking Penguin, 1986, p. 428.

[5]"As that ancient retiree from the Research Department of the British Foreign Office reportedly said, after serving from 1903 to 1950: 'Year after year the worriers and fretters would come to me with awful predictions of the outbreak of war. I denied it each time. I was wrong only twice.'" Cited by Richard Betts in *World Politics,* October 1978.

Intelligence failures, it thus transpires, are not a CIA monopoly; they are not even a monopoly of the intelligence community. Despite vast sums spent on armies of securities analysts who have the advantage of a great deal of reliable public information as well as access to managements, no brokerage firm seems to have found a way of gauging the direction of the financial markets. Indeed, the unmanaged Standard & Poor index fund has been beating three-quarters of the mutual funds run by experts. Even throwing darts at a list of securities has at times produced results as good as, if not better than, those of professional analysts. Nor have economists had notable success in forecasting the course of the nation's economy despite the abundance of indicators at their disposal.[6] What can one reasonably expect, therefore, of analysis which deals with concealed and often deliberately distorted data, and with decisions made in secret by inaccessible rulers, accountable only to themselves?[7]

It needs also to be borne in mind that the sins of the CIA with respect to the Communist bloc duplicated those of academic Sovietology. Proceeding from the same premises and employing the same methodology, the overwhelming majority of professors and think-tank specialists were just as guilty as the CIA of overestimating Soviet strength and stability and of interpreting Soviet actions in defensive terms.[8]

This much conceded, it is possible nevertheless to isolate cer-

[6]At the end of 1994, reporting on the steady growth of the U.S. economy during the preceding 12 months, the *New York Times* wondered: "Why were most forecasters, who as recently as this summer were predicting a much leaner expansion and higher unemployment, so far off the mark?" *New York Times*, December 13, 1994.

[7]The paradoxical aspect of British and American intelligence failures is that if treated as advice rather than predictions, they were often perfectly correct. Germany, indeed, did not have the capacity to wage a prolonged war. The Soviet Union should not have spent so much of its limited resources on the military, nor should it have installed missiles in Cuba or invaded Afghanistan. Similarly, North Korea would have spared itself a humiliating defeat by staying out of South Korea, and Saddam Hussein by giving up his claims to Kuwait.

[8]Good examples of this kind of thinking, common to the academic and intelligence communities, are two treatises by Raymond Garthoff, *Détente and Confrontation*, 1985, and *The Great Transition*, 1994, both published by the Brookings Institution in Washington, D.C.

tain recurrent blunders on the part of both intelligence producers and consumers, avoidance of which would go a long way toward improving the intelligence process. The two most common of these are "mirror-imaging" and political interference.

Mirror-Imaging

Mirror-imaging is the tendency to interpret the actions of others in one's own terms. The analyst looks at the situation which his subject confronts and asks himself, "What would I do if I were in his shoes?" The propensity to think in this way derives from a mixture of deficient imagination and, where other nations are concerned, ethnocentricity. The approach assumes that in every situation requiring choices, one choice is the most "rational" and therefore the most likely to be made.

The trouble with this premise is that "rationality" applies only to the means, not to the ends.[9] The person engaged in mirror-imaging, however, assumes that all human actions tend toward the same end—namely, his own—and that, by placing himself in the position of an adversary, he can anticipate the adversary's behavior. It is, without a doubt, the most common error of intelligence-estimating, much more prevalent in political affairs than in military ones, since in warfare the end is always the same—victory—and thus the means can be more reliably calculated in terms of their "rationality."[10]

The more imaginative the analyst, the better versed in the cultures with which he deals, the less likely he will be to attribute to others his own values and objectives. Unfortunately, in this respect the typical U.S. analyst is at a particular disadvantage, being the product of a political culture that disapproves of the notion that other people are "different," since that notion has commonly been used to justify racial and ethnic discrimination. Deeply embedded

[9]The adjective *rational* derives from the Latin *ratio* which meant "reckoning" or "calculation" and was used in accounting. It defines the ways of attaining a desired result with the least effort and expense.

[10]Mirror-imaging is more common in Anglo-Saxon countries with their prevailing utilitarian ethos. The Japanese and German intelligence services suffered more from a poor understanding of the American and British psyches.

in this country's ethos is the belief that fundamentally all peoples are the same—that is, like white, middle-class Americans—and if given a chance will behave like white, middle-class Americans. What is usually meant by this is that people act out of enlightened self-interest, unaffected by strong passions or convictions, and desire to improve their lot and to live in peace with the rest of humanity.

The following remarks by a scholar who has had close connections with the intelligence community may be overly censorious but they describe a genuine phenomenon:

> The typical [CIA] officer was brought up in a nice American suburb during the 1960's. . . . He has never done manual labor, and has never been personally close to anyone who has lived by it. He has never had to struggle for his next meal, and has never known anyone who has. He has no idea of life under arbitrary power. He has never served in the armed forces, much less has he known danger. He has traveled abroad as a tourist, but has never lived or transacted business abroad. His upbringing did not acquaint him with passion of any kind. It taught him to distrust the notion that anyone can believe in anything. He does not attend church or synagogue, nor does he argue about religion. He is a pleasant fellow, neither aggressively patriotic nor aggressively anything, and is uncomfortable with anyone who is.[11]

Such a person does not understand and therefore is unable to take seriously ideological or religious fanaticism; he interprets behavior that does not serve his conception of enlightened self-interest as either affectation or the result of material want and social injustice.

It is this mindset that has caused the CIA to misread many Communist actions. In 1950, the Agency was convinced that the Chinese would not intervene in Korea because such action would be "irrational": hence it predicted that they would confine them-

---

[11]Angelo M. Codevilla, *Informing Statecraft: Intelligence for a New Century,* Free Press, 1992, p. 103.

selves to the defense of their power plants along the Yalu River. In the early 1960's it could not see any conceivable interest on the part of the Soviet Union in placing nuclear missiles in Cuba since Moscow had to be aware that the United States would not tolerate such deployments: they were simply "too risky."[12] A National Intelligence Estimate (NIE) produced as late as September 1962 argued forcefully against this contingency.[13] The logic behind the gross misjudgment was spelled out in a rare moment of candor by Sherman Kent, a Yale history professor who served as the CIA's Director of National Estimates at the time of the Cuban missile crisis. Kent told his associates that

> his estimate of what was reasonable for the Soviet Union to do was a lot better than Khrushchev's, and therefore he was correct in analyzing the situation as it should have been seen by the Soviet Union.[14]

Mirror-imaging also caused the CIA to construe the massing of Red Army troops in Central Asia in 1979 as designed to protect Soviet assets in Afghanistan. It rejected the likelihood of a political coup accompanied by a full-scale military invasion on the ground that Moscow would not want to jeopardize the SALT II agreement then before the U.S. Senate, let alone risk repeating America's debacle in Vietnam. CIA analysts apparently never contemplated the possibility that Russia might invade Afghanistan precisely to demonstrate that it could win the kind of war that America had lost.

Mirror-imaging also lay behind the stubborn insistence of the U.S. intelligence community in the 1970's that the Soviet Union would not seek nuclear superiority. Persuaded by U.S. scientists, who had largely formulated the American strategy of Mutual

---

[12]Harold P. Ford, *Estimative Intelligence*, revised edition, University Press of America, 1993, p. 103.

[13]Donald P. Steury, in *Sherman Kent and the Board of National Estimates*, Consortium for the Study of Intelligence, 1994, p. ix.

[14]Ray Cline, one-time Deputy Director for Intelligence of the CIA, in Roy Godson, editor, *Intelligence Requirements for the 1980's: Analysis and Estimates*, Transaction, 1980, p. 77.

Assured Destruction (MAD), that nuclear war was unfeasible and that nuclear weapons had only one use—namely, to deter others—the CIA rationalized the observable Soviet buildup beyond parity in a variety of ways: that historic experience had made Russians a paranoid people; that Russia was confronting a Chinese threat; that it sought to make up with superior numbers for inferior quality. So wedded were CIA analysts to the doctrine of Mutual Assured Destruction that they would not even consider an alternative view. Only after being confronted in 1976 with a different interpretation by a group of outsiders, the so-called Team B, whose members were better versed in Soviet political and military doctrine, did the CIA acknowledge the possibility that the Soviet high command was thinking in terms of a first-strike capability.[15]

Political Interference

Ideally, intelligence analysis should be strictly separated from politics: which is to say that it should arrive at assessments without paying attention to the uses to which they may be put and without taking sides in policy disputes. In practice, this ideal is rarely attained. For while the purpose of intelligence is to provide statesmen with objective information upon which to base their decisions, decision-makers are not detached observers but men of action with their own agendas. If reality clashes with their wishes, the wishes usually win out. They welcome intelligence that supports what they are inclined to do and they ignore all else, or, worse still, they exert pressure on the intelligence community to come up with more helpful estimates.

The most glaring example of the political misuse of intelligence was Stalin's refusal in 1941 to heed warnings of Hitler's

[15]That this indeed was the Soviet intention has now been confirmed from Soviet sources: Ford, *Estimative Intelligence*, p. 120. Harold Ford worked for many years in the CIA and in 1977 served as consultant to the Senate Select Committee on Intelligence, which severely criticized Team B for all manner of alleged sins. Both the Team A and Team B NIEs for 1976 have now been declassified and can be obtained from the National Archives. On the Team B experiment, see my article "Team B: The Reality Behind the Myth," in the October 1986 issue of *Commentary*.

impending invasion delivered to him both by his own and by Allied secret services. Stalin had entered into his pact with Hitler with open eyes. Like his patron and teacher, Lenin, he felt that German revanchism represented the best opportunity to get the capitalist powers fighting themselves to exhaustion, which would leave them prostrate and at the mercy of Moscow. To this end, he assured Hitler a safe Eastern front. Expecting a replay of World War I, he was stunned by the rapid collapse of France in 1940, and responded by appeasing Hitler, supplying him with food, rubber, tin, manganese, and everything else Germany required to pursue the war against England. The possibility of Hitler's turning around and attacking so faithful an ally struck him as preposterous, and he dismissed reports to this effect as a British provocation. This, of course, represented a case of blatant mirror-imaging but also, and above all, of political interest overriding objective assessment. It nearly lost Russia the war, and caused millions of additional casualties.

In the United States, flagrant instances of ignoring or tampering with intelligence data occurred under Presidents Kennedy, Johnson, and Nixon. Shaken by Khrushchev's bullying at the Vienna summit conference of 1961, Kennedy chose to demonstrate his toughness by invading Cuba and intervening in Vietnam. In both instances he brushed aside warnings of the CIA. Johnson, too, ignored CIA admonitions about the risks of a massive involvement in Vietnam because he had made up his mind to pursue the war there until victory.

The worst instances of politicization of the CIA occurred under President Nixon, who treated the Agency as a tool of White House policies. Irritated by its independent judgment, Nixon shifted much of the intelligence-estimating authority from the Agency to the office of his National Security Adviser, Henry Kissinger. In this manner, assessments could be reached which justified White House policies. In 1973 Kissinger, now Secretary of State, abolished the prestigious Office of National Estimates, replacing it with an amorphous body of individual National Intelligence Officers, who, acting as individuals rather than as a group, were easier to manipulate. To attain an arms-limitation agreement with Moscow, Nixon and Kissinger disregarded the Agency's skepticism about U.S. ability to verify treaty compliance. According to one Agency veteran, the Nixon White House "brought strong pressure to bear on DCI Richard Helms to change the judgments of the National Intelligence Estimates."[16]

Nixon further politicized the CIA by firing Helms for his independence and refusal to involve the Agency in the Watergate cover-up.[17] Until then, the head of the intelligence agency, like that of the FBI, had been regarded as a civil servant rather than a political appointee. Historians of the CIA agree that these pressures greatly lowered both the quality of its intelligence estimates and its morale.

The practice of pressuring the Agency to come up with politically acceptable estimates continued under President Carter, whose DCI, Admiral Stansfield Turner, is said to have interfered with the estimating process and to have provided his own private estimates to suit the President.[18]

A recent instance of politicizing the intelligence process occurred in connection with the Gulf war. Having decided in late 1989 that he could turn Saddam Hussein around and moderate him, President Bush did not request a CIA assessment of the prospects and risks of such a policy before going ahead with its implementation. According to the CIA's Deputy Director of Intelligence, the NIE on Iraq was produced after the decision to appease Saddam Hussein had been taken and duly ratified it.[19] In order to support that policy, the NIE wrongly concluded that Iraq was too exhausted by its war with Iran to cause trouble before 1992.[20] This judgment was reached despite the fact that satellite imagery clearly indicated a massive buildup of Iraqi forces.

Finally, it is said that an NIE issued in 1990 or 1991 which predicted very accurately the violent breakup of Yugoslavia was

[16]Ford, *Estimative Intelligence*, p. 88.

[17]Ranelagh, *The Agency*, pp. 545–46.

[18]Mark M. Lowenthal, *U.S. Intelligence: Evolution and Anatomy*, 2nd edition, Greenwood, 1992, p. 53.

[19]Douglas J. MacEachin, *The Tradecraft of Analysis: Challenge and Change in the CIA*, Consortium for the Study of Intelligence, 1994, p. 26.

[20]Joseph Nye, *Estimating the Future?*, Consortium for the Study of Intelligence, 1994, p 3.

ignored by policy-makers who did not even want to contemplate such a possibility.[21]

Thus, apart from the difficulties inherent in the process of assessing intelligence data and making forecasts on their basis, the CIA, like its counterparts in other countries, suffers from the added liability of having its estimates rejected or ignored when they do not fit the interests of politicians, their ultimate consumers.

What Can Be Done?

There is little doubt that, before long, decisions will be taken that will significantly transform the Central Intelligence Agency. A presidential committee, headed by ex-Secretary of Defense Les Aspin, has been mandated to come up with recommendations on the subject by March 1, 1996.

Many projects of intelligence reform have been floated in the past, but for the most part they have involved organizational restructuring, which is every bureaucratic establishment's favored way of responding to outside criticism. Current reform proposals, including those emanating from the recently retired DCI, Robert Gates, also focus on splitting up and distributing the constituent parts of the CIA without touching on the profounder causes of its shortcomings. Whatever the merits of organizational changes, they are best left to insiders. Without denying their utility, it may be doubted that the performance of the CIA (or its replacement) will greatly improve unless attention is given to the intellectual and political environment in which it operates.

The following suggestions seek to address the CIA's more fundamental problems:

• One thing should not be changed: a *central* intelligence agency is indispensable. Experience has shown time and again, here and abroad, that the dispersal of intelligence responsibilities among government agencies without a common clearing-house prevents decision-makers from obtaining a reliable overview of a potential enemy's capabilities and intentions.

[21]Charles Cogan, in *Intelligence and National Security*, October 1994, p. 634; Nye, *Predicting*, p. 15.

Senator Daniel P. Moynihan has proposed doing away with the CIA altogether and transferring its functions to the Department of State. This recommendation ignores not only the fact that the State Department is a minor player in the collection and analysis of intelligence, but that it has traditionally spurned an intelligence role, preferring to rely on data obtained through diplomatic channels and being unwilling to have its diplomats treated as spies.

Only an organization separate from the other branches of government, with their vested interests in procuring arms, concluding international treaties, or promoting trade, can act as an "honest broker" and provide the President with disinterested assessments. Its function, in this respect, parallels that of the National Security Council, which came into existence concurrently with the CIA.

• With an estimated staff of 20,000, the CIA is much too large and ought to be *severely reduced in size*. History suggests that intelligence services function best when they are small and are allowed to operate with a minimum of formality. Bureaucratization stifles originality and dilutes dissent, reducing opinions to averages that appear reasonable and yet—since reality is often not reasonable—may be widely off the mark: but bureaucratization inevitably accompanies expansion. The failure of Israeli intelligence in 1973 to interpret correctly the massing of Arab forces has been attributed to its bureaucratization following the Six-Day War of 1967. Conversely, the greatest triumphs of intelligence in this century—the breaking of the German codes by the British and of the Japanese codes by the Americans in World War II—were accomplished by small bands of eccentrics. When he organized the Office of Intelligence Estimates in 1950, Harvard's William Langer said he wanted 20 analysts, and certainly no more than 100. And, indeed, in the first 20 years, the staff of Intelligence Estimates never exceeded 100. Today, the Directorate of Intelligence, the hub of the analytic world, employs 2,500.[22]

• One way to reduce the CIA staff, apart from shifting some of its functions to other government departments, is generously to *reward* good work and ruthlessly *punish* poor performance. Contrary to the Agency's practice, there should be no tolerance of ana-

[22]Discussant in MacEachin, *Tradecraft of Analysis*, p. 33.

lysts who consistently produce flawed assessments or assessments that hedge to the point of being useless. Altogether, the self-protective, clubbish atmosphere that prevails in the Agency needs to be done away with.

Much of the current hostility to the CIA derives from its scandalous indulgence of an incompetent officer, Aldrich Ames, who for nearly 9 years used his position in the most sensitive branch, counterintelligence, to sell the KGB secret documents and betray Russians working for the United States. The U.S. Senate Select Committee on Intelligence has characterized this incident as the "most egregious" case of treason in American history, blaming it on the Agency's habit of being "excessively tolerant of serious personal and professional misconduct among its employees."[23] The charge is underscored by the fact that none of Ames's superiors has been dismissed.

• Analysts should be required to have *profound knowledge and understanding* of the societies with which they deal so as to avoid mirror-imaging. They must be able to identify with the cultures which are their responsibility and, in order to do so, learn to overcome the American aversion to the idea that nations differ in some fundamental ways.

• In the 1930's, Sir Robert Vansittart, acting as a one-man intelligence service, almost alone provided the British government with accurate assessments of Nazi capabilities and intentions, including the likelihood of Germany's rapprochement with the Soviet Union. He succeeded because he knew Germany better than the professionals of the secret service. One month before Pearl Harbor, the American ambassador to Japan, Joseph G. Grew, who had spent nearly 10 years in Tokyo, responded to judgments that the Japanese could not contemplate an attack on the United States by warning against

any possible misconception of the capacity of Japan to rush headlong into a suicidal conflict with the United States. National sanity

[23]U.S. Senate Select Committee on Intelligence, *An Assessment of the Aldrich H. Ames Espionage Case and Its Implications for U.S. Intelligence,* November 1, 1994, p. 85.

would dictate against such an event, but Japanese sanity cannot be measured by our own standards of logic.[24]

So, too, anyone familiar with Communist history and psychology would have known that Moscow could not accept the doctrine of Mutual Assured Destruction, because it had the effect of stabilizing the global power balance in America's favor by eliminating competition in military forces, where the Soviet Union was strong, and shifting it to the political and economic arenas, where it was weak.

Such understanding can be taught, but only up to a point. Beyond that point it calls for wisdom that is an inborn quality: discernment and judgment cannot be institutionalized, but they can be rewarded.

• There is no substitute for *human intelligence* (HUMINT in CIA jargon). Since Admiral Turner's unfortunate tenure as DCI in the Carter administration, reliance on human sources has been severely curtailed in favor of technical means, notably satellite imagery. The preference is, in some measure, understandable: in dealing with informants one can never be certain whether they are not double agents feeding disinformation, or well-intentioned but unreliable sources providing biased information out of grudge feelings against their native country. Cameras, by contrast, neither lie nor distort.

The trouble, however, is that technical means, while generally dependable in the matter of capabilities, cannot penetrate minds and hence are blind and deaf to intentions. Overreliance on technology can cause intelligence to miss what is most important. This, indeed, is what happened in the case of the Soviet Union and Eastern Europe: "Antennas sensitive to millionths of amps, and orbiting cameras that could detect mice on the earth's surface, did not see hundreds of millions of people ready to overthrow the Communist world."[25] Nothing obtained by technical means has provided U.S. and British intelligence with the kind of information supplied by Oleg Penkovsky, Ryszard Kuklinski, or Oleg Gordievsky.

---

[24]Cited in Charles D. Ameringer, *U.S. Foreign Intelligence,* Free Press, 1990, p. 132.

[25]Codevilla, *Informing Statecraft,* p. 125.

In the future, when the United States will confront not one hostile power with a massive nuclear arsenal, but many potential enemies with nuclear weapons and fanatical terrorists at their disposal, human intelligence will be more essential than ever.

• The intelligence community would do well to make greater use of *open sources*. Secret services are habitually reluctant to do so because information obtained by clandestine means enables them to shrug off criticism on the ground that the critics are not privy to classified information. But it is rare for classified data to outweigh what is in the public domain. How much better would British intelligence have understood Hitler's ambitions had it read (and taken seriously) *Mein Kampf*, and how much would U.S. analysts have profited had they studied (and taken seriously) Soviet publications on nuclear strategy or the writings of Soviet émigrés on the Soviet economy.

Quality journalism is not only an essential adjunct to material obtained by intelligence but often a superior product because the information it contains has been collected and sifted by experienced observers on the scene. It has been my experience, while serving on the National Security Council, that although the Intelligence Daily which landed on my desk every morning occasionally provided unique insights, especially on military matters, it added little to what I learned from the press. Like many others in a similar situation, if compelled to choose between relying exclusively on one or the other—intelligence reports or the open press—I would unhesitatingly opt for the latter. The *Neue Zürcher Zeitung* and *Frankfurter Allgemeine Zeitung*, arguably the world's leading dailies, have over the years reported more reliably on political, economic, and cultural developments in the Communist bloc than the CIA. That this is not merely a casual impression has been confirmed by comparisons made by the National Security Council's staff during the Nixon administration.[26]

• To prevent more counterintelligence debacles, the *FBI* should be induced to cooperate better with the CIA. From the

[26]Andrew Marshall, in Roy Godson, editor, *Intelligence Requirements for the 1990's: Collection, Analysis, Counterintelligence, and Covert Action,* Lexington Books, 1989, p. 120.

outset, the FBI has treated the CIA as an unwelcome rival and frequently refused to share information with it. This rivalry is believed to have been responsible for Ames's ability to escape detection for so long. The importance of counterintelligence ought to be upgraded as well: it has been traditionally treated with disdain by the community.

• To the extent that is humanly possible, the White House should resist the temptation to use the CIA as an *instrument of policy*. In the words of a veteran intelligence professional who had occasion to witness White House pressures to bend assessments, "the NIE's ought to be responsive to the evidence, not the policy-maker."[27] This objective might be helped by the creation of a mechanism that would facilitate regular communications between intelligence personnel and policy-makers before crises occur.

• Limits ought to be set to the *legislative branches' powers of oversight* of intelligence agencies. Congress acquired these powers in the 1970's, and though in some measure inevitable—in a democracy based on the separation of powers, the legislative branch is not likely to concede exclusive control over foreign intelligence to the executive—they have exceeded reasonable limits.

The CIA is the only body of its kind in the world that is required to account regularly to the legislature—no fewer than eight congressional committees!—and even to obtain from one of them (the Senate Select Committee on Intelligence) prior approval of clandestine operations. The British secret service, by contrast, is accountable to a single individual, the Minister of Defense.

Given large congressional staffs, even with the greatest precautions the American practice ensures the leakage of classified information, paralyzing covert action. Means should be found to have the CIA report to one congressional committee or, better yet, to one or two of its representatives, and for these overseers to confine themselves to a general audit, without requiring too much detail, as was the case in the first quarter-century of the Agency's existence. With human lives at risk, covert operations surely should be concealed not only from hostile powers but from congressional staffs.

[27]Ray S. Cline, *The CIA Under Reagan, Bush, and Casey*, Acropolis Books, 1981, p. 162.

• Experience indicates that the *Director of Central Intelligence* and other senior intelligence officials can have the greatest impact on policy if they are personally and socially close to the President and other decision-makers. The importance of such a relationship derives from the fact that it enables the intelligence establishment to get a better hearing and better withstand political pressures. This is what happened in the case of DCI Allen Dulles's relationship with Eisenhower and his own brother, the Secretary of State, John Foster Dulles, as well as in the case of William Casey's relationship with Ronald Reagan. An alternative is to treat the DCI not as a political appointee due to be replaced by each incoming adminis-tration—as has been done since Nixon fired Helms—but as a civil-service professional, as is the case with the head of the FBI.

Since its unwelcome but highly beneficial brush with Team B, the Agency has regularly resorted to *outside experts* to evaluate its product. This practice should be maintained and extended.

• The CIA has recently been pressured into accepting the idea of devoting the bulk of its attention to such global issues as pollution, health, natural resources, and endangered species. In 1991, President Bush signed a directive to this effect and the Agency quickly fell into line, creating a National Intelligence Officer for Global and Multilateral Issues. According to Robert Gates, the CIA was planning in 1992 to devote 40 percent of its resources to international economics and only 34 percent to Rus-sia and the other successor states to the Soviet Union.[28] One can only view such a shift of emphasis as a desperate attempt to find a make-believe role for the CIA in the post-Soviet world. *But intelli-gence has only one function: to uncover foreign threats to national security.* International terrorism and nuclear traffic clearly come within its purview. Global economic or environmental problems just as clearly do not: along with other ills afflicting humanity and the earth, they are best left to international organizations.

Although it is at present a fairly peaceful country, *Russia is likely to remain the principal potential threat to the United States* and should, therefore, remain the principal focus of our intelligence. Member states of the so-called Commonwealth of Independent

[28]Lowenthal, *U.S. Intelligence*, pp. 96 and 163.

States, a fictitious political entity if there ever was one, have been unable so far to devise political stability for themselves. Russia in particular lacks a political consensus: its democratic institutions function wretchedly, in an atmosphere of unreality. The mood of its people swings between extremes, one day sinking into abject self-deprecation, ready to welcome a foreign takeover, and the next insisting on being recognized as a global power of the first rank. The Yeltsin government, pressed by reactionary nationalists, is voicing ever-more-menacing threats to its neighbors. The KGB, though renamed and reorganized, remains very much in place. The armed forces, for all their difficulties, are also intact and commanded by generals who have not reconciled themselves to the loss of empire. The United States has mindlessly helped give them what they wanted—that is, a nuclear monopoly—by bullying Belorussia, Ukraine, and Kazakhstan into surrendering their nuclear arsenals. In this manner, the United States has provided Moscow with the means some time in the future to force the separated republics back into the fold. Russia feels isolated, shunned by the world's major military and economic blocs, and tempted to find security in a reconstructed bloc of its own.

All these facts suggest that Russia will for the foreseeable future be a major security problem for the rest of the world. In consideration of these realities, we have retained NATO and refused Russia membership in it. It behooves us also to keep in place a strong intelligence apparatus responsible for giving that country its unremitting attention.

In a world of contending powers, an integrated intelligence service is indispensable. A CIA reduced in size and properly staffed, willing to rely more than heretofore on open sources and human informants, and allowed to operate free of political interference, should be in a position to render decision-makers invaluable advice. But intelligence services are no substitute for the statesman's personal judgment: they have not in the past and are unlikely in the future to provide him with the kind of certainty that he desires. In the end, the insight on which prudent decisions are based is the amalgam of diverse sources of information and experience, distilled by a process cloaked in mystery.

What to Do About

Affirmative Action

ARCH PUDDINGTON

Arch Puddington is a senior scholar at Freedom House. He writes frequently on American race relations.

The thinking behind the policy of racial preference which has been followed in America over the past quarter-century under the name of "affirmative action"[1] is best summed up by former Supreme Court Justice Harry Blackmun's famous dictum that "In order to get beyond racism, we must first take race into account."

The Orwellian quality of Blackmun's admonition is obvious. Seldom has a democratic government's policy so completely contradicted the core values of its citizenry as racial preference does in violating the universally held American ideals of fairness and indi-

---

[1] Affirmative action has, of course, been extended to women and certain other groups, but I will confine the discussion here to race. Affirmative action was devised primarily to promote the economic status of blacks, and the racial implications of the debate over this policy are far more significant than questions arising from preferences for women or other ethnic minorities. I should add that if preference for black Americans is unjustified, there is even less to be said for it when applied to women or to such immigrant groups as Hispanics and Asians.

vidual rights, including the right to be free from discrimination. Not surprisingly, then, where Americans regarded the original civil-rights legislation as representing a long-overdue fulfillment of the country's democratic promise, they overwhelmingly see racial preference as an undemocratic and alien concept, a policy implemented by stealth and subterfuge and defended by duplicity and legalistic tricks.

Americans do not believe that past discrimination against blacks in the workplace justifies present discrimination against whites. Nor do they accept the thesis that tests and standards are tainted, *en masse*, by cultural bias against minorities. Having been taught in high-school civics classes that gerrymandering to ensure party domination represents a defect in democracy, Americans are bewildered by the argument that gerrymandering is necessary to ensure the political representation of blacks and Hispanics. They are unimpressed by the contention that a university's excellence is enhanced by the mere fact of racial and ethnic diversity in its student body, especially when entrance requirements must be lowered substantially to achieve that goal.

Americans, in short, oppose racial preference in all its embodiments, and have signified their opposition in opinion poll after opinion poll, usually by margins of three to one or more, with women as strongly opposed as men, and with an impressive proportion of blacks indicating opposition as well. The contention, repeatedly advanced by advocates of preferential policies, that a national consensus exists in support of such policies has been true only at the level of political elites. Americans do support what might be called soft affirmative action, entailing special recruitment, training, and outreach efforts, and are willing to accept some short-term compensatory measures to rectify obvious cases of proven discrimination. But attitudes have, if anything, hardened against the kind of aggressive, numbers-driven preference schemes increasingly encountered in university admissions and civil-service hiring.

Nonetheless, up until 1995, racial preference in its various manifestations has been impressively resistant to calls for reform, much less elimination. In fact, race consciousness has begun to insinuate itself into areas which common sense alone would suggest should be immune to intrusive government social engineering. To cite but one example of this disturbing trend: Congress has mandated that guidelines be established guaranteeing the involvement of minorities (and women) in clinical research—a form of scientific experimentation by quota.

There is, furthermore, reason to question whether the advocates of race-conscious social policy continue to take seriously the objective of getting "beyond race," a condition which presumably would warrant the elimination of all preferential programs. The late Thurgood Marshall, an outspoken champion of preference while on the Supreme Court, is reported to have blurted out during an in-chambers discussion that blacks would need affirmative action for a hundred years. A similar opinion has been expressed by Benjamin Hooks, the former director of the National Association for the Advancement of Colored People (NAACP). Hooks contends that affirmative action in some form should be accepted as one of those permanent, irritating features of American life—he cited as examples speeding laws and the April 15 income-tax deadline—which citizens tolerate as essential to the efficient and just functioning of society.

Neither Marshall nor Hooks is regarded as an extremist on race matters; their advocacy of a permanent regime of affirmative action falls within the mainstream of present-day liberal thought. The promotion of "diversity"—the latest euphemism for preferential representation—is as fundamental to liberal governance as was the protection of labor unions in an earlier era. And until very recently, liberal proponents of preference clearly believed that history was on their side.

Thus, where enforcement agencies were formerly cautious in pressing affirmative action on the medical profession, the Clinton administration was formulating plans for a quota system throughout the health-care workforce. The goal, according to one memo of Hillary Clinton's task force, was nothing less than to ensure that this health-care workforce achieve "sufficient racial, ethnic, gender, geographic, and cultural diversity to be representative of the people it serves." The task force also had plans to guide minority doctors into specialties while tracking other doctors into general practice. To realize this medical-care diversity blueprint, the task force proposed the creation of a bureaucracy with coercive powers to regulate the "geographic" and "cultural" distribution of physicians and other medical practitioners.

How did America drift from the ideal of a color-blind society to the current environment of quotas, goals, timetables, race norming, set-asides, diversity training, and the like? Those troubled by this question often refer wistfully to Martin Luther King, Jr.'s declaration that he hoped to see the day when his children would be judged by the content of their character and not by the color of their skin. Yet it must be recognized that even when King uttered those inspirational words at the 1963 March on Washington, they no longer reflected the thinking of crucial segments of the civil-rights movement. Already, increasingly influential black activists and their white supporters were advancing demands for hiring plans based on racial quotas. In pressing for such plans (then called compensatory treatment), the civil-rights movement was being joined by officials from the Kennedy administration, as well as by white intellectuals who, going further, announced that black economic equality could never be attained without a wholesale adjustment of standards and the merit principle.

These ruminations were not lost on the Dixiecrat opponents of desegregation, and the charge was soon made that Title VII of the pending civil-rights bill—the section dealing with discrimination in the workplace—would lead to the widespread practice of reverse discrimination. This in turn provoked a series of statements and speeches by stalwart liberals like Senators Hubert Humphrey, Joseph Clark, and Clifford Case, adamantly and unequivocally denying that the bill could be interpreted to permit racial preference.

In order to dispel lingering doubts, Humphrey and other supporters inserted an amendment declaring flatly that the law's purpose was to rectify cases of intentional discrimination and was not intended to impose sanctions simply because a workplace contained few blacks or because few blacks passed an employment test. Armed with this and similar clauses prohibiting reverse discrimination, Humphrey promised to "start eating the pages [of the civil-rights bill] one after another" if anyone could discover language in it "which provides that an employer will have to hire on the basis of percentage or quota."

Under normal circumstances, the insertion of unambiguous antipreference language, combined with the condemnations of reverse discrimination by the bill's sponsors, would have been sufficient to prevent the subsequent distortion of the law's intent. But these protections turned out to be useless against the determination of the country's elites (in the political system, in the media, in the universities, and in the courts) to override them. Having concluded (especially after the urban riots of the late 1960's) that social peace demanded racial preference, political leaders from both parties, along with a growing number of intellectuals and activists, both white and black, began looking upon the antipreference clauses in Title VII as obstacles to be circumvented rather than guides to be followed. The antipreference language which had been added to ensure passage of the Civil Rights Act of 1964 was now not only ignored but treated as though it did not even exist.

Hence there was no serious effort by either Congress or the courts or anyone else to rein in the civil-rights bureaucracy, which dismissed the antipreference provisions with contempt from the very outset. A "big zero, a nothing, a nullity," is how these provisions were characterized by an official of the Equal Employment Opportunity Commission (EEOC) at the time. Federal enforcement officials in general, most of whom were white, were more aggressive in pursuing preferences, and less inclined to reflect on the broader implications of affirmative action, than were many mainstream black leaders of that day, some of whom—Roy Wilkins, Bayard Rustin, and Clarence Mitchell, for example— opposed reverse discrimination on moral and political grounds.

The part played by the EEOC in putting together the structure of racial preference cannot be overstated. In blithe and conscious disregard of the antipreference sections of Title VII, EEOC officials broadened the definition of discrimination to encompass anything which contributed to unequal outcomes. In its most far-reaching move, the EEOC launched an all-out assault on employment testing. The agency's mindset was reflected in comments about "irrelevant and unreasonable standards," "the cult of credentialism," and "artificial barriers."

Yet despite the ingenuity of its lawyers in devising intricate arguments to circumvent the strictures against reverse discrimination—and despite the willingness of activist judges to accept these arguments—the EEOC could never have achieved its aims had it not been for a transformation of elite attitudes toward the problem of race in America.

In 1964, the year the Civil Rights Act was passed, an optimistic and morally confident America believed that the challenge posed by the "Negro revolution" could be met through a combination of antidiscrimination laws, economic growth, and the voluntary goodwill of corporations, universities, and other institutions. But by the decade's end, a crucial segment of elite opinion had concluded that America was deeply flawed, even sick, and that racism, conscious or otherwise, permeated every institution and government policy. Where individual prejudice had previously been identified as the chief obstacle to black progress, now a new target, "institutional racism," was seen as the principal villain. And where it was once thought that democratic guarantees against discrimination, plus the inherent fairness of the American people, were sufficient to overcome injustice, the idea now took hold that since racism was built into the social order, coercive measures were required to root it out.

In this view, moreover, the gradualist Great Society approach launched by Lyndon Johnson, which stressed education, training, and the strengthening of black institutions, could not alleviate the misery of the inner-city poor, at least not as effectively as forcing employers to hire them. Even Johnson himself began calling for affirmative action and issued an executive order directing that federal contractors adopt hiring policies which did not discriminate on the basis of race (or gender); in a process that would soon become all too familiar, court decisions and the guidelines of regulators subsequently interpreted the directive as mandating racial balance in the workforce, thus paving the way for demands that companies doing business with the government institute what often amounted to quotas in order to qualify for contracts.

Little noticed at the time—or, for that matter, later—was that black America was in the midst of a period of unprecedented economic progress, during which black poverty declined, the racial income gap substantially narrowed, black college enrollment mushroomed, and black advancement into the professions took a substantial leap forward. All this, it should be stressed, occurred *prior* to government-mandated racial preference.

Once affirmative action got going, there was no holding it back. The civil-rights movement and those responsible for implementing civil-rights policy simply refused to accept an approach under which preference would be limited to cases of overt discrimination, or applied to a narrow group of crucial institutions, such as urban police departments, where racial integration served a pressing public need. Instead, every precedent was exploited to further the permanent entrenchment of race consciousness.

For example, the Philadelphia Plan, the first preferential policy to enjoy presidential backing (the President being Richard Nixon), was a relatively limited effort calling for racial quotas in the Philadelphia building trades, an industry with a notorious record of racial exclusion. Yet this limited program was seized upon by the EEOC and other agencies as a basis for demanding hiring-by-the-numbers schemes throughout the economy, whether or not prior discrimination could be proved.

Similarly, once a race-conscious doctrine was applied to one institution, it inevitably expanded its reach into other arenas. The Supreme Court's decision in *Griggs* v. *Duke Power, Inc.*—that employment tests could be found to constitute illegal discrimination if blacks failed at a higher rate than whites—was ostensibly confined to hiring and promotion. But *Griggs* was used to legitimize the burgeoning movement against testing and standards in the educational world as well. Tracking by intellectual ability, special classes for high achievers, selective high schools requiring admissions tests, standardized examinations for university admissions—all were accused of perpetuating historic patterns of bias.

The campaign against testing and merit in turn gave rise to a series of myths about the economy, the schools, the workplace,

about America itself. Thus, lowering job standards as a means of
hiring enough blacks to fill a quota was justified on the grounds
that merit had never figured prominently in the American workplace, that the dominant principles had always been nepotism,
back-scratching, and conformism. To explain the racial gap in
Scholastic Aptitude Test scores, the concept of cultural bias was
advanced, according to which disparities in results derived from
the tests' emphasis on events and ideas alien to urban black children. Another theory claimed that poor black children were not
accustomed to speaking standard English and were therefore
placed at a disadvantage in a normal classroom environment. It
was duly proposed that black children be taught much like immigrant children, with bilingual classes in which both standard
English and black English would be utilized. A related theory
stated that black children retained a distinct learning style which
differed in significant respects from the learning styles of other
children. As one educator expressed the theory, any test which
stressed "logical, analytical methods of problem solving" would *ipso
facto* be biased against blacks.

Until quite recently, the very idea of abolishing racial preference was unthinkable; the most realistic ambitions for the critics of
race-based social policy went no further than trying to limit—
limit, not stop—the apparently relentless spread of racial preferences throughout the economy, the schools and universities, and
the political system. Yet it now appears not that the momentum of
racial preference has been halted, but that, at a minimum, a part of
the imposing affirmative-action edifice will be dismantled. Furthermore, a process has already been set in motion which could
conceivably lead to the virtual elimination of race-based programs.

Racial preferences have become vulnerable mainly because of
the sudden collapse of the elite consensus which always sustained
affirmative action in the face of popular opposition. Where in the
past many Republicans could be counted on to support, or at least
tolerate, racial preferences, the new congressional majority seems
much more inclined to take a sharply critical look at existing
racial policies. Equally important is the erosion of support for

preference within the Democratic party. While some newly skeptical Democrats are clearly motivated by worries about reelection, others have welcomed the opportunity to express long-suppressed reservations about policies which they see as having corrupted, divided, and weakened their party.

The revolt against affirmative action has also been heavily influenced by the fact that, as preferential policies have extended throughout the economy, a critical mass of real or perceived victims of reverse discrimination has been reached—white males who have been denied jobs, rejected for promotion, or prevented from attending the college or professional school of their choice because slots were reserved for blacks (or other minorities or women).

There is, no doubt, an inclination on the part of white men to blame affirmative action when they are passed over for jobs or promotions, a tendency which is reinforced by the atmosphere of secrecy surrounding most preference programs. But enough is known about affirmative action in the public sector through information which has come out in the course of litigation to conclude that thousands of whites have indeed been passed over for civil-service jobs and university admissions because of outright quotas for racial minorities. It is also clear that a considerable number of private businesses have been denied government contracts because of minority set-asides.

Another major factor in the change of attitude toward affirmative action is the California Civil Rights Initiative (CCRI), which has already had an incalculable impact. The CCRI was organized by two white, male, and politically moderate professors in the California state-university system. The measure would amend the California constitution to prohibit the state government or any state agency (including the university system) from granting preference on the basis of race, ethnicity, or gender in employment, college admissions, or the awarding of contracts. It would, in other words, effectively ban affirmative-action programs mandated by the state.

Though limited to California, the CCRI is at heart a response to the logical destination of affirmative action everywhere in America: quota systems sustained by the support of elites from both political parties. To be sure, policy by racial classification has grown more pervasive in California than elsewhere in America. White males have been told not to bother applying for positions with the Los Angeles fire department due to the need to fill minority quotas. In San Francisco, Chinese students are denied admission to a selective public high school because of an ethnic cap; for similar reasons, whites, mainly Jews and East European immigrants, are often denied admission to magnet schools in Los Angeles. A *de facto* quota system effectively denies white males the opportunity to compete for faculty positions at certain state colleges. And, incredibly enough, the state legislature passed a bill calling for ethnic "guidelines" not only for admission to the state-university system but for graduation as well. The bill was vetoed by Governor Pete Wilson; had a Democrat been governor, it would almost certainly have become law.

The true impact of the CCRI can be gauged by the degree of fear it has generated among supporters of affirmative action. So long as the debate could be limited to the courts, the agencies of race regulation, and, when absolutely necessary, the legislative arena, affirmative action was secure. The mere threat of taking the issue directly to the voters, as the CCRI's sponsors propose to do through the referendum process, has elicited a downright panicky response—itself a clear indication that the advocates of racial preference understand how unpopular their case is, and how weak.

But a note of caution must be sounded to those who believe that current developments will lead inexorably to the reinstitution of color-blindness as the reigning principle in racial matters. The resilience of affirmative action in the face of widespread popular hostility suggests that even a modest change of course could prove a difficult and highly divisive affair.

There is, to begin with, the fact that affirmative action has been introduced largely by skirting the normal democratic process of debate and legislative action. Affirmative action is by now rooted in literally thousands of presidential directives, court decisions, enforcement-agency guidelines, and regulatory rules. These will not easily be overturned.

There is also the complicating factor of the federal judiciary's central role in overseeing racial policy. Given the emotionally charged character of the racial debate, the critics of racial preference will be tempted to postpone legislative action in the hope that the Supreme Court will resolve the issue once and for all. But while the Court today is less prone to judicial activism than during the Warren and Burger years, and while it may decide to limit the conditions under which a preferential program can be applied, it is unlikely to do away with affirmative action altogether.

The Republicans will face another temptation: to exploit white hostility to racial preference but avoid serious political action to eliminate it. A powerful political logic lies behind this temptation, since getting rid of affirmative action would also deprive the Republicans of a potent wedge issue. Yet one can hardly imagine a less desirable outcome than a prolonged and angry political confrontation over race. Moreover, if responsible politicians who share a principled opposition to preference decline to take the initiative, the door will be opened to racists and unscrupulous demagogues.

An additional obstacle to change is the fact that eliminating affirmative action does not offer much of a financial payoff. Affirmative action is not expensive; its only direct cost to the taxpayer is the expense of maintaining civil-rights agencies like the EEOC.

Claims have been made that affirmative action does represent a major cost to the American economy, but the facts are unclear since neither the media nor scholarly researchers nor the corporations themselves have shown an interest in undertaking an investigation of its economic impact. Indeed, though affirmative action is one of the most intensely discussed social issues of the day, it is probably the least researched. Press coverage is generally limited to the political debate; seldom are stories done about the actual functioning of affirmative-action programs. Nor is there much serious scholarly investigation of such questions as affirmative action's impact on employee morale, the performance of students admitted to college on an affirmative-action track, or the degree to which contract set-asides have contributed to the establishment of stable minority businesses.

Given the truly massive amount of research devoted to racial issues over the years, the lack of attention to preferential policies raises the suspicion that what has been operating here is a deliberate decision to avoid knowing the details of affirmative action's inner workings out of fear of the public reaction.

Opponents of racial preference must also contend with the widespread acceptance of the "diversity" principle within certain key institutions. Here the American university stands out for its uncritical embrace of the notion that, as one recent cliché has it, "diversity is part of excellence." When Francis Lawrence, the president of Rutgers University, came under fire for uttering the now-famous phrase which seemed to question the genetic capabilities of black students, his principal defense—indeed practically his only defense—was that he had increased minority enrollment at Rutgers and during a previous administrative stint at Tulane. True to form, no one bothered to ask how black students recruited under Lawrence's diversity initiatives had fared academically or psychologically, or how the campus racial atmosphere had been affected, or how much standards had been adjusted to achieve the quota. The body count, and the body count alone, is what mattered for Lawrence, and, it would seem, for administrators at many campuses.

The diversity principle is also firmly entrenched throughout government service. Most agencies include a diversity or affirmative-action department, headed by an official with deputy-level status, with intrusive authority to promote staff "balance" and minority participation in contract bidding. So, too, private corporations have accepted affirmative action as part of the price of doing business. Large corporations, in fact, can usually be counted on to oppose anti-quota legislation, preferring the simplicity of hiring by the numbers to the uncertainty of more flexible systems and the increased possibilities of antidiscrimination litigation brought by minorities or by whites claiming reverse bias.

But of course the most serious obstacle to change is black America's strong attachment to affirmative action. Race-conscious policies have had no demonstrable effect at all on the black poor, but they are widely perceived as having played a crucial role in creating the first mass black middle class in American history. The claim here is wildly exaggerated—to repeat, the trend was already well advanced before affirmative action got going. Nevertheless, to many blacks, affirmative action has become not a series of temporary benefits but a basic civil right, almost as fundamental as the right to eat at a restaurant or live in the neighborhood of one's choice, and certainly more important than welfare.

Accordingly, black leaders, who are always quick to condemn even the most modest changes as "turning back the clock" or as a threat to the gains of the civil-rights movement, have now escalated the counterattack in response to the more sweeping recent challenge to affirmative action. When Governor Pete Wilson made some favorable comments about the CCRI, Jesse Jackson compared him to George Wallace blocking the schoolhouse door in Jim Crow Alabama. And when congressional Republicans moved to rescind a set-aside program in the communications industry, Representative Charles Rangel, a Democrat from Harlem, declared that the move reflected a Nazi-like mindset.

It is true that many blacks are ambivalent about preferences, or even critical of them. At the same time, however, they are highly sensitive to perceptions of white assaults on civil rights, and they may well find polemics of the Jackson and Rangel variety persuasive.

Confronted with all these obstacles, some opponents of affirmative action are leaning toward a compromise strategy involving a program-by-program review. This would be a serious mistake; the most desirable and politically effective course would be federal legislation modeled on the CCRI. Such a measure would leave in place the old laws against discrimination but would eliminate all federal programs which extend preference on the basis of race (as well as ethnicity or gender).

The measure could conceivably take the form of a reaffirmation of the sections of the 1964 Civil Rights Act dealing with the workplace, with special emphasis on the clauses explicitly prohibiting reverse discrimination. But whatever the specific shape of the new legislation, absolute clarity would be required on the principal issue: there would be no room for fudging, vagueness, or loopholes on the question of bringing the era of race-conscious social policy to a close. The legislation would therefore also have to include an explicit disavowal of the disparate-impact doctrine, under which the disproportionate representation of the races (or sexes) is often regarded as evidence in itself of discrimination, and which has often led to the imposition of *de facto* quota systems.

The political struggle over this kind of sweeping legislation would be angry and unpleasant. But eliminating both the practice of racial preference and the controversy surrounding it would set the stage for an ultimate improvement in the racial environment throughout American society. On the other hand, an approach focusing on a program-by-program review of the multitude of preference initiatives in an ephemeral search for compromise only guarantees the permanence both of affirmative action itself and of the affirmative-action controversy.

A less sweeping but nevertheless useful approach would be a presidential decree revoking the executive order issued by President Johnson which opened the way to federally mandated quotas. Though (as we have seen) Johnson did not necessarily intend for this to happen, the fact is that his directive became a crucial pillar of the affirmative-action structure. With the stroke of a pen it could be rescinded.

So far as the universities are concerned, the elimination of affirmative action would mean an end to lowering standards in order to fill racial quotas. No doubt this would also mean a smaller number of blacks at the elite universities, but there are perfectly decent state colleges and private institutions for every promising student whose qualifications do not meet the standards of Yale or Stanford. The notion that a degree from one of these institutions consigns the graduate to a second-class career is based on sheer prejudice and myth; for evidence to the contrary, one need look no further than the new Republican congressional delegation, which includes a number of graduates from what would be considered second- or third-tier colleges.

It hardly needs to be added that directing a student to a university for which he is educationally and culturally unprepared benefits neither the student nor the university nor the goal of integration. The results are already clear to see in the sorry state of race relations on campus. Many colleges are dominated by an environment of racial balkanization, with blacks increasingly retreating into segregated dormitories and black student unions, rejecting contacts with white students out of fears of ostracism by other blacks, and then complaining of the loneliness and isolation of campus life. Dropout rates for those admitted on affirmative-action tracks are high, adding to black student frustration. These problems are invariably exacerbated by college administrators, who respond to racial discontent with speech codes, sensitivity training, multicultural seminars, curriculum changes, and other aggressively prosecuted diversity initiatives.

Some have proposed basing affirmative action in university admissions on social class—that is, extending preferences to promising students from impoverished backgrounds, broken homes, and similar circumstances. On a superficial level, this would seem a sensible idea. Blacks would profit because they suffer disproportionately from poverty. Universities would gain from the high motivation of the students selected for the program. And real diversity would be enhanced by the presence of students whose backgrounds differed radically from the middle- and upper-class majority, and whose opinions could not be so predictably categorized along the conformist race (and gender) lines which dominate campus discussion today.

One major caveat is that college administrators, who give every indication of total commitment to the present race-based arrangements, would discover ways to circumvent a program based on color-blind standards. Indeed, they have already done so. Under the terms of the *Bakke* case, which established the guidelines for affirmative action in university admissions, race could be counted as one of several factors, including social class; affirmative action based on race alone, the Supreme Court said, could not pass muster. As matters have evolved, affirmative action on many state campuses, most notably those in California, is based almost exclusively on race and ethnicity.

A similar class-based formula is difficult to envision outside the realm of university admissions. Yet there is no reason to assume that private businesses would respond to the elimination of gov-

ernment-enforced affirmative action by refusing to hire and promote qualified blacks. A return to race-neutral government policies would also enable black executives and professionals to shed
the affirmative-action stigma, since no one would suspect that
they were in their positions only as the result of pressure by a federal agency. The supporters of preferential policies may dismiss
affirmative action's psychological effects on the beneficiaries as
unimportant. But the evidence indicates that the image of a black
professional class having risen up the career ladder through a special racial track is a source of serious workplace demoralization for
members of the black middle class.

The arguments which have lately been advanced in favor of
retaining affirmative action are by and large the same arguments
made more than 20 years ago, when the intellectual debate over
preference began.

Probably the least compelling of these is the contention that
the advantages extended by university admissions offices to athletes, the children of alumni, and applicants from certain regions of
the country justify extending similar advantages on the basis of
race. The answer to this contention is simple: race is different from
other criteria. America acknowledged the unique nature of racial
discrimination when it enacted the landmark civil-rights laws of
the 1960's. Moreover, the suggestion cannot be sustained that out-
lawing preference based on race while permitting preference based
on nonracial standards would leave blacks even farther behind.
Blacks in fact benefit disproportionately from admissions preferences for athletes or those with talents in music and art. No one
objects, or thinks it unusual or wrong for some groups to be over-
represented and others to be underrepresented on the basis of such
criteria.

A similar, but even weaker, argument (already alluded to
above) holds that America has never functioned as a strict meritocracy, and that white males have maintained their economic
dominance through connections, pull, and family. Affirmative
action, this theory goes, simply levels the playing field and actually
strengthens meritocracy by expanding the pool of talent from

which an employer draws. The problem is that those who advance this argument seem to assume that only white males rely on personal relationships or kinship. Yet as we have learned from the experience of immigrants throughout American history, every racial and ethnic group values family and group ties. Korean-American shop owners enlist their families, Haitian-American taxi fleets hire their friends.

What about the claim that affirmative action has improved the racial climate by hastening the integration of the workplace and classroom? While the integration process has often been painful and disruptive, there is no question that more contact between the races at school and at work has made America a better society. But integration has not always succeeded, and the most signal failures have occurred under conditions of government coercion, whether through busing schemes or the imposition of workplace quotas. In case after case, the source of failed integration can be traced to white resentment over racial preference or black fears of being perceived as having attained their position through the preferential track.[2]

There is, finally, the argument that, since black children suffer disproportionately from poor nutrition, crack-addicted parents, wrenching poverty, and outright discrimination, affirmative action rightly compensates for the burden of being born black in America. Yet affirmative action has been almost entirely irrelevant to these children, who rarely attend college or seek a professional career. The new breed of Republican conservatives may sometimes betray a disturbing ignorance of the history of racial discrimination in America. But on one crucial issue they are most certainly right: the march toward equality begins at birth, with the structure, discipline, and love of a family. The wide array of government-sponsored compensatory programs, including affirmative action, has proved uniformly ineffective in meeting the awesome challenge of inner-city family deterioration.

[2] An important exception is the military, where affirmative action is applied to promotions but where standards have not been lowered to enlarge the pool of qualified black applicants.

★   ★   ★

To advocate a policy of strict race neutrality is not to ignore the persistence of race consciousness, racial fears, racial solidarity, racial envy, or racial prejudice. It is, rather, to declare that government should not be in the business of preferring certain groups over others. Because it got into this business, the United States has been moved dangerously close to a country with an officially sanctioned racial spoils system. Even Justice Blackmun was concerned about this kind of thing. In his *Bakke* opinion, Blackmun made it clear that preferential remedies should be regarded as temporary, and he speculated that race-conscious policies could be eliminated in 10 years—that is, by the end of the 1980's.

Affirmative action's supporters grow uncomfortable when reminded of Blackmun's stipulation, which clashes with their secret conviction that preferences will be needed forever. Despite considerable evidence to the contrary, they believe that racism (and sexism) pervade American life, and they can always find a study, a statistic, or an anecdote to justify their prejudice.

If racial preference is not eliminated now, when a powerful national momentum favors resolving the issue once and for all, the result may well be the permanent institutionalization of affirmative action, though probably at a somewhat less expansive level than is the case right now. Alternatively, a cosmetic solution, which eliminates a few minor policies while leaving the foundation of racial preference in place, could trigger a permanent and much more divisive racial debate, with a mushrooming of state referenda on preference and the growing influence of extremists of both races.

It is clear that a bipartisan majority believes that the era of racial preference should be brought to a close. It will take an unusual amount of political determination and courage to act decisively on this belief. But the consequences of a failure to act could haunt American political life for years to come.

Abortion

JAMES Q. WILSON

James Q. Wilson is professor of management and public policy at UCLA whose most recent book is *The Moral Sense* (Free Press). On the issue of crime (see the article beginning on p. 282), Mr. Wilson's books include *Thinking About Crime* and *Crime and Human Nature* (written with Richard J. Herrnstein). He is also the editor of *Crime and Public Policy*.

Abortion is a moral question. Most people, regardless of how they feel the question should be answered or who they think should do the answering, will agree with this. There may be some extreme pro-choice activists who maintain that the decision of whether to carry a fetus to term is purely a matter of taste, but I doubt there are many such persons or that, if confronted with the choice themselves, they would make it in the same spirit in which they decide where to spend their vacation.

Were abortion not a moral issue, then infanticide would not be one, either, because the difference between a 265-day-old fetus and a newborn infant is a matter of but a few hours. We recoil in horror at the thought of deliberately killing a newborn infant, though we may recognize a few circumstances in which that might become a tragic necessity. We must, therefore, recoil in equal horror at the thought of killing an infant that does not differ from the newborn in any respect other than that it receives oxygen and food via an umbilical cord instead of through its nose and mouth. I know of only one philosopher who defends both abortion and infanticide. I find his arguments not only unconvincing but monstrous; I suspect that almost everyone would react in a similar fashion.

The moral debate over abortion centers on the point in the development of the fertilized ovum when it has acquired those characteristics that entitle it to moral respect. This issue is sometimes framed to require one to define a *person* or to decide when *life* begins. I hope to show that it is so difficult to supply a persuasive answer to these questions as to raise the possibility that they are the wrong questions. Each implies that there is a moment at which life has not begun or a person does not exist and then, immediately following it, a moment at which life has begun or a person has come into being. In other aspects of our daily affairs, we do not accord moral respect on the basis of such precise off-on, no-yes distinctions. Rather, we grant greater and greater degrees of moral respect to people to the extent that they conform in their conduct and manner to widely shared standards of what it means to be human. A deranged homicidal maniac who is stalking the streets killing innocent victims is alive and a person, but we have few qualms about the police shooting him down on sight. An elderly man who has been a devoted husband and father but who now lies comatose in a vegetative state barely seems to be alive; an elderly woman who was once a loving wife and mother but who now acts bizarrely under the influence of advanced and irreversible Alzheimer's disease barely seems to be a person—yet we experience great moral anguish in deciding whether to withdraw his life support or confine her to institutional care.

The moral qualms we have about abortion arise, I think, chiefly from the instinctive appeal of the infant, a feeling of compassion and attachment that is as natural as any sentiment that ever enters the human breast. Whatever we mean by life or the value we attach to it, few if any of us are likely to deny that our judgment is at root a moral one or to say that it is irrelevant to the position we take on abortion.

*   *   *

That is not, in general, how the courts see the matter. Though passionate debates and angry confrontations over the morality of abortion are commonplace, the legal rules governing abortion scarcely refer to these moral issues. In *Roe* v. *Wade*, the decision that legalized abortion, the Supreme Court acknowledged that the state had an "important and legitimate interest in potential life," but did not define that interest as a moral one. On the contrary, it went to great lengths to disavow any interpretation of those words that might seem even vaguely moral.

The Court majority ruled that during the first trimester a woman had an unqualified right to terminate her pregnancy at will; during the second trimester the state could regulate abortions only to protect the mother's health; and during the third trimester, when the fetus was viable, the state, "in promoting its interest in the potentiality of human life," might *choose* to forbid abortions, unless the woman's health or life were at risk. Now, if the Court were concerned about protecting life on *moral* grounds, one might suppose that it would not only allow a ban on third-trimester abortions but would insist upon it. But no. In fact, by defining *health* to mean a woman's "well-being," the Court virtually assured that any state law that tried to ban even third-trimester abortions would be open to challenge.

The reason seems clear: if the Court's position were to be even arguably defensible on constitutional grounds, it had to maintain that the fetus was not a person within the meaning of the Fourteenth Amendment. That amendment instructs the states that they may not deprive "any person of life, liberty, or property." As Justice Harry Blackmun, who wrote the majority opinion in *Roe* v. *Wade*, readily acknowledged at the time, if a fetus were a person, then its right to life would be guaranteed. Hence, to uphold a right to abortion, the Court would have had to show that at some stage during its development a fetus was not a person. When it became a person, which surely had to occur some time before birth, an abortion would be an unconstitutional deprivation of life—in short, murder. Since the Court could not establish when a fetus changed from a nonperson to a person, it could not allow the fetus ever to be defined as a person, for then abortions would always be murder. Determined to create a right to abortion based on the assumption that the mother was a person with a "right to privacy" and the fetus was a nonperson with no rights at all, the Court when it came to defining what a state might do during the third trimester allowed the government to "regulate, and even proscribe, abortion," but it did not insist that it do either.

This rights-based view of abortion held sway for two decades and, until somewhat modified by the Court in *Casey* (1992), was reiterated and extended by a series of decisions which not only implicitly denied that abortion was a moral question but struck down almost any state attempt to confront a pregnant woman with either practical or moral arguments about the possible consequences of abortion. In 1983 the Court overturned an effort by the city of Akron to impose a mandatory 24-hour waiting period between an application for an abortion and its performance. In 1986 it overruled a Pennsylvania attempt to require that a woman asking for an abortion be informed about the availability of prenatal care, child-support programs, and adoption agencies. An interesting feature of the Akron ordinance was that it supplied the woman with materials on the physical features of the fetus so that she would know what she was confronting.

In all these cases, the unifying theme of the Court majority was that abortion was a right that a woman alone was entitled to exercise; the state not only could not make that decision for her, it could not even try to influence how she made it.

The result of this doctrinal position was, as Mary Ann Glendon of the Harvard Law School has shown, to make abortion policy in the United States more radical than that in any other industrial nation, with the possible exception of the People's Republic of China.

In virtually every European nation, the right to abortion is either sharply limited or, if generally permitted in the early months of pregnancy, surrounded with constraining regulations in the later months. And in most of these nations, a woman alone cannot decide the matter. In England and Switzerland, for example, two doctors must certify the existence of legal grounds for an

abortion. In Greece and Germany, a woman must seek a second
opinion from a doctor other than the one who is to perform the
abortion. When the abortion is to occur late in the pregnancy,
many nations oblige the woman to present her case to a committee or board for approval. In Israel, an abortion is permitted in the
first trimester, but only when approved by a doctor and then only
when the woman is under 17 or over 40 years of age, the child
was conceived out of wedlock, there is a risk of a genetic defect,
or it is necessary to protect the mother's health. Even Sweden
allows more regulation than does the United States; there, abortion on demand is available, but only until the 18th week of pregnancy, while here it is available for at least 24 weeks.

The difference between the American and European approaches
to the issue arises from how the decision was made and the philosophical framework in which it was cast. Here, the courts decided
the matter; abroad, the legislatures decided it. Here, the issue was
defined in terms of individual rights; there, it was often defined in
terms of moral responsibility. Here, the legal rules were at odds
with public opinion; there, they more closely approximated it.

Americans have made it clear in repeated opinion polls that
they oppose both abortion on demand and a prohibition on all
abortions. A majority will support abortions under carefully
defined circumstances, such as a pregnancy that endangers the
mother's life or is the result of rape, particularly (and possibly only)
during the first trimester. There has been little change in these
views since *Roe* was decided. They seem to reflect an underlying
belief that the fetus is entitled to some degree of moral respect,
especially after it has developed for a few weeks, a degree of
respect that does not preclude taking into account important
competing considerations, such as the health of the mother. In
short, Americans are philosophically at odds with the Justices who
have fashioned their abortion law.

That gap was reduced somewhat by the *Casey* decision in
1992. Then, a bare majority of the Justices reaffirmed *Roe* but
changed its meaning and application. Speaking through Justice
Sandra Day O'Connor, the Court reasserted that a woman has a
"constitutional liberty" to "some freedom to terminate her pregnancy." But the state is now allowed to place restrictions on this

right, even when the fetus is not yet viable, provided those restrictions do not impose an "undue burden" on its exercise. For the first time, the Court seemed to uphold such restrictions as a 24-hour waiting period, a requirement that teenagers obtain the consent of their parents (or, in special circumstances, a judge), and the mandatory provision of written materials about alternatives to abortion.[1] Though the practical effect of the acceptance of these restrictions is uncertain, it is clear that for the first time the official opinion of the Court acknowledges the possibility that the fetus is entitled to some degree of state protection.

But protection on what grounds? There are two possibilities— that the fetus is a person who, like the mother, has rights, or that the fetus is a form of human life that is intrinsically entitled to protection. In a recent book, Ronald Dworkin of New York University Law School and Oxford has made this distinction and assessed its implications.[2]

Dworkin argues that if we think a fetus is a person with constitutional rights, then American opinions about abortion are inconsistent. In particular, the exceptions for rape and incest make no sense. If it is wrong to kill a person, and the fetus is a person, then it is as wrong to kill a fetus that is the product of rape or incest as it would be to kill a newborn infant who was conceived in that manner. If a fetus is a person with rights, then it has those rights whether it is in its first trimester or third and whether it is healthy or deformed.

If, however—Dworkin goes on—our views about abortion are shaped, not by the logic of rights but by the value we attach to human life, then American opinions become more coherent. As a

[1] I say "seemed to hold" because these restrictions were accepted by Justices Sandra Day O'Connor, David Souter, and Anthony Kennedy, but apparently rejected by Justices Harry Blackmun and John Paul Stevens, whose partial concurrence with their three colleagues was necessary to produce the five-to-four verdict reaffirming *Roe*. What state restrictions will in practice pass constitutional muster remains to be seen.

[2] *Life's Dominion: An Argument About Abortion, Euthanasia, and Individual Freedom*, Knopf.

fetus grows it becomes more lifelike, and the more lifelike it is the greater claim it has to our moral respect. If it is horribly deformed (owing, say, to a chromosomal abnormality or a prenatal injury), then it is less human and exercises somewhat less claim on our moral respect. Dworkin argues, I think correctly, that when the great majority of people think about abortion, they think in terms of the value and meaning of life, of the nature of humanity, and not in terms of individual entities asserting rights against one another.

Since Dworkin is a celebrated philosopher who has been strongly identified with "rights talk"—his first book was called *Taking Rights Seriously*—this modification of his views itself deserves to be taken seriously. Most academic political and moral philosophy is about rights; by contrast, most conversations among ordinary people about political and moral issues are not about rights, but about decency, duty, and self-control. As I have argued in *The Moral Sense*, the disjunction between how philosophers define philosophy and how people think philosophically constitutes a major strain in contemporary culture.

It is thus a noteworthy event for one of our leading academic philosophers to suggest that abortion under some circumstances may be wrong because it insults the intrinsic value of human life. But of course this leaves two large questions to be answered: When does the fetus acquire a life that has intrinsic value? And what role shall the government play in protecting that value?

I do not find Dworkin's answer to either question very persuasive. Like most supporters of a woman's right to abort, he finds no clear line that determines unambiguously when life begins. As I have already indicated, I agree with this judgment. Life emerges, or more accurately, the claims that developing life exert upon us emerge, gradually but powerfully. Everyone recognizes the force of this emergence because everyone (or, I suppose, nearly everyone) recognizes that aborting a fetus near the end of its term is morally a far more serious matter than aborting one shortly after it has become implanted in the womb. Similarly, a mother will usually grieve more deeply over the death of her 3-year-old child than over the death of her newborn infant, and more deeply over the latter's death than over the miscarriage of an embryo.

★   ★   ★

Dworkin explains these near-universal reactions by the concept of investment. The death of an infant is worse than that of a
fetus because a greater investment has been made in the former
than in the latter. The investment is of two sorts, biological and
social.

I think this is too narrow a view of the matter. It may be true,
as Dworkin suggests, that the death of an adolescent girl is worse
than the death of an infant because the adolescent's death "frus-
trates the investments she and others have already made in her
life." But I doubt that this is the whole story.

The greater grief a mother experiences at the death of an
infant than at the death of a 10-week-old fetus does not arise, I
think, from the mother's feeling that her carrying the fetus to term
was more costly or constituted a greater waste of resources than
carrying the fetus for only 10 weeks. I obviously cannot speak for
mothers, but I would imagine from what they say that their feelings on the occasion of the death of an actual or potential child do
not reflect lost investment but lost humanity: the newborn infant
is distinctly human, a person whom the mother loves and of
whom she expects a full and mutually rewarding life, while the
fetus is somewhat less fully human. Moreover, the mother sees the
infant but not, ordinarily, the fetus. There are bonds in both cases,
but the bonds are far greater and the loss far more poignant when
the infant has been held in her arms.

Dworkin rejects this line of reasoning. Unaccountably, he
writes that the greater gravity of a late-term abortion than of an
early-term one cannot be explained "on the ground that fetuses
more closely resemble infants as pregnancy continues." To him,
"increasing resemblance alone has no moral significance." He gives
no reason for reaching that conclusion, one that strikes me as
wholly at odds with everything that could plausibly be surmised
about a mother's feelings. Suppose a woman has had, on different
occasions, both an early miscarriage and a late-term one; suppose
that she looked upon the two fetuses: can anyone doubt that the
greater grief she would feel in the second case would to an
important degree be caused by the close resemblance between the
late-term fetus and a live infant?

Nor can the investment theory explain why a young mother might be willing to sacrifice herself for her young child (if, for example, both are in a burning building and only one can be rescued) or how onlookers would react to her refusal to make that sacrifice. There is greater investment in the mother than in the child, but I conjecture that many mothers would tell the rescuers to take her infant first even if that materially increased her chances of dying, and I further conjecture that if she did the opposite—insist that she be taken first and the infant second—most onlookers would feel she had acted wrongly, even cruelly. The onlookers' criticisms would not be moderated by her later explaining to them that nature and society had made a greater investment in her.

I want to assert that it is precisely the degree of resemblance between a fetus and an infant that is of moral significance. We should focus on this point if we believe, as both Dworkin and I do, that because society has an interest in making certain that the intrinsic value of human life is respected, it also has an interest in "maintaining a moral environment in which decisions about life and death are taken seriously and treated as matters of moral gravity."

Before turning to the policy implications of that view, let me take up in general terms what Dworkin thinks the government is entitled to do. Here he makes what, if I understand him correctly, is an astonishing claim.

To him the moral issue concerning abortion has to do with the intrinsic value of human life. I, and I think most people, agree. To him, human life can only have intrinsic value if we think it is, in some sense, sacred. On this, many people will agree, some will disagree. But if fetal life enjoys some degree of moral respect because it is sacred, then, he says, the government of the United States cannot regulate abortions, at least in the early months of pregnancy, without violating the First Amendment prohibition on the enactment of laws respecting the establishment of religion. Since our disagreements about the value of life are at bottom spiritual, the legislature cannot, without violating the separation of church and state, impose one concept of the spiritual on people who have a different concept.

Lest I be accused of misrepresenting Dworkin, let me quote him:

> A state may not curtail liberty, in order to protect an intrinsic value, when the effect on one group of citizens would be special and grave, when the community is seriously divided about what respect for the value requires, and when people's opinions about the nature of that value reflect essentially religious convictions that are fundamental to moral personality. . . . I conclude that the right to procreative autonomy, from which a right of choice about abortion flows, is well grounded in the First Amendment.

But abortion is not the only case that invokes our concern for protecting the intrinsic, perhaps sacred, value of human life. We also oppose infanticide and homicide for these reasons. Why do we allow the legislature to pass laws prohibiting them? Given the criteria Dworkin sets forth in the statement cited above, it can only be that "the community" is not "seriously divided" about these matters. But suppose it were. Suppose this were 1944, not 1994, and lynchings were commonplace in certain parts of the country. People were then "deeply divided" over what respect, if any, was due to the life of a black man. Some people genuinely believed that only vigilante justice could maintain a society based on the (to them) necessary principle of white supremacy. Should people who disagreed with this view—who felt that the life of a black man was entitled to as much respect as the life of a white one—have been forbidden from enacting their views into law because to do so would have violated the separation of church and state?

Or suppose that a legislature is trying to decide whether to enact the death penalty. The legislators will be deeply divided over the issue. Some will think that all human life, even that of convicted murderers, is sacred; others will argue that the life of a victim deserves great respect and the life of the murderer none at all. Lest there be any doubt as to the religious basis of some of these views, both sides will quote from the Bible. Can the legislature vote for the death penalty (or even vote against it!) without violating the First Amendment? If the views of former Justice William

Brennan opposing capital punishment had prevailed, would he have been placing the Eighth Amendment (barring cruel and unusual punishment) at war with the First Amendment?

Suppose, finally, that American armed forces were to conquer a nation in which many people practiced infanticide. (There may not be many such places now, but at one time there were.) Suppose, further, that the conquest was defensible on moral and legal grounds. If the President were to order his commanding general to make infanticide illegal in the occupied land and to stamp out its practice by whatever means seemed appropriate, would he be acting contrary to the spirit of the First Amendment to the Constitution?

There is perhaps one legal doctrine that may appear to be analogous to Dworkin's position on abortion. The courts have refused to allow the government to conscript as soldiers men who are, on religious grounds, conscientiously opposed to war. In doing this, the courts have given the widest possible meaning to the phrase "religious grounds," so that it is not necessary that the objector actually believe in God. But this is not really analogous at all. The courts have not held that war and conscription are impermissible because the community is deeply divided over the rightness of war and that this division reflects spiritual attitudes toward life. Nor have the courts struck down on these grounds any declaration of war.

I believe that the reason Dworkin is unwilling to allow legislation restricting abortion (except, perhaps, in the last trimester) is that, contrary to the implications of his moral argument, he is at heart a person who sees this issue entirely in terms of rights. A woman's right to "procreative autonomy" is trump. He suggests that this right ought to be exercised with due regard for its moral seriousness, but then rejects virtually every legislative enactment that would have the effect of stressing its moral seriousness or heightening a woman's moral awareness. Though he allows in principle for some (unspecified) preabortion restrictions before the fetus becomes viable, in practice he is against almost every law that has been passed with the intention of influencing—just influencing, mind you, not dictating—how a woman should make her decision. Dworkin opposes a requirement that the spouse be notified or that a waiting period occur before the abortion takes place. (He supports a required waiting period before buying a gun, but not one before having an abortion!) Even a 24-hour waiting period might, in his view, make it more costly for some women to have an abortion and thus might deter them from doing so; therefore, such a brief period must be unconstitutional.

I wish to take more seriously than Dworkin the moral approach to abortion and see where it might lead us. To some people, it requires one to ban all abortions because life begins at the moment of conception. This position has the apparent virtue of drawing a bright, clear line. But I am not convinced that such a bright line can in fact be drawn because I am not convinced that there is such a thing as the "moment of conception."

Long before conception, each female egg and each male sperm is alive and each contains within it, encoded in DNA, human life. Though the production of a human being cannot begin until the egg and the sperm are united in the zygote, the elements (some would say the blueprints) of human life already exist. Conception does not summon forth life where none existed before; it permits life to begin developing toward its infant form. If the penetration of the egg by the sperm is the crucial moment, then one must oppose not only abortion but many kinds of contraception, since some of these—such as the IUD and some birth-control pills— prevent the already fertilized egg from becoming implanted on the wall of the uterus. That is the position of the Catholic Church, and it has the merit of complete consistency.

It is consistency purchased at a high price, however, for it requires one to believe that contraception is immoral. I do not think most people anywhere believe that or can be made to believe it. Nor do I believe it. A sperm and an egg, whether separate or just joined, do not arouse the moral sentiments that we associate with human life. It is just as well that people feel this way, because not every zygote becomes an embryo. Many fail to implant on the uterine wall; of those that do implant, perhaps no more than half survive for 2 weeks. According to one expert (Arthur Hertig), only about one-third of all zygotes survive.

Nature flushes away a large fraction of fertilized eggs. If we think that it is the moment of conception at which sacred life begins, then we should be searching for ways to induce more frequent implantations and expressing our anger at how an unfeeling nature is defying our moral beliefs.

But if the line is not drawn at conception (or implantation), then where? Surely it must be drawn well before birth, since the fetus is viable many weeks before a normal delivery. Yet I doubt that a sharp line can be drawn at all. Embryonic and fetal development does not proceed by crossing lines; it is a continuous process governed by no fixed blueprint but by the iteration of many succeeding cell divisions, the outcome of which it is impossible to foretell.

But life in general is filled with circumstances in which the alternatives are not clearly defined. I cannot define twilight, but that does not mean that I cannot tell the difference between night and day. Our inability to draw a line should no more disable us from making moral judgments about a fetus than it prevents us from making such judgments about children or adults. We cannot specify in advance, for all cases, when a promise is so binding that it must be obeyed whatever the circumstances and when circumstances permit one to ignore it. We have an obligation to act fairly, by which I mean treating equals equally, but we cannot draw clear lines that specify over all or even most cases what constitutes an equality of condition that requires equality of treatment. Though we cannot make the specifications, we nonetheless feel, and usually feel quite strongly, that keeping promises and acting fairly are moral obligations.

Though no line can be drawn, we can identify, I think, the rough stage in embryonic development when, if we are made unmistakably aware of it, our moral sentiments begin to be most powerfully engaged. People treat as human that which appears to be human; people treat as quasi-human that which appears quasi-human. Imagine a room on the walls of which are arrayed, in chronological order, exact color photographs of the human embryo, suitably enlarged, from first fertilization, through early cell divisions and implantation, through the emergence of various human, or humanlike, features, and on to the complete fetus the day before normal delivery. There would be 266 photographs in all, one for each day of embryonic or fetal development. Suppose we then ask a variety of people, but perhaps especially women, to examine these photographs and to tell us in which one, or in which small cluster of them, they first see what appears to be "a baby." Having examined such pictures, most people, I speculate, would select those that represent life at around 7 to 9 weeks after conception.[3]

In the first and second weeks of pregnancy, all that is visible, and just barely visible, is a fertilized egg, or zygote. By the fourth week, some organs begin to appear and function, but in no recognizably human form. In the fifth week, a creature is visible, but one that is not materially different from a mouse or pig. By the seventh week, distinctly human arms and legs are evident, and not only the eyes but the eyelids are visible. In the eighth, though the fetus is but an inch and a half long, the fingers are distinct and the genital organs, though still unsexed, have appeared. At the end of the eighth week, doctors stop calling what they see an embryo and begin calling it a fetus. By the tenth week at the very latest, the fetal face has a clearly human appearance.

It would be even better to view motion pictures rather than stills. A pregnant woman will feel fetal movement after 18 or 19 weeks of pregnancy—a feeling, I am told, that is an inexpressible source of wonder and joy—but in fact the fetus has already been moving—flexing, jerking, and hiccuping, too gently for the woman to sense it—since the ninth or tenth week.

Now, my speculation may turn out to be incorrect. At the very least, the viewers' responses to these pictures will cover a range, with a few saying "it's a baby" as early as the fifth week and a few withholding that judgment until perhaps the tenth week. I would be astonished if any withheld that judgment for as long as the end of the first trimester (roughly, the twelfth week).

Suppose, now, that a woman considering an abortion were

[3]Readers not familiar with the magnificent color photographs of embryos and fetuses made by Lennart Nilsson should examine his *A Child is Born*, Dell, 1990.

brought into this room and shown these pictures. She would be told something of this sort: "You are X weeks pregnant, as near as we can tell. The embryo now looks about like this (pointing). In another week it will look like this (pointing). You should know this before you make a final decision."

Some will complain that this exercise would put a woman under moral pressure. Yes, it would; that is exactly why I think it should be done. The problem with deciding on an abortion without a visual encounter with the fetus (or embryo) is that one is relieved, to a degree, of any sense of the extent to which another life may be at stake.

I do not propose this exercise because I am convinced that no woman, seeing the pictures, would agree to an abortion. There are many considerations that will enter into her decision, and some will, on balance, lead her to abort. Nor do I assume that most women now make this decision lightly or unthinkingly. I propose this procedure because it is likely to induce every woman to make a fully informed moral decision.

She will, of course, already be generally aware that abortion is a grave step and vaguely aware that another life may be at stake. But these sentiments will, of necessity, be somewhat vague or unfocused. She will be keenly aware of whatever is at stake in her personal circumstances—her married or unmarried status, her career plans, her economic or social position—that may incline her to abort. She will not be as keenly aware, I suspect, of what is at stake in the development of the fetus. We all find it easier to prefer an outcome we value and can visualize to one that we value but cannot visualize. Being required to see—literally, see—both sides of the issue makes the moral issue clearer and heightens the sense that the choice is, inescapably, a moral one.

All of us are in asymmetrical moral positions of this sort at one time or another. We worry more about a stray cat when it is at our doorstep than when it is out of sight. We may have a policy about giving to a beggar, but no policy quite prepares us for a personal confrontation with one. A pilot will find it easier to drop a bomb on a building in which women and children are hiding than to place a bomb in that building having first seen the women and children in it. A soldier may find it less troubling to shoot an enemy he cannot see than one with whom he has suddenly come face to face. A business executive finds it simpler to "downsize" his firm than to fire a veteran employee who is standing before him. For our moral sentiments to provide a useful guide to our actions, it is often necessary for us to experience, and not simply imagine, those sentiments and the conditions that evoke them.

Some abortion clinics defer to—or play on—this asymmetry in the woman's feelings. A woman goes to a clinic for a pregnancy test; a day or so later she telephones to get the result. The clinician begins by asking, "Will pregnancy be good news or bad news?" If the woman says, "Bad news," the clinician will immediately ask, "Do you want to terminate?" The stage of fetal development is never mentioned. The word "abortion" is never used. She is simply scheduled for a "procedure."

The alternative that I am suggesting is, in effect, followed when a doctor has reason to think that a woman is carrying a seriously deformed fetus. In a famous case in 1962, Sherri Finkbine of Arizona followed this procedure when, knowing she had taken thalidomide, she saw pictures, or at least heard vivid descriptions, of the horribly deformed babies that had been born in Europe to women who had also used the drug; unable to obtain an abortion in Arizona, she got one in Sweden. (The fetus was badly deformed.) My procedure does not prejudge the outcome; it only clarifies the moral choice. I suppose some women (I imagine very few) would abort what appeared to them to be a normal human baby. But at the very least they would not do it in feigned innocence or real ignorance.

The theologian Paul Ramsey once described what the current situation now entails:

> In this instance, the darkness of the womb makes unnecessary resort to a mortician's art to cover the grim reality. As long as we do not see the deaths inflicted or witness the dying, the direct killing of nascent life has only to be compared with the greater or lesser convenience of other solutions in an antiseptic society.

Shine the photographer's light into the dark womb, and things change, not perhaps as much as Ramsey would have liked—he was a stern and uncompromising foe of abortion—but to some material degree. Even after viewing the photographs, a woman might elect an abortion long after the fetus had become distinctly babylike. Her life might be in serious danger, or delayed fetal abnormalities might appear. But I believe—or, at any rate, I very much hope—that only such grave circumstances would lead to abortions much beyond the eighth week.

And that includes abortions when the mother has been the victim of rape or incest. In a purely rights-only perspective on abortion, a pregnancy resulting from rape violates a woman's right not to become pregnant against her will. That violation would justify an abortion even at a late stage in the pregnancy. But a moral perspective would suggest that, if there is to be an abortion, it ought to be before the fetus appears human, which is to say precious, innocent, vulnerable, appealing; if the woman waits beyond that point, then a moral perspective would suggest that the baby, however conceived, should be carried to term ánd, if the woman wishes, put up for adoption.

Some readers will note that my position on abortion is rather similar to that of certain philosophers, such as Aristotle, and medieval theologians, such as St. Thomas Aquinas, who suggested that a fetus does not become a person until it is "ensouled" or "vivified." Aristotle suggested that movement, or quickening, occurs in the male fetus after about 40 days and in the female one at about 80 days, although he immediately added that this was only a rough estimate. Apart from the questionable distinction between the two sexes, it is my conjecture that Aristotle, who was the greatest biologist of premodern times, based his judgment on an inspection of actual fetuses. According to modern embryological research, Aristotle was roughly correct to find that the fetus acquired human features and began to move at (to take the midpoint between 40 and 80 days) 60 days: about 8 or 9 weeks.

Aristotle's view on this matter influenced Aquinas, though the two thinkers came to very different conclusions. Aquinas argued that the human, rational soul was not present immediately after conception. Drawing presumably on Aristotle's concept of quickening, Aquinas suggested that only a human form with human organs could contain a human soul. Before a fetus was a person, it was an animal. A newly conceived embryo was alive, but to Aquinas and those who followed him it did not become a rational, divinely created being until it had been formed by the soul, much as soft wax is formed by a seal. Thinkers holding this view might regard the abortion of an unsouled fetus as a sin, but only the abortion of a souled one as murder.

This was the theory of "mediate animation," which gained the approval of many Church authorities. As early as the 4th or 5th century, long before the time of Aquinas, St. Jerome had written that "seeds are gradually formed in the uterus, and it is not reputed homicide until the scattered elements received their appearance and members." Jerome, like St. Augustine, did not claim to know for certain when the fetus received a soul; only God could know that. But aborting an ensouled fetus was regarded as far more grave a matter than aborting an unsouled one. By the 12th century, both the theologian Gratian and Pope Innocent III were prepared to say that it was not homicide to kill a fetus until after it had been ensouled. This view received the support of Gregory IX in his decretals, but at the same time he made clear that aborting any fetus, however young, was a sin for which penance was required. Some Catholic theologians even suggested that killing an unformed fetus in order to save the life of the mother might not even be a sin, much less a homicide.

By the 19th century, however, Church doctrine on this matter had begun to harden. The reasons, it has been suggested, were twofold. First, modern biological science was casting doubt on Aristotle's theory of embryological stages; in the newer view, the embryo was biologically alive from fertilization on. Second, abortion was apparently becoming more commonplace; rare events might be met with equivocal theology, but routine events required clear rules. One by one the exceptions permitting abortion were eliminated and the penalty of excommunication was extended to women who procured an abortion. By the end of the 19th century, abortion was being condemned, and one Vatican ruling even suggested that an ectopic, or tubal, pregnancy (which physicians knew constituted a serious threat to the life of the mother) could not be surgically ended.

In 1930, Pius XI issued an encyclical that denied there were any grounds for allowing abortion at any stage in fetal development. The Bible does not mention abortion, but to Pius it seemed clear that killing a fetus violated the commandment against killing; every life was sacred, and since embryos were alive, every embryo was sacred. When uncertain knowledge and rare events permitted complex judgments, the Church uttered them, but when events— greater knowledge, common events—forced its hand, the Church drew a clear line and stuck to it.[4]

But was drawing such a line really necessary? John T. Noonan, Jr., a profound historian of Church doctrine from whose writings I have drawn much of the account that appears above, thinks it was. The central question is, "How do you determine the humanity of a being?" To Noonan there is only one possible answer: if you are conceived by human parents, you are human. He recognizes that for several centuries some important Catholic theologians and even some popes gave a different answer, but on reflection all these other answers had fatal weaknesses. Viability is not a guide to an embryo's humanity, since viability can be determined by the skill and resources of modern science; in principle, any fetus might be made viable. Nor is the capacity for having sensory experience a determinant of humanity, because the fetus long

[Jewish teachings about abortion are at least as complex as Catholic thinking. Though some people speak confidently of "the Jewish position," my amateur reading of the summary accounts reveals considerable differences among the authorities. It seems clear that abortion to protect the life of the mother is permitted. Abortions for other than therapeutic purposes are treated as morally grave matters, but there is no codified position as to what consititutes "grave." One modern rabbinical authority describes elective abortions as "akin to homicide," while another would permit them if there were a good reason. Among such reasons is the anguish of the mother at the prospect of a deformed child. See the *Encyclopaedia Judaica,* 1971, Volume I, pp. 98–101, and David M. Feldman, *Marital Relations, Birth Control, and Abortion in Jewish Law,* Schocken, 1974, Chapters 14–15.

before birth has such experiences, and some adults, owing to neu-
rological damage, might stop having experiences without ceasing
to be human. I agree with these views.

Noonan also rejects the test I have proposed, but for reasons I
do not find convincing. He acknowledges that the grief of a
woman over the miscarriage of a fetus is not as great as the grief
she would feel over the loss of a child, but he opposes any test
based on such feelings because "feeling is a notoriously unsure
guide to the humanity of others." He grants that a mother is more
attached to an infant she can see than to a fetus she cannot, but
says that "sight is even more untrustworthy than feeling in determining humanity." He reaches these conclusions by way of this
analogy: since people are known to discriminate against others on
the basis of color, race, religion, and language, then feelings and
sight are unreliable guides to what is human and thus deserving of
respect.

But this is not, I think, a proper analogy. There is no doubt
that our feelings about others are sometimes hateful or that seeing
the other person does not always draw us to him. But these consequences of the natural human tendency to prefer our own kind do
not apply, except in the rarest of cases, to our own offspring. Quite
the contrary: that we are led by nature to prefer our own kind, and
especially our own children, is the surest reason for believing that
we will cherish them, and cherish them the most when we can
see and touch them.

Many couples give birth to infants who are not like them in
color, configuration, or expression. The Mendelian laws of inheri-
tance ensure that many blond parents will have a black-haired
child and many dark-skinned parents will have a fair-skinned one.
It may be that some parents become especially fond of babies who
are "just like them," but I am aware of no evidence that parents are
inadequately attached to infants who differ physically from them.
Indeed, I am forcefully struck by how many parents will lavish
care and affection even on babies born with terrible deformities
or incurable illnesses. Far from being an unreliable guide to affection and moral respect, sight and touch, and the feelings they generate, are the surest possible guarantees of love and care when it
comes to infancy.

In sum: saying that a human being with full and absolute claims on our moral respect exists from the "moment" of conception is not consistent with either modern science or natural sentiments; the Catholic Church itself long recognized that a difference exists between a formed and an unformed fetus; whether the forming of a fetus has natural or supernatural causes does not alter the greater feeling a parent has for a fetus the more fully formed it is; and the struggle to sustain a clear, simple line as the sole basis for a judgment about the morality of abortion does not accord with either the sentiments or the practices of most decent people. Therefore, one should try to clarify the moral issue in ways that draw on the natural respect people have for innocent life by making them, and especially pregnant women, more fully aware of the presence of that life and of the claims it makes on us.

I have yet to discuss how, if at all, the law should take account of this position. If my experiment were carried out and there developed a consensus as to when an embryo became a baby, should the law recognize this and ban abortions after that period? I believe that it should, provided there were exceptions for grave and special cases (such as a severe deformity), and even then only after the woman had obtained the advice and consent of disinterested and expert parties. But before voting for such a law, I would prefer to wait and see what would happen if my procedure were followed.

For it to be be followed, the Supreme Court would have to change its position. The necessary changes are prefigured in the language of the *Casey* decision. It rejected the trimester framework of *Roe*; it reaffirmed the state's legitimate interest in "the protection of potential life"; and it explicitly held that even though a woman alone must choose whether to abort before the fetus is viable, the state is not prohibited "from taking steps to ensure that this choice is thoughtful and informed." Even in the earliest stages of pregnancy (I would have said, *especially* in the early stages), the state "may enact rules and regulations designed to encourage her to know that there are philosophic and social arguments [I would have said, moral arguments] of great weight that can be brought to bear in favor of continuing the pregnancy to full term." But having said that, the Court then went on to rule out any regulations that would create an "undue burden" or present "a substantial obstacle" to a woman seeking an abortion. I suspect that my procedure would fail the undue-burden test, though I can find no philosophical argument in *Casey* as to why it should.

I would much prefer the Court to give greater latitude to state and federal legislatures to define a policy in this area, one that takes as its first principle the protection of human life. This is what the French statute, passed in 1975, does. It states that "the law guarantees the respect of every human being from the commencement of life. There shall be no derogation from this principle except in cases of necessity and under the conditions laid down by this law." The law goes on to specify the circumstances under which the principle can be violated, describing them as matters of "necessity." As it turns out, "necessity" means that a woman who, during the first 10 weeks of pregnancy, finds herself in "distress" is entitled to terminate her pregnancy after she has received government-mandated counseling. But the final decision is hers.

Mary Ann Glendon has endorsed the general principles of such an approach, pointing out, rightly, that it elevates moral considerations over purely personal preferences or individual rights, and that even though an elective abortion remains available during the first 10 weeks, "the way in which we name things and imagine them may be decisive for the way we feel and act with respect to them." Her Harvard colleague Laurence Tribe dismisses such a view; to him, a policy that is a mere formality is a meaningless hypocrisy, whereas one that has any effect "disempowers and disrespects women." To him, even a moderate regulation of abortion "trivializes women." This is too much even for Ronald Dworkin, who chides Tribe for being a prisoner of his rights-only mentality.

Several people, including President Clinton, have said that abortions ought to be safe, legal, and rare. So long as the issue is dominated by pro-choice activists like Tribe who see the matter largely if not entirely in terms of women's rights, abortions will be safe, legal, and commonplace. No restrictions at all will be possible because, by constraining a woman's choice, they will "disempower" or "trivialize" her.

I do not think that there is any possibility of a consensus among pro- and anti-abortion activists, and as long as the matter is defined in terms of rights, the pro-abortion activists will win. For hardly any politician is willing to vote against "rights." By contrast, the American people are less preoccupied with rights and more respectful of life. Even though they are ultimately willing to let a woman make the final decision, they want to ensure that it is a morally constrained and fully informed decision.

I wish that this nation could start afresh, formulating *de novo* a legislative policy on abortion based on the fundamental premise that abortion is a moral question but not one that invariably admits of only one answer in all circumstances. Most other nations have done just what this country seems incapable of doing. This is the price—and I think it a very heavy price indeed—we have paid for turning so important a matter over to Justice Blackmun and his colleagues.

What kind of people are we that we cannot say, legislatively, that human life is precious, that an infant's life is perhaps the most precious of all, and that we want to ensure that women are placed in a "moral environment in which decisions about life and death are taken seriously and treated as matters of moral gravity"? Many women, perhaps most, already treat this matter as a morally grave issue, but many do not—it is for them a form of birth control—and even those who do may not always clearly see, and thus fully sense, what is at stake. Let them see it.

What to Do About

Crime

James Q. Wilson

When the United States experienced the great increase in crime that began in the early 1960's and continued through the 1970's, most Americans were inclined to attribute it to conditions unique to this country. Many conservatives blamed it on judicial restraints on the police, the abandonment of capital punishment, and the mollycoddling of offenders; many liberals blamed it on poverty, racism, and the rise of violent television programs. Europeans, to the extent they noticed at all, referred to it, sadly or patronizingly, as the "American" problem, a product of our disorderly society, weak state, corrupt police, or imperfect welfare system.

Now, 30 years later, any serious discussion of crime must begin with the fact that, except for homicide, most industrialized nations have crime rates that resemble those in the United States. All the world is coming to look like America. In 1981, the burglary rate in Great Britain was much less than that in the United States; within 6 years the two rates were the same; today, British homes are more likely to be burgled than American ones. In 1980, the rate at which automobiles were stolen was lower in France than in the United States; today, the reverse is true. By 1984, the burglary rate in the Netherlands was nearly twice that in the United States.

In Australia and Sweden certain forms of theft are more common than they are here. While property-crime rates were declining during most of the 1980's in the United States, they were rising elsewhere.[1]

America, it is true, continues to lead the industrialized world in murders. There can be little doubt that part of this lead is to be explained by the greater availability of handguns here. Arguments that once might have been settled with insults or punches are today more likely to be settled by shootings. But guns are not the whole story. Big American cities have had more homicides than comparable European ones for almost as long as anyone can find records. New York and Philadelphia have been more murderous than London since the early part of the 19th century. This country has had a violent history; with respect to murder, that seems likely to remain the case.

But except for homicide, things have been getting better in the United States for over a decade. Since 1980, robbery rates (as reported in victim surveys) have declined by 15 percent. And even with regard to homicide, there is relatively good news: in 1990, the rate at which adults killed one another was no higher than it was in 1980, and in many cities it was considerably lower.

This is as it was supposed to be. Starting around 1980, two things happened that ought to have reduced most forms of crime. The first was the passing into middle age of the postwar baby boom. By 1990, there were 1.5 million fewer boys between the ages of 15 and 19 than there had been in 1980, a drop that meant that this youthful fraction of the population fell from 9.3 percent to 7.2 percent of the total.

In addition, the great increase in the size of the prison population, caused in part by the growing willingness of judges to send offenders to jail, meant that the dramatic reductions in the costs of crime to the criminal that occurred in the 1960's and 1970's were slowly (and very partially) being reversed. Until around 1985, this reversal involved almost exclusively real criminals and parole vio-

[1] These comparisons depend on official police statistics. There are, of course, errors in such data. But essentially the same pattern emerges from comparing nations on the basis of victimization surveys.

lators; it was not until after 1985 that more than a small part of the growth in prison populations was made up of drug offenders.

Because of the combined effect of fewer young people on the street and more offenders in prison, many scholars, myself included, predicted a continuing drop in crime rates throughout the 1980's and into the early 1990's. We were almost right: crime rates did decline. But suddenly, starting around 1985, even as adult homicide rates were remaining stable or dropping, *youthful* homicide rates shot up.

Alfred Blumstein of Carnegie-Mellon University has estimated that the rate at which young males, ages 14 to 17, kill people has gone up significantly for whites and incredibly for blacks. Between 1985 and 1992, the homicide rate for young white males went up by about 50 percent but for young black males it *tripled*.

The public perception that today's crime problem is different from and more serious than that of earlier decades is thus quite correct. Youngsters are shooting at people at a far higher rate than at any time in recent history. Since young people are more likely than adults to kill strangers (as opposed to lovers or spouses), the risk to innocent bystanders has gone up. There may be some comfort to be had in the fact that youthful homicides are only a small fraction of all killings, but given their randomness, it is not much solace.

The United States, then, does not have *a* crime problem, it has at least two. Our high (though now slightly declining) rates of property crime reflect a profound, worldwide cultural change: prosperity, freedom, and mobility have emancipated people almost everywhere from those ancient bonds of custom, family, and village that once held in check both some of our better and many of our worst impulses. The power of the state has been weakened, the status of children elevated, and the opportunity for adventure expanded; as a consequence, we have experienced an explosion of artistic creativity, entrepreneurial zeal, political experimentation—and criminal activity. A global economy has integrated the markets for clothes, music, automobiles—and drugs.

There are only two restraints on behavior—morality, enforced by individual conscience or social rebuke, and law, enforced by the police and the courts. If society is to maintain a behavioral equilibrium, any decline in the former must be matched by a rise in the latter (or vice versa). If familial and traditional restraints on wrongful behavior are eroded, it becomes necessary to increase the legal restraints. But the enlarged spirit of freedom and the heightened suspicion of the state have made it difficult or impossible to use the criminal-justice system to achieve what custom and morality once produced.

This is the modern dilemma, and it may be an insoluble one, at least for the West. The Islamic cultures of the Middle East and the Confucian cultures of the Far East believe that they have a solution. It involves allowing enough liberty for economic progress (albeit under general state direction) while reserving to the state, and its allied religion, nearly unfettered power over personal conduct. It is too soon to tell whether this formula—best exemplified by the prosperous but puritanical city-state of Singapore—will, in the long run, be able to achieve both reproducible affluence and intense social control.

Our other crime problem has to do with the kind of felonies we have: high levels of violence, especially youthful violence, often occurring as part of urban gang life, produced disproportionately by a large, alienated, and self-destructive underclass. This part of the crime problem, though not uniquely American, is more important here than in any other industrialized nation. Britons, Germans, and Swedes are upset about the insecurity of their property and uncertain about what response to make to its theft, but if Americans only had to worry about their homes being burgled and their autos stolen, I doubt that crime would be the national obsession it has now become.

Crime, we should recall, was not a major issue in the 1984 presidential election and had only begun to be one in the 1988 contest; by 1992, it was challenging the economy as a popular concern, and today it dominates all other matters. The reason, I think, is that Americans believe something fundamental has changed in our patterns of crime. They are right. Though we were unhappy about having our property put at risk, we adapted with the aid of locks, alarms, and security guards. But we are terrified by the prospect of innocent people being gunned down at random, without warning and almost without motive, by youngsters who afterward show us the blank, unremorseful faces of seemingly feral, presocial beings.

Criminology has learned a great deal about who these people are. In studies both here and abroad it has been established that about 6 percent of the boys of a given age will commit half or more of all the serious crime produced by all boys of that age. Allowing for measurement errors, it is remarkable how consistent this formula is—6 percent causes 50 percent. It is roughly true in places as different as Philadelphia, London, Copenhagen, and Orange County, California.

We also have learned a lot about the characteristics of the 6 percent. They tend to have criminal parents, to live in cold or discordant families (or pseudo-families), to have a low verbal-intelligence quotient and to do poorly in school, to be emotionally cold and temperamentally impulsive, to abuse alcohol and drugs at the earliest opportunity, and to reside in poor, disorderly communities. They begin their misconduct at an early age, often by the time they are in the 3rd grade.

These characteristics tend to be found not only among the criminals who get caught (and who might, owing to bad luck, be an unrepresentative sample of all high-rate offenders), but among those who do not get caught but reveal their behavior on questionnaires. And the same traits can be identified in advance among groups of randomly selected youngsters, long before they commit any serious crimes—not with enough precision to predict which individuals will commit crimes, but with enough accuracy to be a fair depiction of the group as a whole.[2]

Here a puzzle arises: if 6 percent of the males cause so large a fraction of our collective misery, and if young males are less numerous than once was the case, why are crime rates high and rising? The answer, I conjecture, is that the traits of the 6 percent

[2]Female high-rate offenders are *much* less common than male ones. But to the extent they exist, they display most of these traits.

put them at high risk for whatever criminogenic forces operate in society. As the costs of crime decline or the benefits increase; as drugs and guns become more available; as the glorification of violence becomes more commonplace; as families and neighborhoods lose some of their restraining power—as all these things happen, almost all of us will change our ways to some degree. For the most law-abiding among us, the change will be quite modest: a few more tools stolen from our employer, a few more traffic lights run when no police officer is watching, a few more experiments with fashionable drugs, and a few more business deals on which we cheat. But for the least law-abiding among us, the change will be dramatic: they will get drunk daily instead of just on Saturday night, try PCP or crack instead of marijuana, join gangs instead of marauding in pairs, and buy automatic weapons instead of making zip guns.

A metaphor: when children play the schoolyard game of crack-the-whip, the child at the head of the line scarcely moves but the child at the far end, racing to keep his footing, often stumbles and falls, hurled to the ground by the cumulative force of many smaller movements back along the line. When a changing culture escalates criminality, the at-risk boys are at the end of the line, and the conditions of American urban life—guns, drugs, automobiles, disorganized neighborhoods—make the line very long and the ground underfoot rough and treacherous.

Much is said these days about preventing or deterring crime, but it is important to understand exactly what we are up against when we try. Prevention, if it can be made to work at all, must start very early in life, perhaps as early as the first 2 or 3 years, and given the odds it faces—childhood impulsivity, low verbal facility, incompetent parenting, disorderly neighborhoods—it must also be massive in scope. Deterrence, if it can be made to work better (for surely it already works to some degree), must be applied close to the moment of the wrongful act or else the present-orientedness of the youthful would-be offender will discount the threat so much that the promise of even a small gain will outweigh its large but deferred costs.

In this country, however, and in most Western nations, we have profound misgivings about doing anything that would give prevention or deterrence a chance to make a large difference. The family is sacrosanct; the family-preservation movement is strong; the state is a clumsy alternative. "Crime-prevention" programs, therefore, usually take the form of creating summer jobs for adolescents, worrying about the unemployment rate, or (as in the proposed 1994 crime bill) funding midnight basketball leagues. There may be something to be said for all these efforts, but crime prevention is not one of them. The typical high-rate offender is well launched on his career before he becomes a teenager or has ever encountered the labor market; he may like basketball, but who pays for the lights and the ball is a matter of supreme indifference to him.

Prompt deterrence has much to recommend it: the folk wisdom that swift and certain punishment is more effective than severe penalties is almost surely correct. But the greater the swiftness and certainty, the less attention paid to the procedural safeguards essential to establishing guilt. As a result, despite their good instincts for the right answers, most Americans, frustrated by the restraints (many wise, some foolish) on swiftness and certainty, vote for proposals to increase severity: if the penalty is 10 years, let us make it 20 or 30; if the penalty is life imprisonment, let us make it death; if the penalty is jail, let us make it caning.

Yet the more draconian the sentence, the less (on the average) the chance of its being imposed; plea bargains see to that. And the most draconian sentences will, of necessity, tend to fall on adult offenders nearing the end of their criminal careers and not on the young ones who are in their criminally most productive years. (The peak ages of criminality are between 16 and 18; the average age of prison inmates is 10 years older.) I say "of necessity" because almost every judge will give first-, second-, or even third-time offenders a break, reserving the heaviest sentences for those men who have finally exhausted judicial patience or optimism.

Laws that say "three strikes and you're out" are an effort to change this, but they suffer from an inherent contradiction. If they are carefully drawn so as to target only the most serious offenders, they will probably have a minimal impact on the crime rate; but if they are broadly drawn so as to make a big impact on the crime rate, they will catch many petty repeat offenders who few of us think really deserve life imprisonment.

Prevention and deterrence, albeit hard to augment, at least are plausible strategies. Not so with many of the other favorite nostrums, like reducing the amount of violence on television. Televised violence may have some impact on criminality, but I know of few scholars who think the effect is very large. And to achieve even a small difference we might have to turn the clock back to the kind of programming we had around 1945, because the few studies that correlate programming with the rise in violent crime find that the biggest changes occurred between that year and 1974. Another favorite, boot camp, makes good copy, but so far no one has shown that it reduces the rate at which the former inmates commit crimes.

Then, of course, there is gun control. Guns are almost certainly contributors to the lethality of American violence, but there is no politically or legally feasible way to reduce the stock of guns now in private possession to the point where their availability to criminals would be much affected. And even if there were, law-abiding people would lose a means of protecting themselves long before criminals lost a means of attacking them.

As for rehabilitating juvenile offenders, it has some merit, but there are rather few success stories. Individually, the best (and best-evaluated) programs have minimal, if any, effects; collectively, the best estimate of the crime-reduction value of these programs is quite modest, something on the order of 5 or 10 percent.[3]

What, then, is to be done? Let us begin with policing, since law-enforcement officers are that part of the criminal-justice sys-

---

[3]Many individual programs involve so few subjects that a good evaluation will reveal no positive effect even if one occurs. By a technique called meta-analysis, scores of individual studies can be pooled into one mega-evaluation; because there are now hundreds or thousands of subjects, even small gains can be identified. The best of these meta-analyses, such as the one by Mark Lipsey, suggest modest positive effects.

tem which is closest to the situations where criminal activity is likely to occur.

It is now widely accepted that, however important it is for officers to drive around waiting for 911 calls summoning their help, doing that is not enough. As a supplement to such a reactive strategy—comprised of random preventive patrol and the investigation of crimes that have already occurred—many leaders and students of law enforcement now urge the police to be "proactive": to identify, with the aid of citizen groups, problems that can be solved so as to prevent criminality, and not only to respond to it. This is often called community-based policing; it seems to entail something more than feel-good meetings with honest citizens, but something less than allowing neighborhoods to assume control of the police function.

The new strategy might better be called problem-oriented policing. It requires the police to engage in *directed*, not random, patrol. The goal of that direction should be to reduce, in a manner consistent with fundamental liberties, the opportunity for high-risk persons to do those things that increase the likelihood of their victimizing others.

For example, the police might stop and pat down persons whom they reasonably suspect may be carrying illegal guns.[4] The Supreme Court has upheld such frisks when an officer observes "unusual conduct" leading him to conclude that "criminal activity may be afoot" on the part of a person who may be "armed and dangerous." This is all rather vague, but it can be clarified in two ways.

First, statutes can be enacted that make certain persons, on the basis of their past conduct and present legal status, subject to pat-downs for weapons. The statutes can, as is now the case in several states, make all probationers and parolees subject to nonconsensual searches for weapons as a condition of their remaining on probation or parole. Since three-fourths of all convicted offenders (and a large fraction of all felons) are in the community rather than in prison, there are on any given day over three million criminals on

[4] I made a fuller argument along these lines in "Just Take Away Their Guns," in the *New York Times Magazine*, March 20, 1994.

the streets under correctional supervision. Many are likely to become recidivists. Keeping them from carrying weapons will materially reduce the chances that they will rob or kill. The courts might also declare certain dangerous street gangs to be continuing criminal enterprises, membership in which constitutes grounds for police frisks.

Second, since I first proposed such a strategy, I have learned that there are efforts under way in public and private research laboratories to develop technologies that will permit the police to detect from a distance persons who are carrying concealed weapons on the streets. Should these efforts bear fruit, they will provide the police with the grounds for stopping, questioning, and patting down even persons not on probation or parole or obviously in gangs.

Whether or not the technology works, the police can also offer immediate cash rewards to people who provide information about individuals illegally carrying weapons. Spending $100 on each good tip will have a bigger impact on dangerous gun use than will the same amount spent on another popular nostrum—buying back guns from law-abiding people.[5]

Getting illegal firearms off the streets will require that the police be motivated to do all of these things. But if the legal, technological, and motivational issues can be resolved, our streets can be made safer even without sending many more people to prison.

The same directed-patrol strategy might help keep known offenders drug-free. Most persons jailed in big cities are found to have been using illegal drugs within the day or two preceding their arrest. When convicted, some are given probation on condition that they enter drug-treatment programs; others are sent to prisons where (if they are lucky) drug-treatment programs operate. But in many cities the enforcement of such probation condi-

---

[5]In Charleston, South Carolina, the police pay a reward to anyone identifying a student carrying a weapon to school or to some school event. Because many boys carry guns to school in order to display or brag about them, the motive to carry disappears once any display alerts a potential informer.

tions is casual or nonexistent; in many states, parolees are released back into drug-infested communities with little effort to ensure that they participate in whatever treatment programs are to be found there.

Almost everyone agrees that more treatment programs should exist. But what many advocates overlook is that the key to success is steadfast participation and many, probably most, offenders have no incentive to be steadfast. To cope with this, patrol officers could enforce random drug tests on probationers and parolees on their beats; failing to take a test when ordered, or failing the test when taken, should be grounds for immediate revocation of probation or parole, at least for a brief period of confinement.

The goal of this tactic is not simply to keep offenders drug-free (and thereby lessen their incentive to steal the money needed to buy drugs and reduce their likelihood of committing crimes because they are on a drug high); it is also to diminish the demand for drugs generally and thus the size of the drug market.

Lest the reader embrace this idea too quickly, let me add that as yet we have no good reason to think that it will reduce the crime rate by very much. Something akin to this strategy, albeit one using probation instead of police officers, has been tried under the name of Intensive-Supervision Programs (ISP), involving a panoply of drug tests, house arrests, frequent surveillance, and careful records. By means of a set of randomized experiments carried out in fourteen cities, Joan Petersilia and Susan Turner, both then at RAND, compared the rearrest rates of offenders assigned to ISP with those of offenders in ordinary probation. There was no difference.

Still, this study does not settle the matter. For one thing, since the ISP participants were under much closer surveillance than the regular probationers, the former were bound to be caught breaking the law more frequently than the latter. It is thus possible that a higher fraction of the crimes committed by the ISP than of the control group were detected and resulted in a return to prison, which would mean, if true, a net gain in public safety. For another thing, intensive supervision was in many cases not all that intensive—in five cities, contacts with the probationers only took place about once a week, and for all cities drug tests occurred, on average, about once a month. Finally, there is some indication that participation in treatment programs was associated with lower recidivism rates.

Both anti-gun and anti-drug police patrols will, if performed systematically, require big changes in police and court procedures and a significant increase in the resources devoted to both, at least in the short run. (ISP is not cheap, and it will become even more expensive if it is done in a truly intensive fashion.) Most officers have at present no incentive to search for guns or enforce drug tests; many jurisdictions, owing to crowded dockets or over-crowded jails, are lax about enforcing the conditions of probation or parole. The result is that the one group of high-risk people over which society already has the legal right to exercise substantial con-trol is often out of control, "supervised," if at all, by means of brief monthly interviews with overworked probation or parole officers.

Another promising tactic is to enforce truancy and curfew laws. This arises from the fact that much crime is opportunistic: idle boys, usually in small groups, sometimes find irresistible the opportunity to steal or the challenge to fight. Deterring present-oriented youngsters who want to appear fearless in the eyes of their comrades while indulging their thrill-seeking natures is a tall order. While it is possible to deter the crimes they commit by a credible threat of prompt sanctions, it is easier to reduce the chances for risky group idleness in the first place.

In Charleston, South Carolina, for example, Chief Reuben Greenberg instructed his officers to return all school-age children to the schools from which they were truant and to return all youngsters violating an evening-curfew agreement to their par-ents. As a result, groups of school-age children were no longer to be found hanging out in the shopping malls or wandering the streets late at night.

There has been no careful evaluation of these efforts in Charleston (or, so far as I am aware, in any other big city), but the rough figures are impressive—the Charleston crime rate in 1991 was about 25 percent lower than the rate in South Carolina's other principal cities and, for most offenses (including burglaries and larcenies), lower than what that city reported 20 years earlier.

All these tactics have in common putting the police, as the criminologist Lawrence Sherman of the University of Maryland phrases it, where the "hot spots" are. Most people need no police attention except for a response to their calls for help. A small fraction of people (and places) need constant attention. Thus, in Minneapolis, all of the robberies during one year occurred at just 2 percent of the city's addresses. To capitalize on this fact, the Minneapolis police began devoting extra patrol attention, in brief but frequent bursts of activity, to those locations known to be trouble spots. Robbery rates evidently fell by as much as 20 percent and public disturbances by even more.

Some of the worst hot spots are outdoor drug markets. Because of either limited resources, a fear of potential corruption, or a desire to catch only the drug kingpins, the police in some cities (including, from time to time, New York) neglect street-corner dealing. By doing so, they get the worst of all worlds.

The public, seeing the police ignore drug dealing that is in plain view, assumes that they are corrupt whether or not they are. The drug kingpins, who are hard to catch and are easily replaced by rival smugglers, find that their essential retail distribution system remains intact. Casual or first-time drug users, who might not use at all if access to supplies were difficult, find access to be effortless and so increase their consumption. People who might remain in treatment programs if drugs were hard to get drop out upon learning that they are easy to get. Interdicting without merely displacing drug markets is difficult but not impossible, though it requires motivation, which some departments lack, and resources, which many do not have.

The sheer number of police on the streets of a city probably has only a weak, if any, relationship with the crime rate; what the police do is more important than how many there are, at least above some minimum level. Nevertheless, patrols directed at hot spots, loitering truants, late-night wanderers, probationers, parolees, and possible gun carriers, all in addition to routine investigative activities, will require more officers in many cities. Between 1977 and 1987, the number of police officers declined in a third of the 50 largest cities and fell relative to population in many more. Just how far behind police resources have lagged can be gauged from this fact: in 1950 there was one violent crime reported for every police officer; in 1980 there were three violent crimes reported for every officer.

                                    ★   ★   ★

I have said little so far about penal policy, in part because I
wish to focus attention on those things that are likely to have the
largest and most immediate impact on the quality of urban life.
But given the vast gulf between what the public believes and what
many experts argue should be our penal policy, a few comments
are essential.

The public wants more people sent away for longer sentences;
many (probably most) criminologists think we use prison too
much and at too great a cost and that this excessive use has had
little beneficial effect on the crime rate. My views are much closer
to those of the public, though I think the average person exaggerates the faults of the present system and the gains of some alternative (such as "three strikes and you're out").

The expert view, as it is expressed in countless op-ed essays,
often goes like this: "We have been arresting more and more people and giving them longer and longer sentences, producing no
decrease in crime but huge increases in prison populations. As a
result, we have become the most punitive nation on earth."

Scarcely a phrase in those sentences is accurate. The probability of being arrested for a given crime is lower today than it was
in 1974. The amount of time served in state prison has been
declining more or less steadily since the 1940's. Taking all crimes
together, time served fell from 25 months in 1945 to 13 months
in 1984. Only for rape are prisoners serving as much time today as
they did in the 1940's.

The net effect of lower arrest rates and shorter effective sentences is that the cost to the adult perpetrator of the average burglary fell from 50 days in 1960 to 15 days in 1980. That is to say,
the chances of being caught and convicted, multiplied by the
median time served if imprisoned, was in 1980 less than a third of
what it had been in 1960.[6]

Beginning around 1980, the costs of crime to the criminal

---

[6] I take these cost calculations from Mark Kleiman *et al.*, "Imprisonment-
to-Offense Ratios," Working Paper 89–06–02 of the Program in Criminal Justice Policy and Management at the Kennedy School of Government, Harvard
University, August 5, 1988.

began to inch up again—the result, chiefly, of an increase in the proportion of convicted persons who were given prison terms. By 1986, the "price" of a given burglary had risen to 21 days. Also beginning around 1980, as I noted at the outset, the crime rate began to decline.

It would be foolhardy to explain this drop in crime by the rise in imprisonment rates; many other factors, such as the aging of the population and the self-protective measures of potential victims, were also at work. Only a controlled experiment (e.g., randomly allocating prison terms for a given crime among the states) could hope to untangle the causal patterns, and happily the Constitution makes such experiments unlikely.

Yet it is worth noting that nations with different penal policies have experienced different crime rates. According to David Farrington of Cambridge University, property-crime rates rose in England and Sweden at a time when both the imprisonment rate and time served fell substantially, while property-crime rates declined in the United States at a time when the imprisonment rate (but not time served) was increasing.

Though one cannot measure the effect of prison on crime with any accuracy, it certainly has some effects. By 1986, there were 55,000 more robbers in prison than there had been in 1974. Assume that each imprisoned robber would commit five such offenses per year if free on the street. This means that in 1986 there were 275,000 fewer robberies in America than there would have been had these 55,000 men been left on the street.

Nor, finally, does America use prison to a degree that vastly exceeds what is found in any other civilized nation. Compare the chance of going to prison in England and the United States if one is convicted of a given crime. According to Farrington, your chances were higher in England if you were found guilty of a rape, higher in America if you were convicted of an assault or a burglary, and about the same if you were convicted of a homicide or a robbery. Once in prison, you would serve a longer time in this country than in England for almost all offenses save murder.

James Lynch of American University has reached similar conclusions from his comparative study of criminal-justice policies. His data show that the chances of going to prison and the time served for homicide and robbery are roughly the same in the United States, Canada, and England.

Of late, drugs have changed American penal practice. In 1982, only about 8 percent of state-prison inmates were serving time on drug convictions. In 1987, that started to increase sharply; by 1994, over 60 percent of all federal and about 25 percent of all state prisoners were there on drug charges. In some states, such as New York, the percentage was even higher.

This change can be attributed largely to the advent of crack cocaine. Whereas snorted cocaine powder was expensive, crack was cheap; whereas the former was distributed through networks catering to elite tastes, the latter was mass-marketed on street corners. People were rightly fearful of what crack was doing to their children and demanded action; as a result, crack dealers started going to prison in record numbers.

Unfortunately, these penalties do not have the same incapacitative effect as sentences for robbery. A robber taken off the street is not replaced by a new robber who has suddenly found a market niche, but a drug dealer sent away is replaced by a new one because an opportunity has opened up.

We are left, then, with the problem of reducing the demand for drugs, and that in turn requires either prevention programs on a scale heretofore unimagined or treatment programs with a level of effectiveness heretofore unachieved. Any big gains in prevention and treatment will probably have to await further basic research into the biochemistry of addiction and the development of effective and attractive drug antagonists that reduce the appeal of cocaine and similar substances.[7]

In the meantime, it is necessary either to build much more prison space, find some other way of disciplining drug offenders, or both. There is very little to be gained, I think, from shortening

---

[7]I anticipate that at this point some readers will call for legalizing or decriminalizing drugs as the "solution" to the problem. Before telling me this, I hope they will read what I wrote on that subject in the February 1990 issue of *Commentary*. I have not changed my mind.

the terms of existing nondrug inmates in order to free up more prison space. Except for a few elderly, nonviolent offenders serving very long terms, there are real risks associated with shortening the terms of the typical inmate.

Scholars disagree about the magnitude of those risks, but the best studies, such as the one of Wisconsin inmates done by John J. DiIulio, Jr., of Princeton, suggest that the annual costs to society in crime committed by an offender on the street are probably twice the costs of putting him in a cell. That ratio will vary from state to state because states differ in what proportion of convicted persons is imprisoned—some states dip deeper down into the pool of convictees, thereby imprisoning some with minor criminal habits.

But I caution the reader to understand that there are no easy prison solutions to crime, even if we build the additional space. The state-prison population more than doubled between 1980 and 1990, yet the victimization rate for robbery fell by only 23 percent. Even if we assign all of that gain to the increased deterrent and incapacitative effect of prison, which is implausible, the improvement is not vast. Of course, it is possible that the victimization rate would have risen, perhaps by a large amount, instead of falling if we had not increased the number of inmates. But we shall never know.

Recall my discussion of the decline in the costs of crime to the criminal, measured by the number of days in prison that result, on average, from the commission of a given crime. That cost is vastly lower today than in the 1950's. But much of the decline (and since 1974, nearly all of it) is the result of a drop in the probability of being arrested for a crime, not in the probability of being imprisoned once arrested.

Anyone who has followed my writings on crime knows that I have defended the use of prison both to deter crime and incapacitate criminals. I continue to defend it. But we must recognize two facts. First, even modest additional reductions in crime, comparable to the ones achieved in the early 1980's, will require vast increases in correctional costs and encounter bitter judicial resistance to mandatory sentencing laws. Second, America's most troubling crime problem—the increasingly violent behavior of disaffected and impulsive youth—may be especially hard to control by means of marginal and delayed increases in the probability of punishment.

Possibly one can make larger gains by turning our attention to the unexplored area of juvenile justice. Juvenile (or family) courts deal with young people just starting their criminal careers and with chronic offenders when they are often at their peak years of offending. We know rather little about how these courts work or with what effect. There are few, if any, careful studies of what happens, a result in part of scholarly neglect and in part of the practice in some states of shrouding juvenile records and proceedings in secrecy. Some studies, such as one by the *Los Angeles Times* of juvenile justice in California, suggest that young people found guilty of a serious crime are given sentences tougher than those meted out to adults.[8] This finding is so counter to popular beliefs and the testimony of many big-city juvenile-court judges that some caution is required in interpreting it.

There are two problems. The first lies in defining the universe of people to whom sanctions are applied. In some states, such as California, it may well be the case that a juvenile *found guilty of a serious offense* is punished with greater rigor than an adult, but many juveniles whose behavior ought to be taken seriously (because they show signs of being part of the 6 percent) are released by the police or probation officers before ever seeing a judge. And in some states, such as New York, juveniles charged with having committed certain crimes, including serious ones like illegally carrying a loaded gun or committing an assault, may not be fingerprinted. Since persons with a prior record are usually given longer sentences than those without one, the failure to fingerprint can mean that the court has no way of knowing whether the John Smith standing before it is the same John Smith who was arrested 4 times for assault and so ought to be sent away, or a different John Smith whose clean record entitles him to probation.

The second problem arises from the definition of a *severe* penalty. In California, a juvenile found guilty of murder does indeed serve a longer sentence than an adult convicted of the same offense—60 months for the former, 41 months for the latter.

[8] "A Nation's Children in Lock-up," *Los Angeles Times*, August 22, 1993.

Many people will be puzzled by a newspaper account that defines 5 years in prison for murder as a *severe* sentence, and angered to learn that an adult serves less than 4 years for such a crime.

The key, unanswered question is whether prompt and more effective early intervention would stop high-rate delinquents from becoming high-rate criminals at a time when their offenses were not yet too serious. Perhaps early and swift, though not necessarily severe, sanctions could deter some budding hoodlums, but we have no evidence of that as yet.

For as long as I can remember, the debate over crime has been between those who wished to rely on the criminal-justice system and those who wished to attack the root causes of crime. I have always been in the former group because what its opponents depicted as "root causes"—unemployment, racism, poor housing, too little schooling, a lack of self-esteem—turned out, on close examination, not to be major causes of crime at all.

Of late, however, there has been a shift in the debate. Increasingly those who want to attack root causes have begun to point to real ones—temperament, early family experiences, and neighborhood effects. The sketch I gave earlier of the typical high-rate young offender suggests that these factors are indeed at the root of crime. The problem now is to decide whether any can be changed by plan and at an acceptable price in money and personal freedom.

If we are to do this, we must confront the fact that the critical years of a child's life are ages 1 to 10, with perhaps the most important being the earliest years. During those years, some children are put gravely at risk by some combination of heritable traits, prenatal insults (maternal drug and alcohol abuse or poor diet), weak parent–child attachment, poor supervision, and disorderly family environment.

If we knew with reasonable confidence which children were most seriously at risk, we might intervene with some precision to supply either medical therapy or parent training or (in extreme cases) to remove the child to a better home. But given our present knowledge, precision is impossible, and so we must proceed carefully, relying, except in the most extreme cases, on persuasion and incentives.

We do, however, know enough about the early causes of conduct disorder and later delinquency to know that the more risk factors exist (such as parental criminality and poor supervision), the greater the peril to the child. It follows that programs aimed at just one or a few factors are not likely to be successful; the children most at risk are those who require the most wide-ranging and fundamental changes in their life circumstances. The goal of these changes is, as Travis Hirschi of the University of Arizona has put it, to teach self-control.

Hirokazu Yoshikawa of New York University has recently summarized what we have learned about programs that attempt to make large and lasting changes in a child's prospects for improved conduct, better school behavior, and lessened delinquency. Four such programs in particular seemed valuable: the Perry Preschool Project in Ypsilanti, Michigan; the Parent-Child Development Center in Houston, Texas; the Family Development Research Project in Syracuse, New York; and the Yale Child Welfare Project in New Haven, Connecticut.

All these programs had certain features in common. They dealt with low-income, often minority, families; they intervened during the first 5 years of a child's life and continued for between 2 and 5 years; they combined parent training with preschool education for the child; and they involved extensive home visits. All were evaluated fairly carefully, with the follow-ups lasting for at least 5 years, in two cases for at least 10, and in one case for 14. The programs produced (depending on the project) less fighting, impulsivity, disobedience, restlessness, cheating, and delinquency. In short, they improved self-control.

They were experimental programs, which means that it is hard to be confident that trying the same thing on a bigger scale in many places will produce the same effects. A large number of well-trained and highly motivated caseworkers dealt with a relatively small number of families, with the workers knowing that their efforts were being evaluated. Moreover, the programs operated in the late 1970's or early 1980's before the advent of crack cocaine or the rise of the more lethal neighborhood gangs. A national program mounted under current conditions might or might not have the same result as the experimental efforts.

Try telling that to lawmakers. What happens when politicians encounter experimental successes is amply revealed by the history of Head Start: they expanded the program quickly without assuring quality, and stripped it down to the part that was the most popular, least expensive, and easiest to run, namely, preschool education. Absent from much of Head Start are the high teacher-to-child caseloads, the extensive home visits, and the elaborate parent training—the very things that probably account for much of the success of the four experimental programs.

In this country we tend to separate programs designed to help children from those that benefit their parents. The former are called "child development," the latter "welfare reform." This is a great mistake. Everything we know about long-term welfare recipients indicates that their children are at risk for the very problems that child-helping programs later try to correct.

The evidence from a variety of studies is quite clear: even if we hold income and ethnicity constant, children (and especially boys) raised by a single mother are more likely than those raised by two parents to have difficulty in school, get in trouble with the law, and experience emotional and physical problems.[9] Producing illegitimate children is not an "alternative life-style" or simply an imprudent action; it is a curse. Making mothers work will not end the curse; under current proposals, it will not even save money.

The absurdity of divorcing the welfare problem from the child-development problem becomes evident as soon as we think seriously about what we want to achieve. Smaller welfare expenditures? Well, yes, but not if it hurts children. More young mothers working? Probably not; young mothers ought to raise their young children, and work interferes with that unless two parents can solve some difficult and expensive problems.

What we really want is *fewer illegitimate children*, because such

[9] I summarize this evidence in "The Family-Values Debate," *Commentary*, April 1993.

children, by being born out of wedlock are, except in unusual cases, being given early admission to the underclass. And failing that, we want the children born to single (and typically young and poor) mothers to have a chance at a decent life.

Letting teenage girls set up their own households at public expense neither discourages illegitimacy nor serves the child's best interests. If they do set up their own homes, then to reach those with the fewest parenting skills and the most difficult children will require the kind of expensive and intensive home visits and family-support programs characteristic of the four successful experiments mentioned earlier.

One alternative is to tell a girl who applies for welfare that she can only receive it on condition that she live either in the home of *two* competent parents (her own if she comes from an intact family) or in a group home where competent supervision and parent training will be provided by adults unrelated to her. Such homes would be privately managed but publicly funded by pooling welfare checks, food stamps, and housing allowances.

A model for such a group home (albeit one run without public funds) is the St. Martin de Porres House of Hope on the south side of Chicago, founded by two nuns for homeless young women, especially those with drug-abuse problems. The goals of the home are clear: accept personal responsibility for your lives and learn to care for your children. And these goals, in turn, require the girls to follow rules, stay in school, obey a curfew, and avoid alcohol and drugs. Those are the rules that ought to govern a group home for young welfare mothers.

Group homes funded by pooled welfare benefits would make the task of parent training much easier and provide the kind of structured, consistent, and nurturant environment that children need. A few cases might be too difficult for these homes, and for such children, boarding schools—once common in American cities for disadvantaged children, but now almost extinct—might be revived.

Group homes also make it easier to supply quality medical care to young mothers and their children. Such care has taken on added importance in recent years with discovery of the lasting damage that can be done to a child's prospects from being born prematurely and with a very low birth weight, having a mother who has abused drugs or alcohol, or being exposed to certain dangerous metals. Lead poisoning is now widely acknowledged to be a source of cognitive and behavioral impairment; of late, elevated levels of manganese have been linked to high levels of violence.[10] These are all treatable conditions; in the case of a manganese imbalance, easily treatable.

My focus on changing behavior will annoy some readers. For them the problem is poverty and the worst feature of single-parent families is that they are inordinately poor. Even to refer to a behavioral or cultural problem is to "stigmatize" people.

Indeed it is. Wrong behavior—neglectful, immature, or incompetent parenting; the production of out-of-wedlock babies—*ought* to be stigmatized. There are many poor men of all races who do not abandon the women they have impregnated, and many poor women of all races who avoid drugs and do a good job of raising their children. If we fail to stigmatize those who give way to temptation, we withdraw the rewards from those who resist them. This becomes all the more important when entire communities, and not just isolated households, are dominated by a culture of fatherless boys preying on innocent persons and exploiting immature girls.

We need not merely stigmatize, however. We can try harder to move children out of those communities, either by drawing them into safe group homes or facilitating (through rent supplements and housing vouchers) the relocation of them and their parents to neighborhoods with intact social structures and an ethos of family values.

Much of our uniquely American crime problem (as opposed to the worldwide problem of general thievery) arises, not from the failings of individuals but from the concentration in disorderly neighborhoods of people at risk of failing. That concentration is

[10]It is not clear why manganese has this effect, but we know that it diminishes the availability of serotonin, a neurotransmitter, and low levels of serotonin are now strongly linked to violent and impulsive behavior.

partly the result of prosperity and freedom (functioning families long ago seized the opportunity to move out to the periphery), partly the result of racism (it is harder for some groups to move than for others), and partly the result of politics (elected officials do not wish to see settled constituencies broken up).

I seriously doubt that this country has the will to address either of its two crime problems, save by acts of individual self-protection. We could in theory make justice swifter and more certain, but we will not accept the restrictions on liberty and the weakening of procedural safeguards that this would entail. We could vastly improve the way in which our streets are policed, but some of us will not pay for it and the rest of us will not tolerate it. We could alter the way in which at-risk children experience the first few years of life, but the opponents of this—welfare-rights activists, family preservationists, budget cutters, and assorted ideologues—are numerous and the bureaucratic problems enormous.

Unable or unwilling to do such things, we take refuge in substitutes: we debate the death penalty, we wring our hands over television, we lobby to keep prisons from being built in our neighborhoods, and we fall briefly in love with trendy nostrums that seem to cost little and promise much.

Much of our ambivalence is on display in the 1994 federal crime bill. To satisfy the tough-minded, the list of federal offenses for which the death penalty can be imposed has been greatly enlarged, but there is little reason to think that executions, as they work in this country (which is to say, after much delay and only on a few offenders), have any effect on the crime rate and no reason to think that executing more federal prisoners (who account, at best, for a tiny fraction of all homicides) will reduce the murder rate. To satisfy the tender-minded, several billion dollars are earmarked for prevention programs, but there is as yet very little hard evidence that any of these will actually prevent crime.

In adding more police officers, the bill may make some difference—but only if the additional personnel are imaginatively deployed. And Washington will pay only part of the cost initially and none of it after 6 years, which means that any city getting new officers will either have to raise its own taxes to keep them on the force or accept the political heat that will arise from turning down "free" cops. Many states also desperately need additional prison space; the federal funds allocated by the bill for their construction will be welcomed, provided that states are willing to meet the conditions set for access to such funds.

Meanwhile, just beyond the horizon, there lurks a cloud that the winds will soon bring over us. The population will start getting younger again. By the end of this decade there will be a million more people between the ages of 14 and 17 than there are now. Half of this extra million will be male. Six percent of them will become high-rate, repeat offenders—30,000 more muggers, killers, and thieves than we have now.

Get ready.